THE VISITABLE PAST:
A WARTIME MEMOIR

Leon Edel, Honolulu, 1978, standing beside a portrait drawn by Canadian artist Louis Muhlstock in Paris in 1931 (photo by Barbara Hall).

THE VISITABLE PAST

A WARTIME MEMOIR

LEON EDEL

A BIOGRAPHY MONOGRAPH

PUBLISHED FOR THE BIOGRAPHICAL RESEARCH CENTER
BY THE UNIVERSITY OF HAWAI'I PRESS
2001

© 2001 Biographical Research Center
All rights reserved
Printed in the United States of America

01 02 03 04 05   5 4 3 2

Library of Congress Cataloging-in-Publication Data

Edel, Leon, 1907–1997
    The visitable past : a wartime memoir / Leon Edel.
    p. cm. — (A Biography monograph)
    ISBN 0–8248–2430–X (cloth : alk. paper) — ISBN 0–8248–2431–8 (pbk. : alk. paper)
    1. Edel, Leon, 1907–   2. World War, 1939–1945—Personal narratives, American.   3. United States. Army—Biography.   4. World War, 1939–1945—Psychological aspects.   5. World War, 1939–1945—Campaigns—France.   I. University of Hawaii at Manoa. Biographical Research Center.   II. Title.   III. Series.

D811.E29 A3 2000
940.54'214'092—dc21
[B]

                                                                         00-069068

University of Hawai'i Press books are printed on acid-free paper
and meet the guidelines for permanence and durability
of the Council on Library Resources.

CONTENTS

FOREWORD	vii
ACKNOWLEDGMENTS	ix
INTRODUCTION	xi

PART ONE: TRANSFORMATIONS
I Am Drafted	3
Fort Eustis: Soldiering	11
Camp Ritchie: Military Intelligence	14
Camp Sharpe: Psychological Warfare	22

PART TWO: NORMANDY
Convoy and Landfall	29
Omaha Beach and an Orchard	34
A Month in the Country	38
Liberating Brittany	50

PART THREE: ENTERING PARIS
A Hermitage at Montigny	61
A Pause at Rambouillet	70
A Night in the Préfecture	75
The Hôtel Scribe	81
De Gaulle Triumphant	86
Musings and Memories	94
Carnival Without Masks	98
Captain Miller and the Place de la Bourse	101
Liane and Her Companions	108

PART FOUR: BOULEVARD WINTER
In the rue d'Aguesseau	123
Behind the Lines	126
Searching for Sylvia Beach	129
Edith's Lover in Old Age: Encounters with W. Morton Fullerton	138
Interiors	146
From My Notebook	154
A Parachutist's Story	158
The Performing Arts	160
Hospitals	163
Romances and Show Biz	165
Réveillon 1944	169

PART FIVE: STRASBOURG

A Sudden Panic	177
Farewells	181
A Winter Journey	185
Strasbourg Besieged	188
Street of the Blue Sky	190
Briefings	192
Story of Claude	196
Siege Notes	200
Cannonade	207
A Didactic Moment	211

PART SIX: INFORMAL FURLOUGH

Return from the Front	215
The Avenue Rapp	218
Plans and Proposals	220
An Informal Furlough	223
A Soldier's Tale	229
Miss Nausicaa	231
Reverie in the Avenue Montaigne	237
Terminations	240

FOREWORD

LOUIS S. AUCHINCLOSS

In the fifty years that I knew and corresponded with Leon our concern was almost exclusively with Henry James and his world. This was because our meetings, particularly after his move to Hawai'i, were infrequent, and I rather greedily took advantage of them to avail myself of any precious items that I might till from his encyclopedic knowledge of the subject. There was always a new book or article or even a new discovery dealing with the life of the Master on which I would want the opinion that he always cheerfully offered. To have wasted a meeting on other subjects would have been like gossiping with Isaiah Berlin. So, odd as it now seems, it was not until after Leon's death, at a tributary session at New York University, that I learned that he had served in the army in France in 1944 and 1945, in just the same period that I was serving on a U.S. amphibious vessel in the English Channel. With the result that his vivid memoirs of his wartime years have introduced me to a new and even more intensely interesting Leon.

The memoirs create a wonderful symphony of motifs, some blaring and triumphant, some soft and sad, some with terrible discords, as he relates his meetings and adventures in a France slowly and agonizingly regrasping her liberty as the Nazi boot is painfully extricated from her soil. Leon's role as a technical sergeant in psychological warfare—largely as a reporter of the real war news to people long battered with German propaganda—brought him into contact with every sort of person in the streets of Paris and Strasbourg: resistance fighters, both true and phony, American GIs, bored, homesick and sex hungry, collaborationists and anti-Semites, heroic victims of Nazi brutality, prostitutes yearning for a better life, old friends from peacetime sometimes looking a bit odd in uniform, reporters from Leon's newspaper days, and former professors parched for intellectual diversion. Leon lets them tell their stories: some gruesome, some pathetic, some shameful, some inspiring—all interesting. Peace and victory loom ahead, but in the stormy interval one may always be shot by a sniper. France is like a house that has been partially wrecked by a tornado; the foundations may be intact, but the roof is off and a wall is down and a good many seamy closets have been exposed.

War is notoriously made up of even more boredom than terror, caused by the endless waiting between assignments. Leon, like many intellectuals in uniform, did not always delight in the constant company of men to whom his fields of interest were at best boring and at worst anathema. I myself, after four years in the navy amid the endless chatter of obscenity and sex, developed a distinct aversion to four-letter words. But Leon used his gobs of spare time to make careful note of his companions, and his book is the richer for it. One of the compensations for exposure to philistia is the greater appreciation it gives one of the advantages that in peacetime one tended to take for granted. I and another officer of our LST spent the long hours at anchor waiting for orders to sail reading aloud (taking the speeches in turn) all of Shakespeare's thirty-seven plays, all of Webster and Marlowe, and a sizable chunk of Beaumont and Fletcher. Would we have done that before Pearl Harbor?

Leon had already started before the war on his lifelong study of James and James's world, and the project of the great five-volume biography was forming in his mind. The memoirs are studded with significant glimpses of the Master on his visits to Paris, brought to mind when the author finds himself in one of the areas of his stay. The idea of James and his fiction permeates the memoirs as a kind of beguiling leit-motif to remind the reader that there may still be beautiful things to come after Armageddon, however unlikely it may seem and however unlike any possible post-war world the world of James might be.

ACKNOWLEDGMENTS

MARJORIE EDEL

In August of 1944, as he prepared to enter Paris with de Gaulle, Leon Edel jotted down in his diary a chapter outline for his wartime experiences that matches closely the sequence found in this book. He returned to that outline frequently during the following half-century, although it was not until the mid-70s, when his biography of Henry James was finished, that he began working on these memoirs in earnest.

He clearly wanted to write a wartime narrative. Receiving his draft notice would begin the story, and VE Day would close it. But as he explains in his introduction, his reflections on key moments during the war often led him back to the days of his Paris youth, and to other times scattered through his life as well. His wishes for both the content and the structure of his manuscript have guided its preparation for publication.

Many friends and well-wishers have made this book possible. Frank Karpiel gathered together and typed out the entire manuscript. John Rieder carefully read through the page proofs, as did Peter Nicholson, who also carefully checked the French, including names and geographical locations. And Stanley Schab's editorial and design skills moved the manuscript smoothly through every stage of production. Special thanks to Dr. Richard Virr, Curator of Manuscripts, Rare Books and Special Collections Division, McGill University Libraries, for retrieving from the Edel Archive many of the photographs appearing in this volume.

I want to thank Craig Howes especially for his expert and continual help and his unfailing enthusiasm in the preparation of this manuscript. During the last year before Leon Edel's death, he taped Leon's thoughts on his method and materials. These tapes gave Craig a very special knowledge for his work as an editor.

I also want to thank Ileene Smith who contributed her expert skills in the final editing of this manuscript. Her knowledge of Leon Edel and his work created a book in which one hears the voice of the writer.

Others who have made this book possible through their timely and frequent help include W. S. Merwin and Paula Merwin, Michael Ondaatje and Linda Spalding, Louis S. Auchincloss, Lyall H. Powers, J. D. McClatchy, Marie-José Fassiotto, T. C. Wallace, and Russell A. Fraser.

Earlier versions of sections from this memoir have appeared in *Brick, Hawaii Review,* Lincoln Center's *The New Theater Review, Mānoa,* and *Yale Review.*

INTRODUCTION

REMEMBERING AND FORGETTING

These memoirs deal mainly with events that occurred more than fifty years ago, when I was thirty-five and in the army. Thus, this account of my experiences during the Battle of France begins as the personal war story of an intellectual who was trained as a combat soldier but who saw very little combat. The fighting was left usually to the younger men. I moved in the rear line, and occasionally along the periphery of the front. I was a specialist in what was then called "psychological warfare."

As I began writing, though, I soon found that however much I wanted to confine my narrative to the war, I couldn't escape my childhood and youth. I had lived more in other times than most of my fellow soldiers—and lived also quite a different life. I grew up on an island of British life in the southern part of Saskatchewan in Canada. My schoolmates were Irish, or English, or Scotch, and I was somehow set apart, being Jewish, even though my parents, children of the Russian ghetto, had shoved religion aside. My father was somewhat conformist, mainly because he was gregarious and liked to be with his fellow Jews in the business community. But my mother, while inclined by tradition to certain Jewish ways of thought, was an atheist. In depriving me at home of what they possessed, I was further displaced.

My uprooted parents also seemed to think that if I were "well educated" I would know what to do. The blessings of freedom would suffice. I simply wanted to prolong my youth, and be as idle as possible. I didn't ponder the professions. Instead, I pursued an undergraduate and graduate education in literature, first at McGill in Montreal and then at the University of Paris, which resulted in a doctorate and little chance for employment during the depressed years of the 1930s. Inclined to be literary and absorbed in the arts and in journalism, I proceeded to dream away half a lifetime. It was only after the war, in my mid-forties, that I turned to the writing of my best known work, the life of Henry James, and to establishing a career in letters.

While writing and rewriting these memoirs, I have also become increasingly aware of how the process of remembering is wrapped very seriously, and even uncomfortably, with the process of forgetting. War stories in particular have a way of turning into a triumphal march—a little like the way we tend to forget illness and pain and suffering when health returns. This revelation accounts for the shape of the present book. I have tried to let one kind of story beget another; one moment of experience summon a series of past moments. Forgive me then, patient reader, for jumping around in time, along with so many of the moderns who were my contemporaries. Marcel Proust and James Joyce and many of our poets experimented with scrambled narrative earlier in the century. It's actually the way our minds and memories work.

Let me therefore leap to the end of August 1960, shortly before my fifty-third birthday. I found myself in Paris, footloose for a few days before going on to a conference at Liège in Belgium. Many things were happening that summer, among them work on *The Conquest of London* and *The Middle Years,* the second and third volumes of my James biography. My youthful drift of the 1920s, when with a few francs in my pocket I had wandered across Europe, was by then ancient history. Now on an official academic mission, with an expense account and sufficient personal means for amusement, I could allow myself all the little things I denied myself in my youth.

I had taken a liner across the Atlantic, and booked myself into the expensive Hôtel Westminster on the Right Bank of Paris, not far from the Hemingwayan Ritz. I chose this hotel because it figured in what I was then writing. The sense of place is always important. Henry James had spent several weeks there in 1893 in the rue de la Paix. Indeed, he had been imprisoned in it by an attack of gout. I asked for a room near the top, away from the street noise. I had allowed for a half-century's renovations, but the basic shape and size of the room was still Victorian or Edwardian, and not least in the size of the bathtub. It could accommodate massive male or female Victorian bodies. I could imagine gouty paunchy Henry splashing in it with a big sponge and a large cake of soap every morning.

I looked out at *les toits de Paris,* with their obsolete chimneys and pleasing excrescences of red and brown. The view was peaceful under an end-of-summer sky. I was steeped in what James had called "the visitable past"—and especially when my *café complet* was brought to me at the exact hour I had stipulated: rolls, butter, a croissant, and a big bowl of *café au lait.* I liked the attention Europeans paid to their comforts.

Life without a plan—except for that meeting in Liège. It seemed the purest kind of happiness. How much of my undisciplined youth could I now recover in my quest for moments spent and forgotten?

PART ONE
TRANSFORMATIONS

I Am Drafted
Fort Eustis: Soldiering
Camp Ritchie: Military Intelligence
Camp Sharpe: Psychological Warfare

Spring 1944: Tech Sergeant Edel heads overseas.

I AM DRAFTED

I was thirty-five when I was drafted into the American Army on July 12, 1943. The century's second world war had been under way for almost four years. At the time I was working for a media oddity called *PM*, a newspaper which took no advertisements. It was printed on coated stock and sold for ten cents, a high price in that era of penny sheets—a kind of daily version of *Time*, but more liberal, pro-Roosevelt. I had been through a rather long journalistic apprenticeship starting in high school, when I worked one summer on a small town newspaper in Saskatchewan. Born in Pittsburgh in 1907, I had been taken in 1910 to Canada's western frontier by my Russian-Jewish parents. They had fled Russian pogroms, and in leaving America were fleeing one of the nation's recurrent depressions.

When on June 26, 1943, I received the draft board's notice, the formal presidential summons to serve the land of my birth, I was startled. Early middle age, I had believed, protected me from service. I also believed I had a double nationality. I used my Canadian identification documents in Montreal, and my American birth certificate in New York. But Canada hadn't called me, and in 1943, the U.S. did. I certainly felt I was nothing like a soldier. By inclination I was a pacifist, over-educated for barbaric struggle. I had a doctorate from the University of Paris, and certain literary aspirations. Besides, I couldn't see myself in uniform.

I could claim no exemptions. I was married but childless; I had no apparent physical disabilities. When I looked into the question of age, I discovered that the draft, which had begun with twenty-one-year-olds, was reaching out in both directions. Eighteen-year-olds were now being called, and some of the more up-to-date generals argued a motorized army could call on older men as well. And we now know that given Hitler's massive military force, the American military leadership needed large reserves. If the President wasn't scraping the bottom of the barrel when he summoned me in 1943, though, he was digging down as deep as possible. I thought myself—what with the stresses of deadline pressure, irregular meals, continual smoking, and a certain amount of indiscriminate drinking—to be rather a poor physical specimen, a possible disgrace to any uniform. As a newsman, I at one time had acquired a duodenal ulcer, and more recently was showing signs of a tachycardic heart. Still, I could be considered as ripe as the young for certain kinds of service. How ripe remained to be seen.

* * * * *

On July 9, when I reported for induction, the doctors took my medical history. Naked in the chilly cubbyholes where I was examined, I moved from one doctor to another. My bodily orifices were inspected. I was pounded and tapped—auscultated was their word—and generally pronounced healthy. The ulcer history didn't bother them. I telephoned my newspaper to say I was in the Army's clutches.

I was escorted with some fellow recruits to an army hospital at Fort Jay, on Governors Island off the southern tip of Manhattan, for X-rays. We wore purple hospital robes and swapped stories about draft boards, draft dodging, exemptions, fantasy options. My companions were young —truck drivers, blue-collar workers, and a Brooklyn taxi driver, an Englishman. I was the only "intellectual" among them. One young man, I think a salesman, who knew he was a serious ulcer case, passed around forbidden fruit that might underline his disability—a box of excellent cigars, and a bottle of whiskey. Since we weren't patients, the nurses paid little attention to us. With a wink at me as he lit his second cigar, the young man said, "Good for what ails you, eh?" The idea wouldn't have occurred to my impractical self. Still, I took his suggestion. I cautiously puffed to see what a good capitalistic cigar would do to me, and sipped my whiskey gratefully. The next morning, when we were X-rayed, the young man was promptly dismissed. As for me, I drank the prescribed barium, faced the fluoroscope, and was pronounced fit.

I had mixed feelings, and an inner sense of alarm. Nor was the fear of a possible battlefield softened by the realization that violent deaths also awaited civilians in the bombed cities. I filled out forms. Then we were escorted to a large bare room, where we were lined up and took the oath of allegiance. I had never before taken a loyalty oath. In Canada we simply sang "God Save the King." I felt a bit of a fraud as I repeated

America's solemn words. My former loyalties were profound, and Canada had been in the war since 1939.

I knew little American history. I was well versed, however, in Canada's—the Old Regime when France had ruled; the Franco-British wars, with Wolfe and Montcalm on the Plains of Abraham; the defeat of the Americans in 1812. Earlier came the histories of the adventuring fur companies, the resilience of the Iroquois and the Cree. I shared the general attitude of superiority assumed by Anglo-Canadians toward Americans, and the insistence of the French that they were the only genuine *Canadiens*.

Moreover, I had learned during my Montreal years to dislike America's big business, its politics, its arrogance, and the general national boastings. The British parliamentary system seemed to me tidier, more civilized. In later years, I used to tease Edmund Wilson, a startling Anglophobe considering his saturation in English literature, by saying that in Canada parliament questioned the prime minister, whereas in the United States, it was the American press that questioned the President. As for the American tourists who came to Canada during prohibition, I considered them a bunch of hopeless drunks.

I was, as is said now, a Euro-centered youth. In my childhood I had been taken with my brother to Tsarist Russia, for a fifteen-month visit to my mother's parents in the Ukrainian town of Rovno. I had also met my father's mother—the widowed Grandmother Dina, who wore her mourning perpetually for Judah Leon Edel, whose name I carried. She looked like Queen Victoria. My childhood reading had been Dickens and the *Boys' Own Annual,* which was Anglo-Imperial (all for King, Country, and the Church of England), although Mark Twain, Louisa May Alcott, and Horatio Alger, Jr.'s stories about little American boys rising to success gave me an early sympathetic feeling for some aspects of American life. I had always felt myself, with my exposure to my polyglot parents and their memories of Europe, to be rather cosmopolitan. Though unorthodox, my Jewish upbringing made me feel that warring against the Nazis was self-defense. I also hated Mussolini and Franco, but I didn't consider Stalin as belonging in their cretinous world. I had always regarded him as a Russian tyrant a couple of centuries behind western civilization. A strange and even bizarre personage: a Marxist who thought himself a Tsar.

After taking the oath of allegiance to the U.S.A., I faced a gentlemanly young corporal, who asked me what service I might want to join. "The Army," I exclaimed, adding "Of course!" I was adamant because I felt it would be better to be on firm ground than on an ocean filled with enemy submarines. Nor had I any desire to venture into death-dealing airplanes: it was dangerous enough being on *terra firma*. The polite corporal, a graduate of some prep school, clearly thought I was making a mistake. He considered the Navy the most aristocratic branch of the services. Shipboard offered an exclusive society, while land fighting meant sticking your nose into the earth. But my choice placed me in the mainstream of America's citizen army, which is what I wanted. I was to be a plain GI, participating in a vast common national experience within the history of our twentieth century.

The corporal told me that I was officially on a month's leave "to put my affairs in order." What affairs? I assumed this meant I should make my will. I had no savings, no inheritance. What had I to bestow? And my marriage—seven years of aloofness. My wife too was Jewish, the only child of immigrant parents. We came together in Manhattan out of loneliness, into a disjunctive existence. Our working hours testified to this. I was at the newspaper from 4 p.m. to midnight. She worked in an office from 9 a.m. to 5 p.m. We met at odd hours in sleepiness and fatigue, out of a want of tenderness and intimacy. But our union was essentially loveless. Brief physical couplings quickly settled into distancing and silence. She seemed as forlorn as me. We were probably lonelier together than apart. My tendency towards a sedentary, reflective life did not accord with her fondness for hiking and swimming. I might say of her truly that she was a "good sort." If this sounds condescending, she could say the same of me.

We never managed to create a genuine domesticity out of our three little rooms, the one-person kitchenette, and the narrow bathroom at the top of fifty broad steps in our converted Manhattan brownstone. We had few meals together. We had minimal furniture. The bedroom was narrow and dark, the "living room" served for our limited activities. Its light came from a rectangular side window that looked down on sad backyards, a couple of wizened trees, and the dingy rears of other brownstones. We had a relic of a fireplace. On chilly nights, when we could afford to buy wood, we lit a cheering fire for a couple of hours. But the yellow flames merely created a longing for space and elegance.

A small room was attached to our "living room," I presume for the child we were supposed to have. I used it as my study, with its couple of shelves of books and a large, cheap, second-hand desk, the kind you pick up in New York after any election. Its drawers were stuffed with unfinished jottings. I still nourished the dream of some day becoming a writer. I usually got a running start—when I had an idea—and then lost my pace. My excuse was that my night work offered me little sleep. I didn't have the peace of mind for writing. What I really needed—the time would come for me to see this—was more self-confidence. At thirty-five I had behind me fifteen years of study, of competent journalism. But I had never overcome certain immaturities and provincialisms. I remained a country boy—afraid of girls, afraid of the world.

* * * * *

I went to Martha's Vineyard for a couple of weeks before reporting for duty. My wife couldn't join me—she had to stick to her job—and I confess I preferred to vacation alone. Before leaving Manhattan I looked for some reading, and spotted on a shelf the fat paperback of Tolstoy's *War and Peace.* Just the book for me, I said, laughing. I would choose that! I belonged to another age, and he had gone back for his subject to the Napoleonic era, long before his own time. I told myself the obvious: all wars are simply different forms of killing. Then I wondered at my bookish self, my need for books. I would do better during this furlough to chase girls. Many came to the island in quest of company. But I wasn't the chasing sort. I had a monogamous conscience. My intellect interfered with my senses: I had a Puritan rearing. On the Vineyard I could give myself over to the sensuous calms and crashings of the ocean, the comforting sun-warmed dunes, the call of the seabirds, the quiet descendants of Indians at Gay Head.

I sank into the Tolstoy novel on the beach, or in a deck chair in front of my hilltop inn, caught up in the human relations of his story, interwoven with commentaries on the nature of armies. Above all, there were the great writer's broodings on causality. I arrived at Prince Andrei. "Why are you going to war?" he is asked. Because he "must," he says. But aristocratic Andrei wasn't drafted like me. Finally he says, "I'm going because this life I'm leading here—this life is—not to my taste." Wasn't I—deep down—doing the same? For unknown reasons I now yielded to a national summons which I might have resisted in various ways. I could have fought it on grounds of my pacifism, or sought a medic's job. The draft, however, offered me a chance to escape from everything—everything save the threat of death.

I seemed more than willing to leave it to the government or the Army to take care of my existence. Another voice, however, whispered, "There are moral responsibilities in this life as well as material ones. What of your wife?" As for her, my departure for war could be no excuse for raising the subject of what our marriage meant. This belonged to the future. Now I would go and do my duty, such as it might be. Becoming a soldier was an act of colossal avoidance.

* * * * *

I returned from the Vineyard and spent a few anxious days, mostly alone, deep in my fancies. I sorted my few books, looked into the desk drawer filled with unfinished writings, and closed it promptly. Would I ever see it again? I postponed my farewell to my parents to the last minute. They lived in a small detached apartment in my brother's house in Queens. A longish subway ride. The cars were half empty. I traveled as if I too were empty of all feeling save a melancholy that had seeped into my bones. I tried more agreeable thoughts. The rattling subway reminded me of a little journey four months earlier to Bryn Mawr in Pennsylvania. I had been invited to say a few words about Henry James at the noted women's college—the first occasion when an institution took note of my earlier Jamesian writings. The centenary of James's birth was being observed, and the college took pride in being one of the very few in America that obtained a commencement lecture from the novelist in 1905, during his much publicized return to the U.S. My mind suddenly sees the face of a youngish poet named Wystan Auden, also invited on that occasion to read a recent poem describing his feelings at the Cambridge grave of Henry James. My notes say I found him "a sort of codfish Englishman seeming only half interested and in reality rather bored." But I add "I think this must be a mask. Every now and then a rather likable face pushes through." My talk was brief and full of my earliest affection for James, long before I decided to write his life. I felt it to be an irony that I was leaving for the Army at the moment when a revival in James's reputation was beginning.

The hour spent with my parents. Both had fright in their eyes. Their oldest son was ending up a soldier, and soldiers still meant to them the marauding Tsarist military that killed Jews. Mother was dry-eyed but full of doom; my father's gentle words were a request that I write often and take good care of myself. They kissed me; they cried. My younger brother wasn't present—he was detained at City College, where he taught philosophy. We exchanged farewells by phone.

I awoke early the next day, August 2, 1943, placed a few essentials plus the bulging Tolstoy in a small container. My wife and I had little to say to one another. We silently drank coffee, adrift in our divided selves. I managed to consume a piece of dry toast. I blurted out a good-bye, then gave her a frozen kiss, which she returned. As I descended the long stairway, I heard the door click shut. The subway was noisily crowded. Early morning New York was going to work. I was going to a war. Pennsylvania Station wasn't far away. Twenty minutes later I descended stairs to the lower floor. Draftees drifted in—sad, silent faces. Some of the men fell asleep. I attempted to go on with Tolstoy. But my eyes refused to be attentive.

An hour or two later a Long Island train turned up. My eyes watched passing fields and houses, till I somehow became the train, and its monotonous clatter. Then, at some point in the early afternoon, for a split second I saw a small pool of water, gleaming in the middle distance. A single moment of brightness, piercing the day's frozen feelings. Years later in the Hague, I would seek out Vermeer's view of the city of Delft. A painted little patch of yellow wall, which Proust mentions in his great novel of remembrance, reached out for my eyes. And suddenly, so too did that little reflecting puddle, glimpsed at the first hour of military initiation. Memory at work.

At Long Island's Camp Upton fate intervened. I recognized a man behind a desk. He was drafted from my newspaper, where he worked in the legal department. He left his desk, told me to stick to this line, and he would take care of me. "We must put down every particular," he said, "It can make a great difference." My education, my journalism, the languages I speak, all aspects of my career, my Franco-Canadian background. He lingered over details. What was my salary at the paper? The Army needed to know. He particularly emphasized my being a linguist. He kept others waiting—"There, we've got you properly identified." He wished me luck. After this—it was now late afternoon and I was exhausted—we were conducted into a classroom. "A little exam," said a fat staff sergeant, "You're back in school." He handed me a printed form.

I'd never taken an IQ test before. I started plodding through the questions, answering them in their sequence. Later I learned this was a mistake. You were meant to skip around. No time to ponder. Before long a buzzer sounded. I was only half finished. I knew I'd failed. I asked an officer if I would be able to take it again. He said yes. I should apply as soon as I got to the next camp.

The following morning we're once more on a train. I now have a duffel bag full of gear. I'm dressed in khaki. My external transformation seems complete. I have the outer appearance of a soldier: my military education is about to begin.

FORT EUSTIS: SOLDIERING

My recollections of Fort Eustis in Virginia are as fragmentary as those of my childhood. A narrow barracks: bunks, footlockers, a row of unpartitioned toilets, a small shower room in which we jostle one another under cold spray. We feed in a large wooden building filled with clattering plates and buzzing flies. Sticky flypaper dangles from the ceiling, but makes no apparent dent in the fly population.

During our first days we drilled all afternoon in a steaming field of stubble under a southern sun. Our drill sergeant was foul-mouthed and sadistic. We marched non-stop in various formations, and were dressed down brutally if, blinded by sweat, we stumbled or took a wrong turn. I developed foot blisters. They burst in their warm unguence, and the liquid soaked my socks and leaked into my hard new shoes. At the end of the day the medics taped the raw areas for my next day's marching. I moved in a twilight world. The sweat poured constantly into my eyes. Having been robbed of any vestige of independence, I was in a world of private despair. I wanted to weep, but I swallowed my grief. On some evenings, I wrote a few sentences to re-establish my relations with next of kin, wife, brother, parents. But I didn't disclose my devastation. I was reared to the stiff upper lip.

My evenings ended early. I could have ventured occasionally on a camp pass to nearby Hagerstown, where the young pursued girls or found prostitutes and spent a few hours in the local bars. I did go once, and found the town as depressing as the camp. Also my libido was at zero level. The girls were too young, and I never had an eye for the professionals who smiled expertly. After a couple of drinks in one or another beer hall, I returned to the camp. The sortie wasn't worth the trouble. In my state of fatigue and melancholy I could not rise to even this modest bit of freedom. For lack of anything better, I climbed into my prized upper bunk ahead of lights out. A lower bunk would have been claustrophobic and smothering, subject to the body movements of the soldier above. Near the ceiling I got a certain sense of space and privacy. I quickly fell into a deep sleep.

We graduated from compulsive drills. We'd go on long marches, sometimes at night when it was cooler. The officers recognized that the shorter men were left behind, so we were pulled from our plodding places and put at the head of the column. Our short legs now set the pace. The world became long avenues of parades. A rhythmic tramp of boots, occasional snatches of marching songs, as we marched into the nights.

I continued to rationalize our new life style. What the young called "chicken shit" was a reality, a part of the Army's need to make us obedient, to bind us to every command and to one another. A nation can't have a questioning army. When you fight a deadly enemy, especially the Nazi SS—supermen of cruelty, evil, and toughness, who are taught to crush humans as we crush insects—you haven't time on the battlefield for complaint or debate. In the barracks, I found myself arguing that there was a grand purpose in the apparent senselessness. I predicted we would achieve survival better armed with all that now seemed irksome and impossible. The younger men didn't agree. "You talk all right," they said, "but it's still chicken shit."

Though occasionally I was called "an old fart," I took that as a term of affection. Most of the time my mates listened to me when I spoke up. My being older—I turned thirty-six at Fort Eustis—made me a sort of father figure. I avoided preaching. As barracks orderly, I devoted much of my time to conserving the hot water. I walked up and down the row of sinks, turning the taps off when the recruits were being wasteful. They cursed me when they were shaving, yet I was a hero at the end of the day. The tank was full of hot water at shower time, enough for most of them to get a good wash instead of the chilling douche of the late afternoon.

We lost little time in getting down to the killing business. The bayonet drill forcibly brought this home: a big sign said "If you don't know, you get killed." The officers gave us very little instruction. Perhaps little was needed. I made a mental record of the words of one older officer: "You're here to be taught how to kill. That's a primary function. If you learn that you'll know what to do when the time comes." A row of straw-filled sacks. Our bayonets were fixed—I forget the details. The officers said they wanted us to imagine the enemy in that row of stuffed sacks. We had to advance in hate and madness, we must scream. We must remember the enemy is threatening us—if we don't defend ourselves, we are lost. So we parry, thrust, withdraw. Don't drive the bayonet too hard or push it in too far; it's not easy to pull out if it gets stuck. Remember you may need the weapon to continue jabbing. I push out of my mind the spurt of blood, the spilling of guts. Who can envision that?

The reader may imagine that we practiced all that we were supposed to learn, and all that was supposed to toughen us. In reality, we were given lessons for a day or two and then proceeded to something else, because we had a crowded schedule. We did some crawling around obstacles. We were told at some point that we were being trained for anti-aircraft. We spent a couple of days learning about ack-ack guns, but didn't individually handle them. The bayonet drill, after a couple of repeats, was suspended.

An evening came when it was my turn to do guard duty. For the first time I wore all my gear. I was in fatigues. I put on my helmet. I carried not only my rifle and bayonet but a gas mask. I was to do a certain period of duty during the night, get a couple of hours sleep, and then do a second round till dawn. I was given a lonely stretch to walk and told to stay awake. When I set out, my shadow suddenly rose before me, as if I had been filled with hot air. It was portentous, massive, swollen. If I were shot I'd collapse like a pricked balloon. No mirror could have shown me my transformed self or my vulnerability better than the deliberate movement of my shadow in the moonlight.

* * * * *

I remembered to have my second try at my IQ test. This time I had no difficulties. I was relaxed and had my wits about me. I sailed through it. Then, a few weeks later, at the end of my twelfth week of basic training, I received a sudden summons to camp headquarters. The officer who handled my papers welcomed me solemnly, and said I was being transferred to a camp in Maryland. He described it as a hush-hush camp. This was mystifying, yet I felt an enormous sense of elation. There was suddenly a feeling of escape, a portent of change. By rousing myself from my passivity, and passing my exam, I thought I'd made something happen. An officer gave me a large sealed envelope addressed to "Camp Ritchie Military Reservation at Cascade, Maryland." Someone told me this meant I was going to the Blue Ridge Mountains. It was now October. I had been at Eustis since July.

CAMP RITCHIE: MILITARY INTELLIGENCE

The train sped northward through the autumn's russet, yellow and brown, a blaze of impressionism. During the past three months I had read no newspapers, so I worked my way through the *New York Times* and a copy of *PM*. The news seemed to have stood still during my basic training. The Germans were still bogged down in Russia. Stalin was still promising a great offensive westward, while clamoring for a second front. There were still assorted battles in the Pacific. I suppose this is what the French mean when they say *plus ça change, plus c'est la même chose.*

A young private first class met me at Harrisburg, capital of my native state, and escorted me to his jeep. We set off for Maryland, and the Blue Ridge Mountains. We reached Ritchie in the dark. Under weak lights strung along a main drive I recognized that I was indeed in an unusual camp. Marching in orderly fashion were half a hundred men, all in German uniform. They were not goose-stepping, but moving briskly, with an officer at their head.

"Prisoners of war?" I asked.

"Nope," my driver said, "They're our men in German uniforms."

"You mean American soldiers in Nazi drag?"

"Yep."

No further explanation. We drove past them.

At the barracks the driver handed me over to a sergeant with a well-trimmed John Barrymore mustache. The mustache had a name—Staff Sergeant Sagi, company clerk. He said, with a respectful note in his voice, "I used to read your stuff in *PM*." He was quiet-spoken, friendly. I told him I liked upper bunks. "No problem," he replied. In the barracks, my ears picked up a conversation in French with a Parisian accent, and another in Italian. I also heard some German. Sagi spoke to a nearby GI in a language unknown to me while I was settling in. He was quick to notice my questioning look. "You'll hear quite a bit of Hungarian," he said, "and we've also some Russians, Serbs, Czechs, and I believe a Ukrainian or two." He went off and came back in a few minutes—"If you're squared away, I'd like to take you to the mess and we can have a talk."

"Our barracks is a Tower of Babel," I said, as we reached the mess hall. Sagi replied the entire camp was that way. "It's like being in Hollywood," I said. "What were those marching Germans doing near the gate?" "Oh, that bunch," said Sagi. "We've several American companies wearing Nazi uniforms." I told him I thought they were prisoners of war. He laughed. "More likely you'll end up *their* prisoner. When you go into the woods for some creeping and crawling they'll probably capture you and give you a rough time. They help make things real. Everything here is based on a reality principle." He explained that Ritchie was one of the nation's most important intelligence centers. Also, since this was a many-nationed war, and Hitler had drafted men wherever he had conquered, the army had an acute need for intelligence-trained linguists.

From the first, Sagi proved a friendly companion. In civilian life he was a nightclub waiter; his manners reflected a cultivated courtesy and observant attentiveness. There was something of an anxious-to-please maître d' about him, even in the way he suggested we might dine together. He had a velvety voice, low yet always clear and precise. In the mess hall he took charge, and demonstrated that one didn't need to follow army style—that is, accept all one's food on a single plate, eat fast, and leave the crowded dining hall as quickly as possible. By coming in toward the end of the meal, we were able to have a leisurely and civilized repast. We made several trips, buffet-style, and enjoyed the savory soup, excellent roast beef and vegetables, and a well-baked apple pie with ice cream. Sagi demonstrated there were subtle European ways of establishing a continental pace in the army. He knew how to bend the rules and take care of personal comfort. It was a useful lesson.

Bit by bit he gave me a menu for my forthcoming stay. For the first six weeks, I would be a part of the slave labor, although ash and trash would automatically go to the brawn boys, usually groups of African Americans who weren't linguists. After this period I would join the aristocrats. No menial tasks; no wearing of fatigues. You dressed like a soldier on parade—with necktie, clean shirt, and Eisenhower jacket—and went to class eight hours a day. There were no tests or exams. You simply learned your stuff and were judged by your performance. Sagi enjoyed the idea that a great democracy's army reverted to a rigid class system. He said it was logical enough—you couldn't have politics on a battlefield.

On the whole, I enjoyed the period of our enslavement. I spent most of it doing KP, as a result of the sergeant overhearing me say to one of my broom handlers that our job was to move little piles of dust from one room to another. Irony is not appreciated by sergeants. This one was proud of his little world of floor sweeping and blackboard washing, of lining up the desks and getting rid of candy-bar wrappers and petty trash that the recruits generously sprinkled in classrooms. The sergeant felt I was mocking his goldbricking detail that worked minimally in the evening and had the daylight hours free. The next day I found myself reassigned to the mess hall, washing huge oatmeal tubs bigger than myself, and cleaning grease traps. Soon a cheerful red-cheeked young Pennsylvania Dutch farmer intervened as I struggled to get my arms around a tub. With a few deft movements, he lifted it as if it were a ballerina. He tossed it into the air, hosed it down, made it spotless. He returned every morning to help me in this chore. During the second week I was transferred to the officers' mess. Here I ended up doing decorative table settings, and seeing that flowers were replaced in the vases. The punitive sergeant who had banished me from the dust of the classroom had unwittingly bestowed upon me the pleasures of the palate. We ate excellent seafood, oyster, crab cakes with piquant sauces, and clams in their natural or chowder varieties.

The polyglot life of the barracks exposed me again to Europeans. I considered myself half European by birth and education, and the European young, now in American uniforms, made me feel how empty and culturally pallid the youngsters had been in the earlier camp. As might be expected, we had a number of German Jews, intellectuals who had been thrice uprooted, first in their flight from Nazism, and then from the Netherlands, Belgium, France, Spain, or Portugal to America. There were some talented German writers among us, a bit arrogant and aggressive, but always imaginative and intelligent.

I was, as usual, put off by a certain Germanic heaviness, an excessive use of cultural references and German philosophy. My preference was for a soldier like Sagi, who was close to the realities of life. My French, rusty since my student days in Paris, revived, and I felt happy with the Gallic intellectuals who possessed an abundance of verbal acuteness. The

Germans in Nazi uniforms were Jews, Catholics, Protestants—some very cultivated, others of peasant stock. Whenever we parted after an evening of beer drinking, they used to say "We'll be seeing you," adding a sinister tone to their words. They did indeed see me during field exercises when they played Nazis and captured me. The Italian GIs showed much depression. Italy had come apart in 1943, and was being reconquered. It looked as if their linguistic proficiency might not be used. Back to the infantry.

* * * * *

Early in November I shed the fatigues of my slave period and became a member of Camp Ritchie's thirteenth class. We had to appear always in proper dress and to look smart. Rules of status were as rigid as all army rules. We lived by the clock of our privileged position. Fifty-minute classes from 8 a.m. to 6 p.m., ten-minute breaks, an hour for lunch. We were given doctrine, methods, meanings, and practices of military intelligence. Theory was buttressed by field exercises. Our young instructors were highly specialized. Occasionally, an older soldier offered us the sense of an actual battlefield. Our lessons in geography—or rather topography—were consistently educational. We gathered information by studying maps or aerial photos. Suddenly the nature of the land, the contours of the roads along which we marched, the softness or hardness beneath our shoes, the vegetation, the birds fluttering away from us when we disturbed them, represented an environment. We were taught to dig foxholes and to crawl into them. All this was a particular revelation to the city-bred, and even to someone like myself, long removed from the Canadian prairies.

I also found myself involved in a sort of twentieth century "science" of warfare that had a lively appeal, especially with its sleuthing component. Like police or spies, we were sent out to capture one of our "Germans" and get information about enemy positions. We were instructed in the German order of battle, the details of enemy uniforms and ranks, the nature of enemy weapons, how to practice stealth in the woods and avoid capture, and how to watch for mines and recognize booby traps. We would be taken to lonely spots, usually on dark nights, and asked to watch wooded areas a mile or two distant. "Did we see anything?" the loudspeaker queried. Some of us did. A glimmer of light.

Yes, said the voice, we had seen the lighting of a single match. We would be made to listen to the firing of German weapons—their guttural or explosive noises. It was astonishing how quickly this raucous night-music fixed itself in my memory.

Late in November we were told to be ready for a nocturnal exercise. We would be summoned at 11 p.m., given a portion of a map and a compass. Operating in pairs, we were to be dropped somewhere in the neighborhood, and were to find our way back by morning to Camp Ritchie. The exercise was sprung on us toward the end of a day of heavy rain accompanied by blustery winds. I laid out my warmest underwear, my fatigues, and a pair of heavy leather Army boots. I decided on a light supper, and caught some sleep during the evening.

The gusty winds and continual rain were still rattling the barracks at 11, when we were given our torn map. We had a brief look at it before crawling into the truck. I made out letters at the bottom edge—

ANT. . . . . . N. . .

My partner, a Southerner, spelled it out for me—Antietam, the site of a Civil War battle the South lost—and said the N probably was from the word "National" that had been torn away. Many of the old battlefields were now national parks. In one corner of our map fragment I also saw a long thin wavy line labeled—

. . . tam Creek

—thus Antietam Creek. We would be near Hagerstown, the sizable town we sometimes visited on our excursions from camp. We huddled in the truck, which bumped its way through the storm. One man said the exercise was certainly "spontaneous," and another said they must have chosen the weather on purpose to give us experience. We all agreed that it was the kind of night we would have liked to spend in our bunks.

The drive was short, probably about five to ten miles, and when we were dropped we found ourselves on a straight narrow road. In the semi-dark the road gleamed wetness; water was pouring across it. The wind swept through us. We took our bearings with difficulty. The Antietam Creek was to our right—we could distinguish a considerable watery surface—and the water seemed to be nibbling at our road. We were in a wooded area, ideal conditions I suppose for testing our ability to handle ourselves in the wilds. We weren't supposed to light matches or use a flashlight. In all that wetness and wind it wouldn't have helped much if we tried. Our map was all but unreadable and bewildering. We had descended a hill before we left the truck, and we decided we should climb back up it.

We started at a good pace. My boots were a great help: the ground felt firm and secure. My companion kept talking about the Civil War. Suddenly I noticed the water spilling higher across the road. I could see it running through the vegetation on either side, and among the bottoms of the tree trunks. I turned around, and when my eyes got more accustomed to the scene, it was clear the entire woody area was being flooded. The water was suddenly up to my ankles. I was alarmed. "Let's get out of this!" I shouted to my companion. I said something about staying in the road's center and not slipping into the fast-disappearing ditches. The flooding creek seemed to be reaching out to take possession of everything—trees, land, road, and us. Simultaneously we began to run toward the rise in the road. Soon the water was halfway up to my knees. We splashed through as we ran, like swimmers about to plunge into an ocean. My heart began to participate in the race. It was beating very fast. I was frightened.

In distance the race was comparatively short; in time, it seemed an eternity. As we got to higher ground, the water gave way to a trickle and the road emerged again. As we neared the crest, we could hear a rough-voiced loudspeaker splutuering and coughing words that finally told us, amid the sound of rushing waters, that the military exercise was canceled. We were to make our way back to trucks waiting for us on the higher road. Then there was a sudden splash of floodlights. The entire scene was illuminated. Men silhouetted along a crossroad were waving flashlights. We were breathing heavily when we reached them, and when an officer checking our names waited for mine, I could only gasp and stammer. I could see the terrain we had covered and beyond it. The entire lower woodland was now filled with water. The army trucks that carried the floodlights revealed in the distance a couple of vigorous swimmers struggling in the water. Sheets of rain filled the air around us. We were kept waiting a long time—until about 3 a.m. Finally, the trucks took off for camp. It was good to get out of our wet clothes and crawl into our bunks. I fell asleep very quickly.

The Hagerstown newspaper next morning had a full account of the entrapment of Camp Ritchie troops in the flash flood, and reported that the body of one soldier was recovered near the creek. The death of a fellow soldier sent a shudder through us. It told us that no matter how well we were trained, we were children of chance, and that armies are ruled by the unexpected. I looked at a large-scale map of the region, and realized how fortunate we were to have been dropped near high ground. At the battle of Antietam, long before, General Lee lost 8,000 men and General McClellan more than 11,000. That had been a ferocious battle. All we had was a little skirmish with nature, but the name "Antietam" continues to startle me when I hear it. After more than fifty years, I can still see the panorama of the flooded landscape under the klieg lights, the sense of the swollen relentless water of a creek that had been originally a thin line on a torn map.

* * * * *

We graduated from Camp Ritchie on December 23, 1943. My "diploma" was a mimeographed sheet with a modest seal of the U.S. Military Intelligence Training Center. We were given prompt leave for the Christmas holidays. I motored to New York with four fellow graduates. We talked, smoked, joked, and dozed. At intervals we exchanged rumors that we would soon be organized into companies with a distinct war mission beyond the primer of military intelligence we had just acquired.

I emerged from a longish nap and saw the first signals of dawn in the cold sky. Soon we were curving into Manhattan's mid-town tunnel. After entering an empty Fifth Avenue, we stopped at the 42nd Street library, where in a very few days we would meet for our return. After the familiar subway ride, I wearily climbed the fifty steps of the old brownstone near the park. My wife, informed of my impending arrival, greeted me warmly. We breakfasted on poached eggs and muffins. Aside from a certain warmth in our reunion, the distance between us had widened. I judged she liked the idea of having a husband in the service, defending the U.S.A. against the fascists. I confessed to her I enjoyed the army. It was almost as if I had simply changed jobs, though I was pledged to secrecy about details.

We visited friends, went to the movies, attended a New Year's party. I spent some hours with my brother, his wife, and two-year-old son in

Queens. I visited with my aging parents, who wished I were back in civilian clothes. Mother had faded, yet she was still witty, harsh, domineering. She rode roughly over others' feelings. My father seemed shrunken, yet he remained his gentle self; he tended to love people and to trust them, whereas mother distrusted everyone and everything. They wanted to know what I was doing. I told them I'd passed through the marching and shooting, and seemed on the way to an army desk. They were not reassured. Soldiering meant wounds and cruelties—death. Father spoke of the doom of Jewish youths drafted into the Tsarist army. Drunken officers and rank and file soldiers considered Jew-bashing fair game; few Jews emerged whole from their training. They were killed or crippled en route to wider slaughter. Simon Edel escaped to the New World in 1903, and he spoke of American liberties as if they were the elixir of his long hard life.

CAMP SHARPE: PSYCHOLOGICAL WARFARE

We drove out of New York in the dark of the new year, a starry winter world. Our feasting was behind us. We reached Ritchie before dawn, in time for a sleepy slow-motion reveille. It was January 2, 1944. Sagi confided we would be leaving this camp the next morning. We were divided into two Mobile Radio Broadcasting Companies. The name emphasized radio, although we were in reality being transferred from intelligence to Psychological Warfare. Our captain introduced himself at reveille. He and the commander of the second company used the phrase *esprit de corps*. His pronunciation of the French cliché indicated he was not a linguist. In civilian life he led a jazz band; his presence among us was due to his radio experience.

I left Camp Ritchie with distinct regrets. It had been a lively little Europe, a glance back into my own cosmopolitan roots. We settled down for a long drive. After an hour we stopped. We were at Camp Sharpe, a mere fifty miles from Ritchie, parked in a muddy hollow at the bottom of a slanting road, just outside the national park of Gettysburg. The barracks were probably thrown up in 1918, after America joined the first world war, and were filled with dust and cobwebs. The windows looked as if mud had been smeared across them. Mice and rats had left their deposits. As usual, I took hold of an upper bunk and dumped my duffel bag on it.

The next morning found us in a grimy assembly hall. We sat on folding chairs and wore our fatigues. Our instructor was in a well-tailored captain's uniform. He was a European whose manner was aristocratic—Hans Habe, a Hungarian, tallish and strong-featured, fluent in French and German. His English was heavily accented. Our linguists said his name was the equivalent of his initials, HB—"Ha-bé." This was his pen name: his real name was Hans Bekessy. I had heard of a successful book he published when France was defeated, *A Thousand Shall Fall*.

Sartorially, Habe seemed determined to get away from army monotony. A white silk handkerchief hung out of his breast pocket; he wore a jeweled tiepin in his regulation necktie. A watch chain was visible when he unbuttoned his jacket. His hair was dyed brown with a touch of russet at the edges. When he ran his fingers through it, several gold rings flashed. There was something old-fashioned about this foppish man, who had an absent, far-away look in his gray eyes.

Once he started describing the nature of psychological warfare, he revealed a strange mix of Anglo-French words and expressions. "I'm here," he said, "to tell you some dopes." He spoke of "changement" and "groupment." He told us "how many innumerable" things he had to cover. He was forced to "condensate." Having condensated, he offered "a few additional datas." He was certainly a dapper newsman, and he took distinct pleasure in all the deceptions that could be practiced in print—the uses of words like "alleged," or "virtual," or the making of flat statements while inserting the word "probably" where the eye will let it pass. His family, I was told, wielded power in Budapest through publication of various scandal sheets.

He spoke about opposition within the army to psychological warfare. Old army hands regarded us as superfluous. Bullets, not words, were the staples of combat. However, the military had to reckon with the comparatively new media of broadcasting. Nations listened to one another as never before, and talked to one another over the heads of armies and parliaments. A special kind of communication was required if we were to reach our fighting enemy, our occupied allies, or newly liberated populations. This was the supreme and not very secret mission of psychological warfare.

The usual procedure would be for us to follow the tanks into a town or city and take possession of radio stations and printing presses. Our German linguists would conduct careful and searching interrogations. Counter-intelligence would screen enemy civilians who might be of assistance to us. Enemy broadcasts would be carefully monitored, so we would know what the Germans were saying to still-occupied areas, as well as to recently liberated ones. We French linguists would preach avoidance of panic, caution the French to stay off the roads, and circulate among civilians. Above all, we were to deliver to these areas sober and objective news using radio stations and street posters. Public address systems were also an important tool. Loudspeakers could be used in liberated towns to give out the latest Allied news.

Addressing the enemy required being more delicate than the daily newspapers. Though we had to hammer the German fighting man with a series of distinct ideas, the messages themselves had to be gentle, sympathetic—without betraying our hypocrisy—and above all as truthful as possible. Propaganda was usually associated with lying. Manipulated by Goebbels, Hitler's pronouncements continued to contain a great many lies; at this stage, they could be contradicted by indirect discourse. Instead of mocking Germany's air force, we could speak casually about having bombed a certain target. Gradually the prisoners would begin to tell us that Germany was not being sufficiently defended. Again and again, Habe enjoined us to be sensitive to the enemy's feelings. Our leaflets must be persuasive without being coercive. We had to treat our enemy as equals. They were soldiers. We were soldiers.

Commercial broadcasting had ratings; we would get ours from the war prisoners. They had been instructed not to discuss military matters if captured, but they hadn't been told not to comment on our radio programs. German POWs lit up with pleasure when asked about their preferences. They liked Marlene Dietrich's singing of *Lili Marlene*. They admitted to enjoying American jazz. Bit by bit a rough poll emerged, the reactions to our programs of our audience on the other front. Large numbers of prisoners would let us draw a fever chart of German morale.

Habe also dwelled in some detail on "black" stations. On a special wavelength, these installations pretended to be Nazi stations. Designed to spread rumors and gossip that we avoided in our regular broadcasts, black stations would offer false "good" news on a given day, make quite a fuss about it, and then announce shortly after that the news was unreliable, causing a letdown, and increasing mistrust of German stations. Handled by specialists in deceit, these stations also offered ambiguous entertainment and propaganda jokes. Those of us in regular psychwar came to consider them a dirty business.

* * * * *

We waited for some sign of our departure overseas. One very obvious signal turned up during April. We woke one morning to find two massive gleaming army trucks, one at each barracks of the Second and Third Mobile Broadcasting Companies. These were broadcasting and printing trucks especially constructed for us. I remember our astonishment, and our attempts to calculate the expenditure of taxpayer money to provide us with these chic visions of what a mobile radio broadcasting unit needs on the battlefield. It was a corporation executive's dream—an assembly of transmitters, microphones, and printing presses, ingeniously laid out within the narrow confines of the deluxe vehicles. The trucks, with their sleek chrome and plastic interiors, seemed like pieces of Hollywood science fiction, though of course we didn't dare say that.

Some of us noticed empty shelves and drawers carefully installed in one part of the ponderous vehicles. Our officers said this section provided storage space that we might need later for office supplies. In whispered tones, we told each other that here was heaven-sent accommodation for extra personal luggage. I bought a luxurious sleeping bag. This seemed to me the most practical item I could think of, and I placed it in the admirable conveyance. Our promotions arrived right after our custom-made vehicles. I emerged as a Technical Sergeant. The army thus labeled me a "specialist."

The activating of our two companies and our equipment was followed by a secret operations order from General Eisenhower. Order No. 8, dated March 11, 1944, was mainly designed to imply to the "old boys" of the Army that they had to accept the presence of an auxiliary arm dedicated to the use of broadcasts, leaflets, and other media services. His definition read as follows: "Psychological Warfare is the dissemination of propaganda designed to undermine the enemy's will to resist, demoralize his forces and sustain the morale of our supporters." In a model of explicitness, the Supreme Commander told his high officers that "The successful outcome of Psychological Warfare demands centralized control and coordination of propaganda themes and aims." He added that "any departure from this principle can only lead to ineffective or disastrous results." Subordinate commanders were told that whenever a specific use of propaganda was desired, the Psychological Warfare Branch at the appropriate headquarters would be consulted. Above all, Eisenhower ordered that "Army groups will ensure that all possible assistance is given to the execution of approved Psychological Warfare plans." Small wonder that among the heads of our branch, Eisenhower's order ten weeks before D-Day came to be called "The Psychological Warfare Charter."

In its stripped down form, then, our mission was to inform, comfort, and convince. In certain situations, in limited battle, we would be using vocal persuasion—a human, rather than bestial behavior. We would be substituting words for gestures. We would employ our vocal cords, aided by microphones and loudspeakers and various kinds of print, to send messages rather than death-dealing missiles. It invoked the principle of inquiry and negotiation, a tremendous step from the training given to us to go into a vocal rampage during bayonet drill. As I prepared to be convoyed to battlefields, then, I could at last rationalize my presence in the Army. I was now a "media soldier."

PART TWO
NORMANDY

Convoy and Landfall
Omaha Beach and an Orchard
A Month in the Country
Liberating Brittany

The liberation of Rennes, August 4, 1944. Inside the Mairie. Leon Edel, with M-3 and helmet, is photo center; the American soldier to his left is Morris Bishop (photo by Lawrence Riordan, Psychological Warfare Division, Office of War Information).

CONVOY AND LANDFALL

Our warship sailed late in the afternoon of a balmy spring day in 1944. The Third Mobile Broadcasting Company mingled with hundreds of newly trained and equipped Europe-bound soldiers. As we passed the Statue of Liberty, I felt the nobility of The Lady but also that we were surrendering the very few liberties left us. We belonged, entire—and to the death—to the U.S.A. I went to the rear of the vessel, and looked for a long time at New York's obtrusive and arrogant skyline, fading into the sad gray sky. We seemed at that moment a lone ship braving an ocean infested with German shark-submarines. I remembered the kindly, still young manager of the Canadian Press Bureau in Rockefeller Center, under whom I had worked a couple of years earlier. An experienced journalist, he wanted to be nearer the European scenes of war as a London-based correspondent. We had given him a drunken send-off party in 1941. He never reached his destination. "Lost at sea in enemy action" was the phrase that ultimately reached us. He disappeared into the sullen winter Atlantic.

When I first descended into the hold, and saw the tiers of bunks rising to a great height, I felt a touch of panic. The thought of being wedged into a narrow space, with men above and below me, made me shudder. The image in my mind was a torrent of water pouring into the hold. I wasn't much of a swimmer, and knew it would take a miracle to survive. Fortunately, I sought and found an upper bunk. Counting six rows as I climbed, I deposited my equipment in the seventh space, just below the ceiling. Beneath me was a murmur of voices, much coughing, a certain amount of shouting. The ship rocked us on the ocean, as if we had been returned to our cradle. When night came, a thousand men or more drew breath almost in silence.

The morning after our somber and seemingly lonely departure I climbed on deck to find that we were no longer alone. During the night, ships from various directions had fallen into line. We looked like an Elizabethan Armada, without the fancy sails and trimmings of the past.

The old theory of safety in numbers seemed to be generously applied. We were perishable human cargo, and the American war machines were assembled on a theory of abundance.

The ship's loudspeakers gave us a dull recital of daily news. When I told the Navy man in charge that we had aboard an entire company of news experts, he said "Be my guest." I could have access to the microphone whenever I wanted. He was ready to accept a daily roundup of events, some synthesis and commentary. I asked him whether we didn't have to go through channels and get proper permissions. He said if I stuck to the news he didn't think anyone would object.

I began at once, typing up news summaries and anonymously describing, as vividly as the dispatches permitted, the continuing battles around the world. From where I broadcast, I could see the men gathered near the loudspeakers. The occasion to do something useful for myself and my impromptu audience helped to reduce the monotony of our voyage, as well as to calm many anxieties. I actually looked forward to my daily hours in the little office the Navy gave me, and enjoyed my communion with the microphone. At the end of the day, I compared my commentaries with the official ones received during the night. Some came close to what the correspondents were sending the American newspapers. The date of the Cassino battle, which I reported on, helps me fix the time when we were at sea. The battle ended May 11–12. Polish, British, and American troops figured in the victory. I stressed in my commentary the Allied unity and power that broke the Nazi defenses.

Aside from this personal diversion and patriotism, I did a goodly amount of reading during our voyage, including for the first time Stephen Crane's *The Red Badge of Courage*. Though it certainly mirrored the psyche of the young around me—their fear and courage, their military bravado and potential cowardice—as a middle-aged reader thoroughly unenamored with military life, and with no romantic illusions to lose, I found the book thin. I also read a number of detective stories, and certain trashy novels I can no longer recall.

I also brooded on my own past. I remembered the long hours spent at my typewriter in the Agence Havas, where I wrote news stories that didn't interest me, yet which had to be exact and knowledgeable. One night I amused myself by listing all the newspapers I wrote for in Montreal between the ages of sixteen and twenty. Why had I done so much hackwork, when I wanted to do so many things? Need of money; my father never made enough.

We zigzagged from New York to the Azores, followed the coast of Spain, and made a northward diagonal up the west coast of Britain to Scotland. Our landfall was Glasgow. The train waiting for us took a long time to get down to a quiet town, Clevedon, near Bristol, where a many-roomed mansion was turned into a barracks. There were six of us in a ground-floor room that looked out on a garden. Fuel was rationed; hot water was available three times a week. We showered on such days between drops of hot and cold. Our clothing was everywhere in our room, hanging from the moldings or stuffed into duffel bags. We slept on straw paillasses covered with army blankets.

In the evenings we were free. I used to go for a walk to recover my sense of privacy. I was lonely, and self-consoling in my loneliness; otherwise I was surrounded by talkative fellow-soldiers, whose life consisted of articulation of their loneliness, a good deal of excrementary language, talk about sex, and chronic complaints about army discipline. What did you expect? I used to ask my fellow soldiers. Cushions, sheets, electric blankets, the kind of coddling they had in their middle-class homes? They responded it was all chicken shit in the Army. "That's what war is," I replied.

However much they complained, my fellow soldiers were enjoying the ride away from their generally mundane lives. They liked being taken care of. I could see even then how they, like the veterans of 1918, would look back after the war and call it the happiest time of their lives. I too enjoyed having no responsibilities. I could think my free thoughts as long as I obeyed orders. I tried to be the traditional good soldier, obedient and cautious.

Such were some of my reflections as I walked through the tidy little streets of Clevedon, which is situated among green hills running down to a winding bay, where tides cover and uncover rocks and sand. The best houses were built of stone, and designed to offer all possible protection against the sea damp and thick coastal mists. The people seemed quite as indestructible. I greeted the Britons as if they were my neighbors.

One evening I came back in the darkening light to our billet. At the entrance, I saw our commanding officer and an American major beside him. I approached, saluted, and suddenly saw the major, full-face. He acknowledged my salute, but his arm also was extended for a handshake. He was Louis Huot, an old fellow journalist. We had both been down and out in Montreal in the early 1930s, working for a small newspaper to earn a few dollars a week. Dapper as ever, Huot grinned at me from under his handsome lengthened mustaches.

"The long arm of coincidence," I said.

"Yes, Doc, it almost wrenches one's arm out of the socket."

(I had been "Doc" in Montreal, because the staff knew I had received a Sorbonne doctorate.)

Huot looked very handsome in his officer's uniform. He was a bit older than I, and much more sophisticated. A man of the world, while I tended to be withdrawn and meditative. I learned with surprise that he was the head of psychological warfare in Patton's Army; in other words, our chief. The captain treated him with a certain amount of awe, and also beamed at me. He liked having a man in his command who knew a significant officer. I wondered whether Major Huot would make a difference in my role in the Third Mobile Broadcasting Company.

"I'll be seeing you, Doc," he said, as we parted that evening.

A few days later, we were abruptly shipped from Clevedon to London, and put through a series of crash lectures, mostly by executives from the National and Columbia Broadcasting Systems, and by journalists from *Time, Life, Newsweek,* and some of the major newspapers as well. After fifty years, I no longer can recall that they told us anything of significance. I do remember one high "personality" with an attractive manner talking to us about the French underground, which he literally translated as *souterrain,* where the French would use *résistance* and *clandestin.* We judged ourselves more qualified to lecture him.

During one weekend in London, we were instructed to wander in London parks and carry out a covert opinion poll. We weren't supposed to ask direct questions, but simply to be friendly, and ascertain how these people, enjoying what proved to be a dazzling spring day, felt about certain elements of the war. I took pleasure in the casual talk with many sorts of persons, and was even invited by a war widow with a baby to come home with her for a cup of tea. She seemed disappointed when I politely declined. Perhaps I had shown too much sympathy. That evening, when we swapped our day's experiences in our billet, I discovered I was rather naive compared with the younger generation. Most of the men had a pleasant day for themselves. They then invented their answers to the questions. These, in due course, were evaluated and fed back to us to show how scientific our poll had been. Perhaps the invented answers did represent a consensus. The opinions of the GIs were probably as good as any other.

During our stay in London we were quartered in a series of bungalows in a suburb. I distinctly recall awakening on June 6, 1944 to the roar of planes, flying hour after hour in a straight single line toward the French coast. We knew before it was officially announced that D-Day had come. Within twenty-four hours we were on our way back to Clevedon, where I was told that Major Huot had chosen me to be a member of a small team from psychwar that he would lead into Normandy at once. The long arm of coincidence was putting me into the war zone sooner than I expected! That's what comes, I said, from knowing too many journalists. I was wrong. Huot was an adventurer. He was giving me a chance to share what turned out to be one of the happiest adventures of my service overseas.

OMAHA BEACH AND AN ORCHARD

Our orders came four weeks after D-Day. I remember a cross-country drive at dawn from Clevedon to somewhere near the coast around Bournemouth. We were three officers, including Major Huot, a couple of tech sergeants like myself, and ten enlisted men. We spent the better part of a day covering the engine of our jeep with thin layers of beeswax, to protect it from salt water. Then we paraded into a vast shed beside a huge freighter. At dawn we climbed aboard. The big ship seemed to crawl across the Channel, a dirty sprawling vessel. The sea was calm. On the third day, we sighted what had already become famous as Omaha Beach, although from our deck it looked very ordinary.

I searched the high ground for any evidence of landing battles. There were some burnt-out tanks and other exploded vehicles. The stevedores of the beaches, most of them African Americans, came aboard and unloaded our vehicles on what they called "ducks" and "rhinos"—different types of landing craft. The men were relaxed, and worked with ease and skill. We saw our jeep lifted aloft, and deposited neatly on the craft that would take us ashore. Then in the afternoon came the moment when we found ourselves clambering like pirates down the net ladders. I carried my pack, gas mask, rifle; I wore my munition belt, which had eighty rounds. The rhino was simply an enormous platform, rocking gently on the waves. At dusk we chugged slowly toward the sandy shore, and our vehicle splashed off the platform into the water. We were on Omaha Beach as if on a peaceful excursion.

We promptly set about removing the beeswax we had so laboriously spread over our engine forty-eight hours earlier. The twilight was deepening into darkness, and the sky lit up from time to time in gashes of blood-red flame. Officers arrived to lead our little cavalcade. I heard no shooting. There were no enemy planes. I must have suppressed a great many feelings—a mingling of fear with the consciousness that we were driving across a place of bloody battle. Tense and silent, peering into the dusk, we moved over the pitted roads very slowly.

At a crossroads we came on multiple signs, a series of names concocted to confuse the enemy if it turned up in this area. Under the starlit sky, sheeted recurrently in flame, we found ourselves on a hill, in an apple orchard. It must have been July 7, 1944, because we were told we had arrived on D-Day plus 31. In the orchard among the stubby trees we settled down in the dark, in general disorder. War correspondents were a short distance from us in another orchard. The major said we'd better eat our K rations and get some sleep. I volunteered for guard duty. In my middle-aged awareness of being face to face with actual war, I had a wide-awake nervous system.

The orchard was at the top of a long slope. I saw the gleam of a narrow stream to our right. Beyond it, cows moved like ghostly hulks, making guttural noises. The animals had been moved into an adjoining field to make room for soldier-animals like us. At the bottom of the slope, I saw dimly a typical two-story French country house. It was dark and shuttered.

I inspected the area of my night duty, remembering how frightened I had been by my own shadow the first time I mounted guard at Fort Eustis. My metamorphosis was complete. No longer my civilian self, I was some kind of military creature. All was country silence—only an occasional distant rumble, and a flashing magenta sky. I might have been in a theater where someone was monkeying with the stage lights. They came on briefly, and then the enveloping darkness returned. My job was to stay awake, and be prepared in case an enemy tank lumbered into our field or orchard, or some enemy planes swooped over to do a little machine-gunning. No one told me what to do.

I knew where I was. It was Normandy—the Normandy I had known during my student days in France in the late 1920s. Somewhere beyond, men were being killed, planes were tumbling out of the air, towns were in flames, citizens being shot by Nazis. Jittery, filled with chaotic imaginings, I heard lowing cattle in the distance. I walked slowly and cautiously around the edge of the orchard for two hours—along the bank of the night-gleaming stream, down to the large country house at the bottom of the hill, and then up again, under large enclosing trees. I remained in a state of nervous alert. My footsteps and senses responded to a heavy darkness, broken by patches of dim light. A sleeping life surrounded me—the young under the apple trees, and the cows in the adjoining field, with their deep reverberating mooing. I could smell the damp earth, the leaves, the river, and the turds, especially when I stepped into them. From the top of the hill, off on one side, a variety of sounds reached me. A match flared in the war correspondents' camp, as someone lit a cigarette. At Camp Ritchie, we'd been taught that a lighted match in wooded darkness can be visible to an enemy miles away. The newsmen apparently weren't briefed. Little details like this one passed through my mind. "This is war," I kept saying to myself, "you're really in a war." In the distance, in the intermittently lit up sky, I saw the reflection of a battle—the livid flames of Saint-Lô.

A month earlier, this had been occupied territory. Now the Germans were defending themselves along our horizon. Were enemy soldiers lurking in the woods? Would a plane suddenly start sputtering above our orchard? I continued my slow-paced watch. As we had crossed it at sunset, moving from dune to solid earth, Omaha Beach had been a scene of desolation filled with funereal emotion. Night sounds accompanied these visions, and I kept recalling my clambering down the rope net, loaded with my heavy gear and gas mask, and stepping on the gently heaving platform. *Treasure Island* came into mind, and I was a boy again.

My first acquaintance with Normandy had occurred in 1929 or 1930, when I spent a few weeks in a student hostel, a modern farmhouse set in these fields and orchards. The hostel had been established by a French banker, in memory of a son lost in the first war. I repeated to myself some of the familiar place-names—Carentan, Caen, la Haye-du-Puits—and in particular Bayeux, at the narrower part of the Channel, where the British troops were landing, and where Allied engineers were creating an artificial harbor. History beckoned as well. This part of Normandy on one side, and England's West Anglia on the other, had seen William set sail in 1066 to defeat Harold at Hastings.

I had seen the Bayeux tapestry, 231 feet of hemstitched linen, displayed in the Louvre in the 1930s—medieval knights in armor, grim archers, little cramped figures needle-sewn in eight-tone colors to preserve scenes of the Norman conquest. Below the paneled episodes, the anonymous stitcher, or stitchers, included peripheral events. In particular I recalled a group of soldiers—they seemed almost caricatures—tense figures with penises erect, advancing on cowering females, as if their cocks were spears. I could almost supply a sound track—the clang of armor, heavy swords, chain mail, and rapine. The Normans had to cross thirty miles of water to fight the Battle of Hastings, where Harold met his defeat and died in the fighting. Our modern armies thought nothing of traveling 3,000 miles across the Atlantic. A thousand years of history had changed the ways we traveled and fought, and yet nothing was changed.

A tap on my shoulder. A young corporal said he was to relieve my watch. I curled up under an apple tree and slept.

A MONTH IN THE COUNTRY

The bright sun made me squint. Naked soldiers were splashing in the stream, shouting the water was ice cold. Their voices told me they were having more pleasure than chill. I slid out of my fatigues, dropped them on the grass, stepped on the muddy ledge of the river, and was speared by iciness. The stream was deep right up to the bank. Gleaming buttocks, flying arms, floating pink penises. The men frolicked, and I, a city boy, a poor swimmer, bathed among the young. I found a foothold and a cake of soap. It was purifying to wash away the dirt of that old Liberty ship. Then I hoisted myself onto the grass, and used a military green towel to dry myself. Army green camouflage seemed drearily artificial beside natural greens. I pulled on my fatigues, turned my helmet into a sink, and shaved; my tiny mirror reflected a grinning fragment of my face.

Bathed in the sunlight, I surveyed the shining places I had guarded like a ghost during the night—the lively river, the shuttered house, the chewing, dumb-eyed animals. A smell of bacon and coffee wafted down from a field kitchen that had appeared magically overnight at the top of the orchard. I felt very much at home in this verdant landscape. We were encamped on its lower part, while the war correspondents were on the hilltop. But they resented the inaction, while we had a sense of vacation—a stay in the country.

True, the battle of Saint-Lô raged on some miles away, one of a series of struggles to determine whether the enemy could keep us bottled up in our peninsula, the Cotentin. (I would learn we wouldn't budge until General Patton landed all his tanks.) And soon, precise instructions came for the digging of latrines and essential points of defense—trenches of comfort and mounds of safety, in case an enemy should arrive in the field. But there was no sign of the enemy, and although jobs and contrived duties, which the men rightly called chicken shit, were assigned, our major was enough of a worldly man, a realist, to keep us only busy enough to preserve morale.

We gave him no trouble. Reveille was a formality, and roll call was easily dispensed with—we were so few in number. Customary calisthenics were set aside in favor of swimming. We slept soundly in our residences, regulation pup tents. We explored the farm, played games, took long siestas. The farmer said he was delighted to host an army that brought its own supplies and spoke French. For four years, he had surrendered almost everything to the Nazis. They treated civilians ruthlessly, took the greater part of his produce, and carted away such cider as he couldn't conceal to be converted into industrial alcohol in Germany. The farmer was hospitable. He fed us Calvados, and looked on in horror when our men drank it like whiskey.

Within the general frame of our organized life, I led a sedentary existence. I created a hammock between two shade trees, and spent wondrous afternoons. I read novels, from Walter Scott to F. Scott Fitzgerald, from Jane Austen to Edith Wharton, in the small print of the special Army editions. I freely meditated and indulged in rambling reveries, filling the woods around me with erotic dryads. I lived in a miniature Darwinian world of creeping, crawling things—buzzing flies, bees, beetles, butterflies, accompanied by whirring and twittering birds. The air was balmy; there were gentle breezes. The rustic life evoked agreeable recollections of my early years in Saskatchewan. I would wake from an afternoon dream and think myself back in Yorkton, where I was a boy during the first war, and where the trees were stunted maples, offering little shade during the brief torrid summers. Normandy was all slope, hedge, field, riverbank—and tall trees, such as I hadn't known in my Canadian childhood. The prairie was tableland, and the horizon seemed always to have been drawn by a straight-edged ruler.

In the late afternoons, we sometimes returned to our stream for a pre-dinner swim. Refreshed, we bargained with a mess sergeant for a few steaks, which we cooked on the grassy bank, dressed out with items from our K-rations. We sang, chattered, told stories. The prolonged European twilights gave us a sense of living, in very long days, an idyllic pastoral life. We had expected to be plunged into stresses and dangers, but were being allowed, during this hiatus between preparedness and battle, the calm of Normandy's streams and fields.

* * * * *

After forty-eight hours in our encampment, Major Huot confided that he was moving into the handsome country house. Some nuns were living in the rear, and the Mother Superior had the keys to the place. I readily understood the major's desire to domesticate himself, even in a transitory military situation like ours. He had always loved luxury and style. Later, in Paris, he would invite me to expensive restaurants, where he could display his culinary skills, and mix his own salad dressings while in deep consultation with the maitre d'. He also learnedly and a bit pedantically discussed wines with every *sommelier*. I wasn't surprised when I saw his eyes light up as he inspected the facade of the low-slung country house. Like many officers, he must have seen himself issuing commands from a handsome abode. He had earlier arranged for two tents to be set up on the lower pasture—one as our news tent, and the other as his office—and had signal corps men install phones. When he telephoned me from next door, I could hear him without using my receiver. Now, doubtless, he would set up communications in the spacious rooms of the absent landowner's residence.

Presently, the major asked me to supply some men to move him and his British opposite—psychwar was Anglo-American in the field—into the house. The officers arrived with a pile of luggage. One of the youths I chose for the job whispered, "We're being turned into bellhops." Another was more emphatic. He said he wasn't in the U.S. Army to be a batman to a limey. I warned them to stop complaining, or I'd report them for disobedience. They carried the bags and gear lazily and dumped them higgledy-piggledy in designated rooms. I went with them mainly to get an impression of the interior, with its comfortable furniture and spacious fireplaces. When we came downstairs, the major and the Briton were on the walk, smoking cigarettes and chatting briskly. At this moment, another remarkable coincidence. A jeep was swinging onto the gravel, and drew up beside the house. From it emerged a lanky one-star general; his star gleamed. He moved slowly, disengaging his long limbs from the small frame of the jeep. We briskly saluted.

Very quietly, he addressed the major.

"Are you moving in?"

Erect and precise the major replied, a bit hesitantly—

"Sir, we thought we would open up this house. The keys were available. It was shuttered and rather gloomy."

The general paused as if in meditation. Then he snapped—

"Major, are you aware that General Eisenhower has issued explicit orders? It's not our Army's policy to occupy houses of French civilians."

The major's face went brick red. He groped for something to say. The one-star didn't give him a chance.

"Major, I want you out of this house at once. I'm sure you can find accommodations elsewhere."

The general's long legs swung back into his jeep. We saluted once more, as his vehicle moved into the nearby road. When it was gone, the major offered a feeble embarrassed smile.

"I guess, sergeant, we'll reverse our procedure."

I turned to the two men, and said "On the double!"

This was a mistake. I could hear the men shouting and laughing as they climbed the stairs. The general had confirmed their hostility to the duty assigned them. With a show of alacrity they appeared at the upper windows, and before I could stop them, down came duffel bags, val-packs, and briefcases. At one moment I heard a sound of breaking glass.

* * * * *

On that same day I visited the group of nuns who occupied rooms at the back of the mansion. They had been installed there by the landowner, who had fled to Paris with his family when the fighting started. The nuns took care of the house—there were I think seven or eight of them. I found only one when I came to their little verandah. Inside, Ursule told me, was the Mother Superior, a large woman in a rocking chair. I wasn't introduced. Ursule expressed pleasure we could communicate in French. She had never studied English. She was plain-looking, a farm girl with red cheeks, and never looked directly at me, but rather at my boots. She had a certain spinster pertness, and promptly took an interest in my welfare. After we had talked for a while, she offered to do my laundry. She tried to do such chores to keep herself from idle thoughts. But she would need soap, since the Germans had commandeered all fats. I said I would supply soap for my laundry, and any other needs she and the other nuns might have. She then went inside to obtain permission from the Mother Superior.

To show my gratitude, I supplied sweets from the field PX. Sister Ursule, who always lowered her eyes, said she was praying for me. I told her I hoped she would pray for all the American soldiers who had come so far to drive out the Germans. Oh yes, she said, her prayers embraced all suffering humanity. But since she had made my acquaintance, she was bound to have particular feelings toward me. There was an undercurrent of flirtatiousness in her courtesy. She told me the sisters fled on D-Day, making their way by side roads to Bricquebec, the village nearest to us. She described the nunnery in Cherbourg, and to my surprise mentioned that the nuns were responsible for a little museum in memory of the Normandy writer Barbey d'Aurevilly. I astonished her by knowing who he was—Jules-Amédée Barbey d'Aurevilly, a poet, novelist, and critic. He had cut a distinct figure in Paris in the 19th century. The author of such novels as *Impossible Love* and *An Old Mistress,* he had been a tempestuous, flamboyant character. The nuns spoke with awe of the decadent poet. For Ursule he represented "Literature," and she added, "He was a good Catholic." It was clear that he wasn't included in the nun's reading, but he was a local celebrity, and they did their duty to maintain regional glory.

On another occasion, Ursule gave me a small St. Christopher medallion, a kind of additional assurance beyond prayers of saintly intervention in my behalf. I put the St. Christopher in my wallet. After a while I forgot it was there. Discovering it long after, I said to myself that if I were more religious, or more superstitious, I might consider that I had been quite properly and faithfully protected. I could never get the nuns to tell me how they lived under the Nazis. "We managed to get by," Ursule said, looking at my boots. And then, as an afterthought, she added, "You know, many of the German soldiers were good Catholics. They were devout and they respected us." She offered a modest smile: "I would say they were very correct."

* * * * *

A heavy-set German émigré, a Lutheran, asked whether he could join me in a shared shelter. Since I hadn't paired off with anyone else, I agreed, though I didn't warm up to his personality or his manners. He had been clinging to me ever since we sailed from Southampton. He had singled me out by informing me he used to read my reportage in *PM,* the glossy Manhattan sheet sometimes called leftist by conservatives because it supported President Roosevelt. We set up our pup tent, joining the single sheets of canvas each of us carried to form two sides, a crawl-in for the night. I would have liked a more cheerful and less interrogative partner. He was crude, literal-minded, practical, alert, and obsessive. An ideal army man one might say—certainly obedient, and if anything too servile. He made awkward attempts to find out my supposed leftist leanings. I told him I wasn't accountable to anyone for my political opinions.

After a while I began to believe he might be one of the Army's counter-intelligence men, acting as an informant on his fellow soldiers. One day he asked a question which determined my need to confront him. In his assumed casual manner, as if he had just had a thought that needed clarification, he wondered how I would feel if we ran into some French resistance guerrillas, and discovered they were a bunch of Communists. My first reaction was to laugh. "I'd start shooting right away," I said. Then I turned serious: "What kind of question is that?" What was he fishing for? Didn't he understand the French Resistance was on our side, composed of men who wanted to get rid of the Germans on French soil? These men had built up a successful underground composed of many political shades, and I was sure we'd be hearing about them, and perhaps from them, when we moved into the heart of France. Then I told him bluntly I felt he was trying to find out whether I was a Communist, and that he was probably a member of the army's counter-intelligence. "After a while," I said, "you probably will want to know also whether I'm a homosexual."

His face turned crimson, and he swallowed hard.

"I suppose I should tell you," he said weakly, "but you must promise not to tell the boys—I'm supposed to keep an eye out for subversives."

I rejoined that I was tempted to inform our men he was a half-baked spy. He looked at me sheepishly, but with an arrogant curl of his lip.

"I hope, sergeant, you wouldn't do that. I'm simply following orders."

I took a few days to decide whether to report him to counter-intelligence. I finally told him I wouldn't, but that he had better make sure of the line of questioning he used if he thought he was on the track of real subversives. I also told him I was particularly opposed to this in an army in zones of battle, and that I'd keep an eye on him. My final question was, "Shouldn't you be looking for Nazis in our midst?"

* * * * *

One evening, I came back to the pasture to find a neighboring farmer searching for me. He was in a state of panic. One of his cows was stuck in mid-stream, and was taking in too much water. He wanted a couple of soldiers to help pry the cow loose, and get it back into the pasture. I said he should be glad she wasn't drinking Calvados. "*Mon capitaine*," said the farmer, "this is not a joke." Cows were dumb. If they got stuck in a stream, they drank too much water and died. If the Germans hadn't taken away his horses, he would have used them to pull the errant cow safely to shore. I called for volunteers, and several GIs promptly joined the rescue party. It seemed an amusing diversion on a quiet evening.

When I saw the cow stranded in the center of the rushing stream, I realized it was slipping on the muddy bank. Every time it took a step, it splashed back into the stream. The farmer tied a rope around its middle, and we began our struggle with animal inertia. The cow wouldn't budge. The farmer used a big stick to beat the animal, but this didn't prove helpful. We adjusted the rope. Some of our men waded into mid-stream. We surrounded the animal. For the better part of half an hour, our task seemed endless and futile, so great was the cow's innocent resistance, and so slippery was its foothold. Then we marshaled our combined strength and gave a fine old-fashioned heave-ho. The cow gripped its way as we pulled landward, and with a loud bellow strolled off onto the grass of the pasture.

The farmer embraced me. Tears of relief rolled down his cheeks. He said it was as if we had rescued a member of his family. He escorted us to his kitchen, but what with our wetness and our muddy feet, we decided we would have the Calvados he proffered on his doorstep. I said it was an important achievement; any form of life rescued during a war contains a message. Life isn't cheap. I would recall this evening again and again as I came on dead cows and horses on some of the battlefields.

*****

There were fifty-five newspaper and magazine correspondents in the big tent at the top of the rise—an assemblage of well-known byliners attached to Patton's Third Army. I heard one newsman say, "It's a helluva thing to be squatting in an orchard when we're supposed to be winning a war." The press identified itself with commanders and generals, and only occasionally with soldiers. Its camp was strictly off limits to us.

The newsmen had to submit all they wrote to censorship, to remove details that might help the enemy. They were handsomely accommodated. We envied them. I also took a snobbish attitude toward these members of my own profession. I could readily describe their behavior in that tent without visiting it. They drank, they swore, they swaggered. They were vocal in their criticism of the delay, almost as if the war was being fought for their benefit. They were the guys with pencils, notebooks, and typewriters, who described what they saw—the soldiers in action, the civilians in agony. We were the guys with the guns. To me, the big tent seemed like the usual alcoholic press club one might find in many cities, now transferred across the Atlantic, and set up among the apple trees of Normandy.

Ernest Hemingway turned up in the big tent around the middle of July. I had seen him in the late 1920s, during his younger days in Paris. He was then round-faced, brawny, handsome in a large way. Sometimes he moved along the Boulevard Montparnasse a trifle tipsy; at others, he seemed submerged in a damp alcoholic depression. I recalled one occasion in Brentano's, the bookstore near the Opéra where I was browsing. Suddenly I heard a voice exclaim, "D'ye know what I got out of that book—Camels!" I turned round, and saw the young wonder of the literary world. He was holding a condensation of Lawrence of Arabia's description of the desert war of 1914–1918, in which camels played their versatile roles both as transportation, and when necessary, as food.

Hemingway breezed in with a captured set of binoculars around his neck and a Nazi map case slung over his shoulder. He had been writing about the Royal Air Force for *Collier's*, a weekly, which meant he didn't have to file a story every day like other newsmen. The young looked at the novelist-journalist with a distinct awe. He was a celebrity, whose picture and adventures appeared constantly in *Time* and *Life*. Long before, he had written a novel whose title declared *A Farewell to Arms,* but Hemingway never could say that farewell. Arms and violence played a continuing role in his existence—in his love of bullfighting, his chase after big game, his pursuit of human struggle and extinction. He had reported the Spanish Civil War up close, and in *For Whom the Bell Tolls* he had turned it into a kind of Western.

Now he was in Normandy. The British Air Force landed him near Cherbourg, where he lived in a handsome rural house reserved for important Army personnel. After surveying the wreckage of the port, he was transported to our big tent and attached to Patton's armored forces. I think he must have been given a distant view of Saint-Lô. One anecdote had it that while he was on the periphery of the battle a shell exploded a few feet away. Neither Hemingway nor the two-star general he was speaking to bothered to turn their heads to look at the crater. The general asked why he had come when he didn't have to, and Hemingway replied, "I got war fever like the measles." Such stories floated around our camp.

As I write this, I have surrounded myself with biographies of Hemingway to find out where in Normandy the novelist went. The books do not give a coherent account, and the events he recorded in letters seem to place him all over Normandy. He visited a few infantry areas near Saint-Lô, and then went on to Mont-Saint-Michel, where he ate la Mère Poularde's huge omelets. As for our location, one account puts him "in the blackout at night in that big tent in the apple orchard with other correspondents in their bathrobes," and another mentions a "gabfest," held "during the night we were lying in this goddamned tent in this apple orchard in the little town called Méhou"—actually Néhou, near Bricquebec, the village nearest to us. But Patton's push isn't mentioned.

While Hemingway was in our camp he decided he didn't want to remain in tank warfare, and especially during the heat of August. Tanks raised too much dust, he said. Instead, he got himself transferred to the correspondents covering infantry actions beyond Saint-Lô. He liked to be involved in man-to-man combat, the kind of fighting that didn't use heavy jolting machines. Hemingway therefore missed the sensational climax of our month in the country. It was Patton who liberated the Cotentin, including Mont-Saint-Michel and Brittany's capital, Rennes, and then started his historic blitz that took him beyond the liberation of Paris to the German frontier.

I heard more gossip about the press on certain evenings toward the end of July from a Cornell professor of French who wandered into our pasture looking for me. He had heard from our major that I was a Francophile. Morris Bishop was in late middle age, a handsome, sturdy, white-mustached man of middle height who wore shorts and army boots. A civilian employed by the Office of War Information, there was something distinctly debonair about him. We sat on the ground next to the river. Our talked rambled to academics we knew and then to French literature—to La Fontaine and Molière, Cocteau, Proust, and Gide. Was I aware, Bishop asked, that we were near Proust's "Balbec," just a few miles away? Bishop wondered what I was doing at my age in the Army. I said that was the way things happen. I refrained from asking what he was doing at his ripe age in the OWI. It was obvious. He liked action.

He was back the next evening, and many others. He seemed to want to escape from the upper orchard and the shoptalk of the press. We lapsed into French. I admired his linguistic accuracy, and his mastery of colloquial words and phrases. I told him I had learned the language by going to the theater and to movies, and by talking with fellow students at the Sorbonne. I had not been an avid reader of French books, though I read much Balzac. I spoke with a certain glibness, yet often without grammatical niceties.

Teaching, Morris Bishop said, was a very good life. It suited him admirably. I explained I had taken my degree after the stock market crash, feeling that I should bring back to America something to show for my residence in France. The depression interfered with my job-hunting and my attempts to get out of journalism. There were no jobs in academe—and I could have added, "especially if you were Jewish." Jews weren't particularly welcome in English departments at that time. But I didn't say it. It might sound like a reproach. He urged me to persevere. I finally asked why late in life he had returned to the Army—he had been in Pershing's army in the first war.

"I dislike fascism," he told me. "You could say I've come back to the Army in my civilian role as a patriot, but also because my language skills are as useful as they were in 1918. Besides, it's nice to get away for a bit from academe. And of course I enjoy being with the young. It makes me feel younger."

Maybe because his name was Bishop, I remembered that I had a miniature chess set. So our meetings ended with me sitting on my duffel bag, and Bishop in a rickety chair I found at the farmhouse, the small peg-board between us, indulging in the strategies of the feudals and their pawns. He played a good steady cautious game; I was often careless, and invariably checkmated. Whenever I think of our month in the country,

I remember the courtly Morris Bishop and our war games on a chessboard, played in peace and tranquillity during the last days of the battle for Saint-Lô.

*****

There were days when we obtained transportation from the corporal in charge of the vehicles for the press camp. On our first trip we decided to drive the thirty miles to Cherbourg. The corporal assured us that the shell-torn road was manageable. We arrived to find the great harbor, to which splendid liners had traveled in the time between the wars, an aquatic ruin. Ship fragments bobbed in the sea, and parts of sunken hulks jutted from the waters. As we walked the shattered streets of the town, the rubble crunched underfoot. We gazed at nightmare houses, the bottom floors shot out, the upper floors open and suspended in midair, the house innards a jumble of hanging toilets and bathtubs, and crisscrossed wires. We were spared the human victims. And here we were, walking about in the bright sunshine, while the indifferent sea, blue and calm, seemed unaware of the horror. We silently drove through the dusk. What was there to say? We felt lucky to have been spared thus far. The night calm of Normandy was untroubled; there were no more livid flashes in the sky.

On another day we decided to visit a neighboring village, a one-street town without ruins. We brought our rations and a supply of cigarettes for barter. Though the houses looked locked and deserted, we saw an elderly man opening the door of a bistro. When we addressed him in French, he looked at us suspiciously. Our French might be a German trick. He softened up after a bit, and said a number of residents had fled, but others were staying indoors with scraps of food, and trying to start life again. Some slept in the fields. They hadn't seen many American soldiers, being distant from the main roads.

We asked whether there was any chance of getting a hot meal in the bistro. When we gave him cigarettes and some powdered coffee, he became hospitable, and let us into his bare establishment. There were a few bottles on the shelves—local wine. Otherwise the place was cheerless and unstocked. He pointed in the direction of the butcher's shop, and said that if we could get some meat, he'd make a meal for us. The butcher brought out a few strips of veal in return for coffee. Entering into the spirit of our improvisation, the bistro-keeper brought up a dusty bottle of a superior vintage, and made us some delicious *escalopes de veau,* serving the meal with a certain amount of flourish, as if times were improving. He apologized for the absence of tablecloth and napkins. When we offered to pay him, he said we had already given him enough, what with the carton of cigarettes and the coffee.

Somehow this informal meal in the narrow bar remains lodged in my memory, as if it had been a gala occasion. I realized how in war one can find individuals trying to continue their lives as if nothing had shaken custom or habit. We sang as we drove back to Bricquebec, warmed with the wine, the seasoned food, and a sense of fellowship.

LIBERATING BRITTANY

The contentment of the countryside had filled my spirit, but a month in the country is inevitably finite. The battle for Saint-Lô ended on July 18, 1944. Patton and his Third Army in the Twelfth Army Group became operational on the 30th, and we were expelled from our little Garden of Eden on August 1. The news was given to us at reveille. I took my final plunge at dawn in our precious cold stream, ate half a dozen pancakes well saturated with maple syrup, and drank more cups of coffee than usual. While I ate, I listened to noisy excitement in the press camp.

It took us a very few minutes to wrap up our pup tents, while a special detail packed our "offices" and disconnected the little-used phones. Sister Ursule brought me the last of my laundry. I assured her I had my St. Christopher, and gave her several bars of soap and a box of chocolate bars. I wished her a safe journey to the little Cherbourg museum, where the nuns would continue to preserve the memory of the dissolute Barbey d'Aurevilly. She again announced she would be praying for me.

During our last moments in the pasture we made a pleasing discovery. Parked in front of the country house was the elegant and expensive ambulatory broadcasting studio and print shop to which we had said farewell in Gettysburg. We told the driver that we wanted to take a last look inside. Immediately, we made for the cupboards and drawers where we had sequestered our contraband. It was all there. I removed my bedroll and packed it with my gear. With continual stops and starts, we rolled down the peninsula where Hitler had hoped to trap us.

We swung abruptly onto a larger highway. What we saw explained in an instant why Patton gave us our rural month—an uncountable number of Patton's tanks filled the highway to the horizon. We were part of Patton's 4th Armored. The tanks made us—a small band of roving vehicles—feel like insects hovering around a railway train. I remembered that Hemingway had expressed contempt for tank war—a large cloud of yellow-white dust hung over the extraordinary procession.

We swung away at the first opportunity for the comfort of unpolluted air. These side roads took us to simple country scenes on the beaches of the Cotentin—the women sunning themselves, swimming, knitting, talking, while the children hopped around the dunes with their little sand pails. When I talked to some of the bathers during brief stops, I mentioned the aggressive assemblage nearby. They shrugged, and said they'd seen plenty of tanks during Germany's four-year occupation. They'd endured air raids, both the Germans' and ours.

The coastal road led us to a small hotel near the gulf that had been carefully checked for booby-traps. The exterior was pleasant enough, but when we got inside, we found wrecked furniture, stripped mattresses, and papers, magazines, and letters torn to bits, as well as many snapshots that told their silent story. They showed the Nazis embracing young French girls of the town. The soldiers grinned beside assorted young women, mostly of school age. Despite frantic attempts to destroy all the evidence—by the Germans? by the French?—enough remained to suggest that in this place at least, sex had triumphed over national feeling.

I managed to get a room for myself on the ocean side. I didn't feel like undressing, given the filthy mattresses, and stretched out in my clothes, carefully placing my new M-3 beside me, in case there might be some treacherous incident during the night. The automatic weapon was assigned to me shortly before our departure. It came with my rank. Long after the war, Morris Bishop, remembering Normandy, spoke of "Edel with his sub-machine gun, which he carried with him everywhere."

It was easy to drift off after our day's drive, with the waves splashing along the beach. The night seemed too brief. After a hasty breakfast, on a pleasant country road moving towards Avranches we got our first taste—or rather smell—of a battlefield. The visible signs: dead horses, their feet often pointing skyward, as in war movies, and a few dead cows nearby, some seemingly asleep, others in anguished positions. The phantom morning light sifted down among tall trees at the far end of the field. A few American soldiers emerged, shrouded in the morning mist. Moving as if in a trance, they were assembling bodies, mostly enemy soldiers. Somehow it all took place in slow motion. That is the form one apparently gives to something frightening, even when it is viewed at a distance, from a vehicle speeding swiftly past.

* * * * *

A few miles further and we were on high ground, high enough to give us a view of the Baie du Mont-Saint-Michel. I looked down steep cliffs as our road wound higher. Far below there was a gleaming spire. I recognized it as the fabled Mont-Saint-Michel. I had seen it as a tourist a few years earlier, before the war began. I later learned that at about that time Hemingway and a few other correspondents were ensconced in a little hotel on the rock, pretending in their particular false highbrow way that they had read Henry Adams's *Mont-Saint-Michel and Chartres*. My own memories of seeing it at sea-level, as a tourist years before, were of quicksands, and the death-racing tides. Then Mont-Staint-Michel seemed a construct of human defiance against nature. Now however I admired the jeweled structure for having withstood the wars of so many centuries.

We descended to wheat fields, mostly stubble, the wheat stacked in the large yellow bundles portrayed in Van Gogh's late painting. At the end of the afternoon we reached our destination: Saint-Aubin d'Aubigné, a village eight miles from Rennes. Major Huot greeted us. He was encamped in a shaded corner of a green buckwheat field with a woman correspondent proportioned like one of Wagner's Valkyries. I admired his penchant for action and romance. He was living out a Hemingway novel of war and sex, now part of the national folklore.

The major and the Valkyrie were having their late afternoon whiskey at a neat little camping table beside a neat tent. We tactfully set up camp in an adjoining field. As I'd done four weeks earlier in the orchard, I announced I'd take the middle guard at 2 a.m. I liked to sink quietly into a new environment. I put on my full regalia—gas mask, backpack, my M-3 dangling from my right shoulder. A large harvest moon supplanted the sun. The stubble fields were uncomfortable for walking. I suppose I should have acquired a pair of wooden clogs, still worn by the farm people. I felt a sense of exaltation at the nocturnal vastness, with stars in space, and the varicolored farmland around us. The stillness was occasionally interrupted by an ambulance speeding wildly on the road, its Red Cross illuminated, on its way from Rennes. Relieved from my guard at 4 a.m., I stretched out for a couple of hours. I was restless, and slept poorly. At reveille I found our vehicles drawn up for departure. The major and the Valkyrie were having their morning coffee in front of their tent. In the morning light, the Valkyrie's hair looked tousled.

The quiet surrounding us was broken by a powerful explosion. Some of the men dove for the vehicles. A second explosion, quite as loud and ominous, again shattered our hearing. A third explosion followed. Then all was quiet. No cannonade. No direct shooting at us. The explosions seemed to come from a distance, from the direction of Rennes. Major Huot appeared, and remarked a bit excitedly, "Maybe a sort of overture for us; but maybe also a finale." He thought it meant the Germans had blown up certain sites in the city. They always tried to do a bit of bombing when they abandoned a town.

We waited for more than an hour. The major returned to his tent, after warning us we might encounter snipers en route to Rennes. Shortly after 11 a.m., his vehicle drove to the head of our line. The Valkyrie was with him. For a while we proceeded peacefully along the narrow road. Instead of snipers shooting at us, small groups at gateways to suburban houses were throwing flowers. They shouted and made V for victory signs, à la Churchill. Some looked as if they were in their Sunday clothes. Others with eager faces were waving Allied flags. We remained watchful, in case we might encounter treachery. Bells were ringing. We moved through the streets of Rennes and presently swung into a large, almost empty square. We were in the Place de la Mairie, in front of city hall, across from a large theater-like building with a curved front. It bore a torn German sign. I read *Kraft durch Freude*—"Strength through Joy"—one of Hitler's popular organizations for young Nazis. A man walked slowly past us collecting swastikas, apparently to dispose of them. Our command car, its top down, was parked in the middle of the square. From where I sat, I looked at the low-slung balcony of the city hall. Two big French windows on either side were wide open. A nearby clock proclaimed noon.

The Mairie, or city hall, at Rennes was a large building ravaged by time and history. Looking for art words to describe it, I would say it was "provincial baroque"—it combined the Gothic with the Roman. Two soldiers were wrapping the French tricolor around the ironwork of the balcony. I was exhausted, and moved into the rear seat, which was filled with our duffels. I sat on one, and pulled out a little notebook to set down a few facts about our liberating Rennes. Morris Bishop, arriving at this moment, exclaimed, "Aha, writing history even before it has happened!" He had just been inside the city hall, and told me the Major was organizing an official celebration in the square. We would provide psych-war sound trucks and microphones. The Germans had fled. De Gaulle officials had ousted the city administrators, some of whom were arrested as collaborators.

I decided to remain and listen to the celebratory speeches. By this time I could see a GI hanging a Stars and Stripes above the French tricolor. I deemed it rather tactless to cover up the French flag. It made us look as if we were now occupying Rennes. The balcony was filled with official-looking persons; our major was talking to some of them. I also watched an American tank taking a position in the far corner of the square, a proper military precaution. A group of French Forces of the Interior (FFI) in parade formation marched past. They were in civilian clothes, and looked like disciplined minutemen. They took up positions around the entrance of the city hall.

The people of Rennes were especially eager to meet American soldiers, who seemed to have arrived from another planet. The men and women passed their hands over the surface of our vehicles. They examined the upholstery, and praised the tailoring of my uniform. They were delighted when I talked to them in French. They said they could hardly believe we traveled so fast. They had thought we were still stuck in the north along the beaches. They had feared street fighting in Rennes. "So had we," I rejoined. One sprightly old lady, erect and smartly dressed, patted me on the shoulder, and then picking up my hand, kissed it. I said she should be thanking America's mobilized industry. "I can't kiss that many hands," she responded with a laugh.

The square was filling up. One of our radio specialists, a gnarled little broadcasting assistant who was always asking our officers for the "lowdown" on our operations, stuck a German pistol into his belt, climbed one of the loudspeaker trucks, and assumed a Napoleonic stance. In his fractured French he kept the people entertained as he boasted about our radio equipment and our remarkable tanks. The crowd laughed and cheered him. This made him increasingly smug and pleased with himself. He continued to spout platitudes.

I was so interested in my conversations with the townsfolk that I was suddenly surprised to discern how many people there were in the square. Apparently the word had been passed along through the city, probably by radio stations still capable of broadcasting after the explosions. Lively young women asked permission to climb on our open car for a better view. I soon found myself surrounded by several, with a couple of boys squatting on the radiator. I had imagined we would encounter a starving populace. However, the crowd looked healthy and energetic. The department of Ille-et-Vilaine is an agricultural area in Brittany, and the farmers knew how to keep sufficient food from confiscation by the enemy.

Presently the crowd began to sing the *Marseillaise.* The Germans had forbidden the national anthem. Now the people kept on returning to it, as if they couldn't sing it often enough. Then the oratory began. Much of it had the amusing drabness and mediocrity of the fair scene in *Madame Bovary,* that ironic reproduction of provincial bombast. The proceedings became more sophisticated when one of de Gaulle's aides arrived. His intonations and vocal expressiveness had become known during the night broadcasts from the BBC. De Gaulle's name was cheered whenever he was mentioned. Roosevelt and Churchill were applauded. One speaker touched depths when he used the word "enslavement." France's four years of slavery under Nazism had ended. The people of Brittany were once again Bretons—and French.

The tone of the oratory expressed feelings no longer suppressed; the audience was constantly awakened to its recovering sense of freedom. The speakers were emphatic that collaborators must be punished, and with the rawness of that wound, the audience was emphatic also. At this moment it would have hanged them on the nearest lamppost. Indeed, during the day there were incidents and near-riots in various parts of Rennes, especially when some forty collaborators were found cringing in a basement. Prostitutes who were assumed to have slept with Germans had their hair roughly shaved—this was their badge of collaborative shame. The more notorious collaborators, when found, required police protection. Shortly before the oratory ended, the crowd became aware of a strange hum in the air, a sound that seemed to come from a distance, like the low quivering of a mass of insects, or some strange murmuring wind. The sound swelled and swelled. And suddenly it soared to grandiose tones. The hum came from behind closed lips, as if the music was forbidden and punishable. It was the marching song of the Resistance, the *Marche Lorraine,* celebrating French courage and the historic spirit of Joan of Arc. Many wept as they sang. Pigeons were startled from the rooftops of the Mairie. A flutter of wings lifted the music into the Breton sky. The spontaneous rendering had the solemnity and beauty of a noble hymn, or the thrill of marching songs of history.

The day of liberation in Rennes seemed to be endless. At 3 p.m. we headed for the offices of *Ouest-Éclair,* the city's largest newspaper, which proved to have a very modern plant with large presses. Assembled to greet us were reporters and printers, led by a chunky figure with wild black hair, spokesman for the liberation press committee. A case of champagne was consumed. Nothing was said about the newspaper having continued to publish under the Germans. We knew that the *Ouest-Éclair* would at the least have to change its name. That was a firm policy already announced in London. But such details came later. Our present aim was to keep news flowing to the people, to avoid silly and dangerous rumors, and to quell possible panics. After several speeches of welcome, Major Huot explained that with shipping devoted to war supplies, American bounty didn't yet extend to newsprint. We offered to edit a series of placards—posters, really—giving the essential daily communiqués. Psychwar's loudspeaker trucks would also broadcast the latest bulletins at street corners. With the restoration of electricity over that weekend, we prepared our first posters, which told of the liberation of all Brittany, including the key ports of Brest, Lorient, and Saint-Nazaire. Even after the newspapers began to appear as a single condensed sheet, the billboards were still issued and plastered around town.

At dusk of this remarkable day Morris Bishop and I found ourselves in a bistro. We ate by flickering candlelight, with empty wine bottles serving as candlesticks, surrounded by inquiring strangers and some of the local newsmen. The bistro's *patron* produced dust-covered vintage bottles from his cellar. We had gone beyond our day's exhaustion into a state of surfeited mellowness, what with our constantly refilled glasses and much civilized talk. We continued to hear what it had been like to live under a foreign dictator's rule, and how the French Resistance endlessly frustrated the occupying forces. Trains ended up on wrong tracks, when they didn't end up as wrecks. Mail was misdirected. The professions went underground. Doctors tried to maintain communal health. Lawyers did what they could to undermine the constant flouting of international law, and kept track of the jurisprudence related to the Germans' iniquities. Writers published clandestine tracts, and kept French poetry and fiction alive in spite of a rigid German censorship. The Resistance wasn't simply a guerrilla war army; it was an entire civilization trying to survive below, behind, and around oppression.

As the candles burned low and began to sputter, a stoutish man, slightly tipsy, stopped at our table and began to make crude remarks about interfering Americans. He was cynical and nasty. Suddenly one of our French companions stood up; he was tall and had long arms. He slapped this man hard on both cheeks. "You god-damned Nazi shit!" he said. The waiters threw the intruder out. Morris Bishop was disturbed as much by the face slapping as by the ungentlemanly behavior of the fascist. Everyone had been so well behaved earlier.

PART THREE
ENTERING PARIS

A Hermitage at Montigny
A Pause at Rambouillet
A Night in the Préfecture
The Hôtel Scribe
De Gaulle Triumphant
Musings and Memories
Carnival Without Masks
Captain Miller and the Place de la Bourse
Liane and Her Companions

A mon grand ami Léon Edel en souvenir de nos passionantes discussions pendant la guerre et la paix.

— Lia . . . Schubert

A HERMITAGE AT MONTIGNY

I had finished our work in Rennes by the middle of August, and wondered what my next assignment would be. One afternoon, wandering through the now-familiar streets, I encountered our instructor at Gettysburg, Hans Habe, now a captain. We adjourned for lunch to a pleasant café. He had complaints. Psychwar was being conducted by too many civilians from national broadcasting companies without a grasp of military propaganda. In his accented English, Habe exploded: "Some of them should be shot and the rest court-martialed!" He was still freewheeling in the Army. His uniform remained admirably tailored, his hair still carefully dyed. His ambition was to found big German newspapers. I would meet him again later, triumphant, in Bad Nauheim and Munich, with still higher rank, the publisher of the sensational dailies he dreamed up. They were sponsored by the American military government.

    Finally my new assignment arrived: travel orders to return immediately to the Cotentin, to a camp at Saint-Sauveur-la-Pommeraye, near Granville. I didn't want to leave Rennes. We had restored the news channels in the city; our posters were constantly read by groups of citizens in the streets. The newspapers were about to resume publication. I had a notion that we would soon be speeding once more cross country, on some further Third Army mission. A return to Normandy at this moment seemed a backward step. A weapons carrier was going in my direction, and I was summoned to get aboard in a hurry. I left without getting a chance to say farewell to Morris Bishop or Major Huot. I would never see the latter again, but learned much later he had recommended me for an officer's commission. I would see Morris Bishop at various times in New York.

    The trip back seemed to me depressing. We passed Avranches. The stench was gone; the cow pasture was filled with bomb craters. The Army engineers had been repairing the roads. We passed long rows of German war prisoners. The new pasture where I arrived in late afternoon lacked the charm of Bricquebec. No orchard or glistening stream, no ruminant cows, no Calvados-dispensing farmer. A couple of large tents set up on a grazed and trampled piece of land. I reported to Captain Fernand Auberjonois, whom I remembered from our work in the office of Havas in New York. An easy-going, smooth-faced Swiss-American, he seemed perpetually young. Our acquaintance had been brief, but he seemed to have remembered me. He had found my name in the personnel list of the Third Mobile Broadcasting company, and arranged for my transfer. It was a repetition of what had happened with Major Huot in England: my old life as a journalist seemed to be guiding my life in the Army. I told Auberjonois I was flattered that he had summoned me, but my voice couldn't conceal a note of regret. I admitted to feeling that I was moving backward. "Hardly," said the captain, "You're to serve on the task force that's going to Paris."

To have been named for a further adventure, and a very great one—the liberation of Paris—and to have the prospect of returning to the beloved city of my youth, was worth any number of steps backward. For now, we would wait in Normandy and edit a printed newsletter, a kind of house organ in French. "For whom?" I asked. Who would be our readers? Certainly not the farmers, the villagers, the soldiers. The captain shrugged—

"Don't you see, it's just window-dressing. We'll play things by ear."

We didn't wait long. On the morning of August 20, we awoke to the startling radio news that the citizens of Paris had taken the war into their own hands. They were attacking the Nazi garrisons. Meanwhile, French workers had called a general strike. Trains stopped running. The postal services were at a standstill. The police had shed their uniforms at the start of the insurrection, so as not to be exposed to German attack. The capital seemed determined to liberate itself. Paris billboards said: "All to the barricades! Organize, defend yourselves, house and street, against the enemy." The network of the French Underground had struck at a logical moment. The Germans were on the run. Their defeats in Normandy and Brittany, and the speed of the Allied advance, had given the Parisians courage.

Orders came swiftly. Our destination was Rambouillet, a few miles outside of Paris, where further orders would be given. We were warned to be vigilant. German tanks were loose in the countryside. There were also snipers—French collaborators who had served the Germans. I was in a jeep with Captain Auberjonois. Our driver was a psychwar corporal, an

American of French descent. Jacques Augier was a rather simple-minded little man, probably in his late thirties, with lizard eyes and mockery in his voice. He regarded the war as a picnic. When had he been so carefree? When could he chase girls more easily? He was light-hearted, fun-loving, and thoughtless, unaware of anything but the immediate orders he carried out.

* * * * *

It was August 21, 1944. I was put in charge of a recon, an army five-seater with a convertible top. Three German linguists rode in the rear. I knew them from Gettysburg: Conrad Kellen, a former secretary of the novelist Thomas Mann; Gerard Speyer, a high-school teacher of singular capabilities; and Oscar Seidlin, a witty and cheerful professor of German from a mid-western university. The captain and Augier, in the jeep, led our little procession. We also were accompanied by our mobile studio and printing press.

We sped along mostly empty roads from Saint-Hilaire to Fougères, northeast of Rennes, and on to Vitré, Laval, and Le Mans. Around noon we reached a wider artery. Moving at high speed, and with so great a sense of freedom and pleasure, it came as a shock to find ourselves being flagged down by a group of French resistants wearing strange mixtures of clothing, and carrying assorted old weapons. They announced themselves members of the FFI. Their leader, in a matter-of-fact voice, told our captain that some German tanks were dug in on high ground about a mile down the road. They had been picking off American vehicles since early morning. I experienced a spasm of fear. I think we were all shaken—this sudden reminder that we were still fighting a war, not enjoying a holiday on the roads to the capital. While the FFI explained the situation, our studio truck passed us. The driver cheerfully waved. Our command car driver, without a moment's hesitation, started at high speed after the truck. It was like a chase scene in the movies.

"Tanks ahead," we shouted, "Tigers ahead!"

The sleek vehicle did an electric turnaround. Meanwhile, we sped back to the French fighters.

The FFI men looked like hardy guerrillas, and they didn't waste much time. We could backtrack, they said, and wait somewhere until those German tanks were knocked out. Or we could take a bypass through the woods. I scanned the FFI faces. Would these strangers lead us to safety or into greater danger? Our officer decided on the bypass. We turned into a muddy road, leading into thick woods. We splashed through puddles over soft terrain. We were totally in the hands of these strangers.

I glanced at our German linguists, who sat impassively in the rear, clearly quite as scared as I was. I remember how my ears suddenly acquired a new dimension—I heard the sounds of our engines, the cracking of branches and twigs, a bird song, a few whispers among our guides. We were soldiers who had not yet had the experience of fearing that guns might open up at any time, and I told myself that a thousand variants of such situations—more dangerous and terrifying—could be told by other soldiers and guerrillas. During the unclocked minutes of our stealthy progress, I learned how blinding fright can take hold while the mind remains active and vigilant. I clutched my weapon. My ears and eyes somehow became centers of the self. And my mouth had a singular dryness.

At such moments, we seem to become a switchboard of charged nerves. I was in a world I had known only in dreams—monsters, shadows, voracious mountains, tempestuous waves. There was no obvious sign of danger. The vehicles crossed the wooded terrain without difficulty. There were stops, starts, silent signals from ahead. At times we turned the engines off and waited. Apparently, the FFI had been guiding vehicles along this route since early morning. There was no wasted motion. We negotiated the wordless trip by gesture—raised arms, hands on lips, signals from the advance guerrillas far ahead.

Suddenly our little journey was over. We climbed up an embankment, crossed a little bridge that put us on an unencumbered highway. Our guides showed us where we were on the map. We parted with friendly handshakes, gave them cigarettes, knowing we owed our lives to their vigilance. We paused for water in a silent little village. The experience had dehydrated us. We did not speak about our fear. Instead we praised the discipline of the French guides, their complete control. After studying the maps, we set out, more cautious than ever.

*****

As the fear diminished, I found myself looking again at the bright rolling countryside—the plowed fields, and the old men and young women at work. By late afternoon we had covered two hundred miles, following the fertile fields in this granary of France, At dark we found ourselves at a bridge the Germans had blown up with a charge of dynamite so generous it shattered nearby houses. As we studied our maps, some FFI men found us. They seemed to be keeping an eye on all the roads in that region. We told them we had hoped to reach the Château at Montigny that night. They escorted us to a side-road that took us deep into the woods. When we emerged, our headlights picked up relics of the feudal age: old houses with thick stone walls; an old gate which once supported a heavy portcullis. Then we saw an avenue of trees, leading to the Château. In the blackness we didn't try to pitch our tents. Our captain located the stables. There was plenty of straw there and a good roof. Our feet crunched broken glass. The blowing up of the bridge had shattered a greenhouse and some barn windows. We spread out the straw, shook the broken glass from the bundles, and made ourselves comfortable.

* * * * *

Roosters signaled dawn. At the end of the avenue we found a clustered village—one hotel, an ancient church, a café, and about a hundred assorted dwellings in short winding streets. We encountered children everywhere, little mouths chewing American gum or sucking American candy. While I was standing there with Augier, a middle-aged man with tired eyes, bushy brows, a full mustache, and a limp approached. His name was Beaufort. He was a schoolteacher in Paris, where he had taught primary school for a quarter of a century. The children told him we had slept in the stables. Why? There were plenty of empty rooms around. Wouldn't we like to stay at his home? He was in the Hermitage, near the Château's stables.

I assured him we were very comfortable in the stables. We had slept in the cow pastures of Normandy and wheat fields of Brittany. He rejoined that it was all the more reason for taking advantage of his invitation. He led us to the solid stone Hermitage, and walked us through an old-fashioned kitchen with a large open fireplace. A long table was being set for lunch, as if for a banquet. "We're basically an orphanage," he said, pointing to the children. "We have many mouths to feed."

He took us up the stairs to a big attic room with several beds in it. On the floor below were beds for a dozen youngsters. This unassuming, middle-aged man had brought groups of Parisian children to Montigny two summers earlier. In the winter he went back to Paris and taught, leaving his wife and others behind to take care of the brood. He had also worked in the Parisian resistance. He brought more children when he returned in the summer. He spoke of this as if it were routine. Wars create orphans.

He began to point them out. This one's father had been deported to Germany, and his mother was in hiding. The whereabouts of the parents of that one were unknown. Little Ninette, aged three with saucer eyes, made friendly faces at me, and reached for my mustache. Young Jean was reading *The Three Musketeers*. There was a sad little Jewish boy of about eight who was musical, and his sister, aged six. They would never again see their parents. Presently we were seated at the long kitchen table, feasting on rabbit stew ladled out of an enormous pot. The children inspected my uniform, counted my ribbons, examined the buttons of my jacket. The wide-eyed little girls watched our every movement; the little boys asked polite questions, with occasional outbursts of laughter.

Our host explained that the war made for a very busy and complex life. There were the German soldiers to be dealt with "on tiptoe." One could never predict when or where they'd turn up with demands and orders. They had a mania about radios, a determination to keep all Allied news from the people. A farmer nearby had hidden a large cache of arms for the Resistance in various buildings. One day his radio broke down. While taking it to a neighbor for repairs, he was stopped by the Germans, who were trying to find out how their food supplies were disappearing into the black market. They searched the wagon, found the radio, and promptly went to the farmhouse, where they discovered the store of automatic weapons. The farmer was taken away by the Gestapo and eventually shot. The Nazis returned and shot the wife and two sons. Two of the farmer's younger children playing in the village escaped. They were among the orphans at our table.

A bright redheaded boy of about twelve gulped his food, and brought out an accordion to serenade us while we ate. The Jewish boy, with curly hair and sad dark eyes, produced his small-sized violin and played a sad ghetto melody. His younger sister clung to him. The teacher whispered that the parents had been "taken away," and then he dropped his voice still lower: "We hid these beautiful children, and I brought them here."

The scene had a kind of Dickensian cheerfulness, in spite of the horror stories about the Nazis. Beaufort was consistently relaxed and jovial. He presided over the feast with informality and a certain dignity. I took away with me an enduring picture of human warmth and generosity. Here we were, strangers from a trans-Atlantic world, drawn into this life almost immediately after our night in the storm-drenched countryside. A thousand years of living lay behind that Château, and the war seemed to have created a particular communal life, a feeling of closeness in adversity.

Near the end of the meal, a priest arrived. He looked at us with laughing eyes. He was tall and direct, a man of strength and simplicity.

"I see you've collected some American soldiers as well as the stray children," he said to Beaufort.

"Our mayor," Beaufort introduced him.

"Acting mayor," the priest said. "You foisted that on me."

No one wanted to be mayor in Montigny during the occupation—no one wanted to deal with the Germans. The priest got the job without being a candidate. He seemed best suited to be the local spokesman and diplomat.

"You Americans," he said, "are really liberating me—you're liberating me from politics." He was going to step down now that the town was free.

* * * * *

We had a long night's sleep in the slant-roofed attic amid the country stillness. I think we would have slept until noon if we hadn't suddenly heard a great deal of commotion below—children's feet on the stairs, a babble of raised voices, and the radio playing very loudly. The BBC was broadcasting the *Marseillaise*. An announcer was proclaiming victory in Paris. The city was free. The French police were in total control. Nothing could contain the patriotism and fervor that swept the city. It sounded like the great revolutions—1789, the first call to arms; 1848, the tide that swept Europe; and 1871, the period of the Commune, after the defeat of France by Germany. Calendar dates imprinted in French history. Haunted dates that proclaimed the Rights of Man.

To the residents of Paris, the city *was* France. Our captain in due course reported that the BBC was distinctly premature. There were still

German holdouts. Snipers were shooting from the rooftops, including curiously enough certain Japanese residents, who considered themselves duty-bound to participate as allies of the fleeing Germans.

We had been ordered to continue immediately in the direction of Rambouillet. Monsieur Beaufort, surrounded by his clamoring extended family, bade us an affectionate farewell. I thanked him warmly, and for a moment he held my hand. Then, after wishing me godspeed, he said—"Remember everyone—but everyone—in Paris will tell you they were in the Resistance. It has become very fashionable."

I looked back as we drove away. The schoolmaster was leaning on his cane, surrounded by a few of his young orphans.

* * * * *

I have re-read my old fragmentary notes of our brief pause at Montigny-le-Gannelon half a century ago, and feel that they describe a fairy tale. Our refuge in the large well-kept barn filled with hay; the wise old wizard or magician, surrounded by war orphans; a spacious Hermitage next to a fairy-book Château of the Lévis-Mirepoix. I still have among my relics a fading postcard I bought in the town. It shows the Château on its height. On the road, a woman in a black dress with a long white apron leads a white goat, and a child in a loose frock and a hat with a curved-up brim leads a younger black goat. I count half a dozen turrets on the Château. The picture is real enough, and yet it evokes a dream of almost too much sweetness and light. It does not convey the hidden suffering of the children.

Beaufort's whispered warning that I watch out for lies, treacheries, deceits, boasts, and avowals kept me brooding during the hours of our journey to Rambouillet. Only later, when I was exposed to the politics of liberation and the ensuing events, did I realize how little, in the midst of triumph and flowers and kisses, Americans understood about how France had been divided. Vichy and Pétain had been a horror, a fascist nest. The younger generation—those not in the Resistance—accepted the form of government the Nazis had imposed to mask their unexpectedly swift triumph in France. The French were emerging from a long nightmare of contradictions and ambiguities. There were other nightmares to come.

* * * * *

Soon we were on the road leading to Chartres and its wondrous cathedral. I sighted on the horizon two unequal spires which I knew well from other years. Even from our great distance, I could see the splendid edifice was filled with light—its stained glass stored away, as it had been during 1914–1918.

After a short stop, we rode out of Chartres into the continuing wheat fields and the yellow sunshine of late afternoon. Off in the distance, across a field, I saw a young girl running toward us. Her beautiful figure swiftly crossed the furrows, her head held high. She was like the figure I remembered seeing on old French postage stamps when I was a boy. *La semeuse*—the sower—scattering grain along furrowed fields. Sturdy, with a round face and the sky in her eyes, she moved with beads of sweat on her forehead and waved us to stop. We did. I went with Kellen and Speyer to meet her.

"Forgive me," she said, "I simply want news. My fellow-workers want news. Is Paris really free?"

We said we believed de Gaulle was on his way to Paris. In a matter of days or even hours, Paris would be free. She smiled her thanks and wished us good luck, this pliant sturdy figure of the earth on which she stood barefoot. I took her strong hand in mine and held it for a moment. She looked into my eyes, then turned and ran back across the field.

Until we reached Rambouillet in the deep dusk, we passed through villages crowded with people—flags waving, cheering, flowers, the V for victory sign, ecstasy over the Allied vehicles rolling along in their unending stream. We saw crushed German tanks, and our own vehicles, shattered and fragmented by the enemy. Not least, by the roadsides we saw the youngest children, born during the occupation. Confused and still indoctrinated, they gave us the Hitler salute.

A PAUSE AT RAMBOUILLET

I awoke on my bundle of damp straw in a large barn near Rambouillet, thirty miles southwest of Paris. I climbed down, and looked out of the large stable door at sheets of water. A stormy rain-drenched morning. The rain beat down on a vast assembly of vehicles and tanks, pieces of artillery, supply trucks, bulldozers, jeeps—all waiting for battle. As the misty veils lifted, I saw an elegant, turreted château in the middle distance. It was as if a gauze curtain had risen at the opera.

I imagined the interior of the château, filled with young, high-ranking officers studying maps, reading intelligence reports. I wished we weren't kept in such total ignorance. Most of us were merely pawns—limited in direction, and expendable.

I found myself thinking of Waterloo, Austerlitz, Gettysburg. Through the thinning drizzle, I began to see old battles. Horses everywhere, splendid cavalry animals, trained, powerful, experienced in combat—replaced in our century by fuel-driven engines. The plumed cavalry were in movie-color costumes. I saw horse-drawn artillery, lances, swords, muskets. Or here were the plodding comic foot soldiers of the Shakespeare plays. The battles faded into the khaki green of 1914. I smelled gas, oil, and the fresh rain. This was the twentieth-century war. The old cruel and terrible wars involved human contact and fierce struggle between man and man and beast and man. The new wars asked soldiers to empty automatic weapons and launch missiles—often at invisible targets. It was a clockwork war, a clash of metals. Did Providence, creating that work of art which became Adam, fashioning him out of dust in an empyrean studio, intend earthy man to be dominated by a machine?

I found myself wondering whether another *War and Peace* could be fashioned out of this Second World War. I was like blundering Pierre Bezukhov. Where were Napoleon and his generals, or Kutuzov, the tsar's Field Marshal? Eisenhower was a modern composite of those leaders who preceded him. An open cheerfulness hid his worry about the lives he had sent into disaster.

Beyond the cluttered assemblages of war machines, fifty war correspondents gnawed at their pencils. Eager to get the preliminaries over with, they were impatient to write their grand stories about the liberation of Paris. Soldiers very early learn the lesson of patience. Closer to the correspondents than I was in Normandy, I met them outside their tents, and was astonished at how little they knew about the campaign, very much like the GIs. Few correspondents were willing to recognize the political dilemma of de Gaulle, and how wisely he was confronting it. He had to contend with the numerous organs of the Resistance, each with its own view about the course France should take. He would have to placate the communists, recognizing that they had fought valiantly. Few recognized the depths of de Gaulle's dedication, patriotism, and idealism, his fundamental belief in *gloire* and national pride, his solid grasp of history. Having "defected" from the Vichy-controlled army, he had refused to become a tool of the Germans.

The situation in Paris as we pieced it together from intelligence reports was as follows: the insurrection had begun in the usual disorder that accompanies an upsurge of rage, frustration, and high patriotism—a general impulsive plunge into urban guerrilla warfare. The war in the streets shifted from hour to hour. Young girls in flowing dresses on bicycles moved from barricade to barricade on rescue missions. The word went out—*Chacun son boche!*—and some of the descendants of Dickens' Madame La Farge proclaimed they had killed their German—those "little gray mice," as they called them, strutting in these exultant days of first possession.

When Eisenhower first received word of the uprisings, he made it clear that the Allies were not to be drawn into a battle for Paris. The Resistance was to be helped; arms were to be supplied. But the Supreme Commander wanted no state of siege, none of the dangers of a pitched battle. In the final hours before the liberation, though, General Eisenhower brought his military plans into harmony with the political plans of General de Gaulle, who at this moment was France's figure on the horse, a kind of modern Joan of Arc.

We enjoyed hours of idleness during our prolonged wait at Rambouillet, while Allied armor cleared the road to Paris and knocked out German positions. The weather had turned fine, the sky acquiring its tender French blue, less intense and more subtle than the more spectacular American skies, or at least those known to me. GIs played cards, threw dice, slept, swapped stories, talked in their macho way about the girls they would have in Paris. Only the correspondents were unhappy.

Most were new to me—the ones I had met in Normandy had moved on with Patton. These men and women were assigned to write the big emotional story—the liberation of a thousand-year-old city. The older correspondents were fixated on the Paris of the 1920s—as indeed I was. Images danced before their eyes of the old Dôme and the Coupole, the Deux Magots, the Flore, the Boulevards Montparnasse and Saint-Germain, the enduring Brasserie Lipp.

In Hemingway's eyes, Paris was the all-important bar at the Ritz. Most biographers heard about his time in Rambouillet from his own boastful letters. The swaggering Ernest had attached himself to a lively group of *maquis,* local guerrillas, and they thought this American "officer" great fun. They liked his bravado and ebullience, his love of weapons, his eagerness to kill Germans. They fed his war bravado and his fantasies by bringing him odd bits of news of German roadblocks along the highway, and such German tank and gun positions as remained visible. Hemingway translated this into "important" military intelligence that would get him more quickly into Paris. Our correspondents felt Hemingway's disregard for Army rules might enable him to scoop them in the news of the liberation. They were also angry over the novelist's blatant carrying of weapons, forbidden to the press. As one newsman said, for Hemingway it was all a "toy war."

At the press camp, I ran into an acquaintance from the Associated Press. Seeing a familiar face in uniform made him explode. Why these delays? What was the army up to? There were only a few German tanks to be mopped up—why didn't we get on with it? His editors had chewed his ass off by cable.

"Look," I said, "are you expecting me to have all the answers? I'm just a sergeant—waiting like you. Be glad you aren't being wasted in some ambush down the way."

Further along, I came on a two-star general surrounded by some correspondents. One of them asked whether the press would get to Paris that day. The general was relaxed and amused—

"I suppose we'd better get to Paris, or some thirty correspondents will have a nervous breakdown."

* * * * *

By dawn, the grandiose battle scenery had melted away. Only a few tanks and scattered service vehicles remained. Our captain came to us shortly after breakfast. We were to leave in the afternoon. I would be in charge once more of the command car and the same German linguists. Once in the city, we were to make for the Hôtel Scribe, a familiar landmark in the rue Auber, across from the Grand Hôtel and the Café de la Paix. There was to be no freewheeling. We were to remain in military procession, bumper to bumper en route. We were in our recon early, in a long line of vehicles. Our driver said there were tanks in the lead, in case we ran into trouble.

The three German linguists were discussing the city. One wondered whether it derived its name from the Greek playboy who started a war by his affair with Helen of Troy. The older professor, who talked with tenderness, as if we were his children, said that Paris was originally a settlement on the island in the Seine where Notre Dame now stands. Here there lived a tribe called the Parisii. Thus the city's name was indigenous: it had nothing to do with Troy. Of the celebrated urban centers immortalized in history, Paris had acquired a particular distinction. It endured. Modernity had been kind to it. And tyrants had respected it as inviolable, although Hitler had wanted it razed.

We spoke of a kind of prevailing logic—the *clarté* in which the French took proper pride. They were a people whose feet were grounded not in fantasy but in actuality—in their attitudes toward the Church, the State, money, and not least sex. Even those of us reared in the immaturities of the new world somehow recognized this as a Continental "maturity." I quoted to the erudite men the outburst of a French officer from *War and Peace.* Having eaten an omelet and a leg of lamb at Pierre Bezukov's house in Moscow, he declares "a man who doesn't know Paris is a barbarian. You can tell a Parisian two leagues off. . . . There is only one Paris in the world." A Frenchman would say that, revealing his insularity as well as his pride. Still, I asked myself, why did Paris have so much meaning for me? Why did I cling to my memories of freshly baked baguettes, carried naked under one's arm? Or the way in which the aroma of French tobacco came to my nostrils at one end of the Dôme, where the cigarettes and cigars were sold?

As we talked, our driver sat at his wheel, a monument of Middle-American patience. At 3 p.m. by the Army's clock, suddenly we were on our way. I had thought our journey would be a matter of an hour or so to cover the thirty miles to Paris, but when we moved out of the farmland and reached the highway we began a series of tedious starts and stops. After an hour or so we settled down to continual slow motion between villages whose names were unfamiliar, and large adjoining fields of truck farming—spreads of cucumbers, onions, radishes, and especially tomatoes. Our pace was so slow that we could leave our vehicles, wander into the fields, and talk with the women—they were mostly women —picking the ripe plants. They had seen many Army columns during the past few days, but knew very little of what was going on. The crops had to be gathered. Vegetables grew, war or no.

Our pace and the sun of late afternoon made us lethargic. The linguists in the rear seat sank into sleep. I kept my eyes open with difficulty and often dozed. A kind of montage of images and scenes danced before my eyes—my first arrival in Paris, which I remembered vividly. This had been in 1928, when I was 21. I had a scholarship that would give me three years in the French capital. Why had I chosen Paris? I went there without a thought of anywhere else. Since I was literary I chose the city of the avant-garde, where James Joyce and Gertrude Stein lived. It seemed then to me the center of the western world.

Near the end of our journey, I discovered the principal reason for our caution. At a hilly point, where the contours of the land placed our vehicle on a height while the vehicles ahead were descending, I saw the front of the procession. Standing up in the leading vehicle, erect as only a practiced soldier could be, wearing a simple khaki uniform with his kepi firmly set on his head, was Charles de Gaulle. We were escorting the heroic general into the capital of France. Many of the stops had apparently been made to allow him to greet cheering citizens. After the thrill of recognition, I experienced a shudder of excitement at my first glimpse of him. This then was the end of his long exile, the end of the patriotic general's journey. Both his arms were raised in characteristic greeting. Children were piling flowers on his car. Young women tried to kiss him. He was formal, smiling, and in complete control. As we drew closer to Paris, the crowds grew. A sort of enchantment spread over our entire procession, even after he was out of our sight. We were now a military parade—or so it seemed—in honor of France's hero, and his four years of leadership of the Free French. For a moment this was no longer a war: it was an extraordinary celebration.

A NIGHT IN THE PRÉFECTURE

Fate was bringing me back to my section of Paris—about a hundred yards from where I had lived for three years, from 1928. Ahead I saw the Porte d'Orléans, the square where long before stood the old Orléans gate to Paris. We were on the Orléans road. Everything was falling into place. My past attached itself to my middle-aged self, to my soldier self. In the distance I could see the Place d'Orléans, where the general was standing upright in his vehicle, slowly moving through the center of the square, surrounded by a vast ecstatic crowd. The cafés I used to stop at on my way to the university, or on my way back home, were in their places. I used to have a snack or a late-night drink in their bars, after an evening in Montparnasse or the old Latin Quarter. At this spot in the mornings, I would climb on the battered old trams that rattled and whined all the way down past Place Denfert-Rochereau, with its massive stone crouching "Lion of Belfort," then past the Observatoire, to the Boulevard Saint-Michel—old Boul' Mich. And down the way was the Cité Universitaire, where I had lived in the Maison Canadienne, a comfortable shelter for young students from Canada, especially from the French province of Québec.

It was at this moment that I had my best view of the adoration of the general. The crowd was pelting him with flowers as his car inched toward the main avenue. Waves of cheering followed upon each other, as American-made vehicles carried de Gaulle to his hour of triumph.

From this point on, all became chaos. The crowds cut off the general from us; his surrounding vehicles were engulfed; our procession was broken up. By the time our recon reached the square, he was disappearing down the Avenue d'Orléans. I told our driver it looked as if we were no longer on parade. If we couldn't catch up, I thought I knew where to go. We reached the lion of Place Denfert-Rochereau, commemorating a battle or a siege of the Franco-Prussian War. The square itself was familiar, and soon we swung into a shuttered Boulevard Raspail.

Landmarks of Montparnasse appeared, and presently we were at the Dôme. The café had been the round-the-clock rendezvous of American tourists and artists for years, especially during the twenties. What I saw would become a familiar sight as we traveled through Paris during that crowded hour—heaped-up chairs and tables, in earthquake disorder, to protect the plate-glass fronts. Slowly we swung into the Boulevard Montparnasse. Across the way from the Dôme was La Rotonde, boarded up. Its interior used to be covered with a multitude of mediocre paintings by artists of the quarter, who bartered their art for a few cups of coffee. La Coupole, that modern, cavernous place once popular with Latin Americans, was also defended by its chairs and tables.

Up ahead, German soldiers poured out of the Gare Montparnasse, pushed on by the rifle butts of the FFI and some troops of General Philippe Leclerc, the man who had led Free French forces across Africa, and who now had led them into Paris. The crowd seemed pent-up, ready for a massacre. The soldiers were putting the Germans into waiting vehicles. My attention was riveted by the prisoners of war. No longer the strutting "master race," they were men in absolute terror, their hands clasped behind their heads, creatures in field gray, looking and acting like scared animals surrounded by hounds. A torrent of violence accompanied them; it was the historic rage and mockery of the crowds around the tumbrels on their way to the guillotine. People spat in the faces of the prisoners. Men and women poked canes and umbrellas in their faces. One German—he looked like a fat little corporal, with a round face and fright in his popping eyes—was suddenly pulled by grasping hands from the top of a tank; he sank under trampling feet.

I took no pleasure in this humiliation of an enemy I thoroughly hated—though I know I would have felt differently were I face to face with Hitler, Goebbels, or Goering. I hadn't lived for four years under the merciless presence of the Nazis. I found myself sympathizing with Leclerc's men, who on the one hand were protecting their prisoners, and on the other had no desire to make any restraining gestures against the crowd.

The shut-in walls on either side of the rue de Rennes seemed to press against us. Storefronts were covered with their metal fretwork. Many windows had old-fashioned shutters of another age. The heavy double doors that opened into the courtyards were tightly sealed. After the terror and disgust of the Gare Montparnasse, we were moving in sinister solitude, very like the woods through which we had passed to avoid ambush. I was staring at the Café des Deux Magots, its glass front cluttered with its furniture. Chairs and tables were piled up around the Café Flore, Sartre's and de Beauvoir's hangout. In the mid-thirties, during the time of the Spanish Civil War, I used to spend evenings there, playing bridge or poker with fellow correspondents. I saw that cozy little street so inaptly named for a warrior—the rue Bonaparte. In the twenties I used to window-shop in it, looking at paintings I could have bought for a few francs, the work of the avant-garde that Gertrude Stein collected. For some minutes we remained in the very center of a trafficless Boulevard Saint-Germain.

Suddenly there was a sign of life. Swinging into the boulevard from a side street, a group of firemen marched—a dozen in proper formation, with a neat swing of their arms, wearing their brass casques. They were preceded now by a black-haired young girl dressed in white, with bouncing breasts. She held high a white flag with a red cross. Our driver swung beside the group. I called out that we were Americans looking for directions. The leader shouted, "*Halte.*"

Impulse triumphed over discipline. They broke ranks, swarmed over our recon, embraced and kissed us. We were the first Americans they had encountered. Their affection dissipated my brooding sense of isolation.

"Is it safe to go by way of Concorde to the Opéra?"

The leader looked at me without answering.

"Or should we go down rue Bonaparte to the Seine?"

"Dangerous. One never knows where the shooting will start!"

He said many Nazis were in civilian clothes; there were also French collaborators who knew they were now outlaws. They were shooting too. I asked about Boul' Mich. Negative. No telling what things were like. Would our best choice be to go to the insurrection headquarters, the Préfecture of Police? The leader thought that might be a good idea. We shook hands, wished each other luck. They sprang back into rhythm. In front, setting the pace, was the dark-haired young woman carrying her flag of mercy. It was she who had told me that they were the medics of the insurrection.

* * * * *

I knew where to find the Préfecture. During my student days, I went to one of its offices on the Île de la Cité to obtain my identity card, which all foreigners had to carry. We proceeded along Boulevard Saint-Germain, and began to see barricades—heaps of paving blocks, laced with barbed wire, sandbags from air-raid shelters, old furniture, entire trees. They obviously had been thrown up in a hurry at the entrances to narrow streets. At the river, Notre Dame appeared, miraculous and dominating, its towers fronting the evening sky. The Cathedral had seen Paris grow and spread into settlements on the banks of the Seine—ripening into this beautiful city, enveloped in its latest state of siege. Those towers had looked on battle scenes, riots, barricades for seven centuries, and now stared undisturbed at vehicles of a new age. To avoid a shoot-out, our journey had brought us to the very ground of the city's origins. Here the tribes of the Parisii had built their first fortifications, and the Gallo-Romans had established their civilization.

The gates to the Préfecture were wide open; one of them was badly banged up. Inside the gates, amid an assembly of battered German vehicles, we parked and were quickly surrounded by police.

"*Les Américains!*"

"We've just come in with de Gaulle."

"He's at the Hôtel de Ville. He came to congratulate us."

"We need information," I said.

"We've got all you want," said a stocky, black-mustached police captain, "I wish we had as big a supply of guns. Come inside."

We entered a long hallway with a large gutted carcass of beef, hanging as if in a butcher shop. The captain said this was a "little thing" they had picked up during the fighting. They seized food wherever they found it, not knowing how long the siege would last. He spoke of dozens of cases of champagne and brandy captured from Germans, and quantities of tinned food. He led us into a large office, brought out some tumblers, and filled them to the top with Armagnac. The shooting we were hearing was the end of the street battles—mainly from individual snipers, and from holdout Nazis who hadn't yet received the cease-fire news.

The captain finally came to the main questions. Why had we come to the Préfecture? And in what way could he be of help? He was curious also about our ease in French. I explained that we couldn't find any safe route to the Hôtel Scribe. Our weapons were the radio, microphones, and printing presses. We were selected for our Army duty because we spoke French as well as other languages.

"The Scribe! That's where Goebbels' propagandists were billeted!"

"We're propagandists too," I told him.

He said he'd have difficulty telling us which way to go. The shooting would go on for hours. In a Paris in which the FFI, the Leclerc men, the collaborators, and the Germans were letting off steam, we would be best off spending the night right where we were. When I repeated I was uneasy about missing our rendezvous, he said, "Call the Scribe."

I had assumed the phones were not working, but after about twenty rings, a ghostly voice said "*J'écoute!*" I felt like a Kafka character calling the Castle. Could I reach some American officers?

"No one is reachable," said the voice, "No one knows anything. Please call tomorrow." The voice hung up.

The Armagnac was soothing, but we were too excited to rest. We started swapping stories. When we Americans broke out of Normandy, the captain told us, French pride had dictated that Paris should attempt to free itself. The police were among the first to strike. The communist faction of the Resistance ordered the barricades more for sentimental than practical reasons. Everyone remembered from their schoolbooks the barricades of 1871, the time of the Commune. On August 18, the railways had gone on strike. That was the day the police took over all the precincts in Paris and barricaded the Préfecture itself. Other elements of the Resistance seized the newspapers and radio stations. Maybe, the captain laughed, there were too many chefs in the revolutionary kitchen: "De Gaulle now has to deal with all these leaders."

Eventually the captain announced our bedtime, and escorted us into a large room with slit-windows close to the ceiling. A few members of the police force were already sprawled in sleep. We found a comfortable spot in the middle of the room, and I stretched out on my bundle of straw. Tucking my weapon beside me, I knew I would be helpless if someone tried to take it from me in the night. Sleep came swiftly.

* * * * *

I awoke hours later to the twittering of birds, my head thick from the Armagnac. My fellow linguists were lost in surrounding bundles of straw. After straightening my uniform, I brushed off the straw, and went out to see how our driver had fared. He was asleep in the front seat of the car, his gun beside him, his car keys probably hidden on him. If there were French guards, I did not see them. The wide square beyond was deserted. Notre Dame stood in its morning splendor, silent and solemn in its permanence.

When I returned, a gendarme asked me to join him in a cup of coffee—*café national,* he said. I felt I couldn't refuse the offer of hospitality. The cop said it was best drunk with Armagnac, and gave me another tumbler. This ersatz coffee was as horrible as usual. I took a few sips, thanked him, and said I had to rejoin my team. I left the tumbler on a windowsill along the way. When I got back to our quarters I found a message from the police captain, saying we could reach the Scribe now without much danger. After a few general handshakes and gendarmic hugs we were off.

We followed the Seine, and then made for the rue de Rivoli. Paris shone in the morning light as if it had been freshly cleaned. Across the river, the buildings had their familiar forms—the much-photographed structures with their high roofs and chimneys, old windows and varicolored facades. Presently we were driving along the Louvre. In the distance, the Eiffel Tower flew the tricolor. There was the Carrousel, and beyond, at the end of the Champs-Élysées, the Arc de Triomphe. A memorial to the great wars of the Republic, it stood ready to celebrate the newest triumph.

We crossed the rue de Rivoli. Nearby was the Théâtre Français, where in my youth I had spent evenings with Racine and Molière. The Théâtre was now an emergency hospital: its columns were sandbagged, and a large red cross hung over the entrance. The wide Avenue de l'Opéra was deserted, divested of its usual traffic. A street of shutters. The rococo Opéra presided over its particular square. We swung past it into the Boulevard des Capucines and descended to the Hôtel Scribe, which with eagerness and a sense of relief we entered. We had kept our appointment—twelve or more hours late.

THE HÔTEL SCRIBE

A revolving door propelled me into the lobby, amid a scattering of café tables, some overturned, and a stale heavy smell of tobacco and whiskey. Facing me, in deep sleep in a chair, was a U.S. major in full uniform, his head cradled in his arms. Beside him, a young second lieutenant—tall, thin, with a long face—seemed in a state between sleeping and waking. His head nodded like a ventriloquist's dummy, his mouth open as if he were a swimmer coming up for air. A few bleary-eyed celebrants sat at tables, drinking what looked like the national coffee. Broken and spilled glasses, and the detritus of the Army PX littered the carpet—bits of food, candy wrappers, peanuts, empty beer and champagne bottles, and occasional pools of vomit. A small swastika flag had been placed in a bottle, doubtless in derision; there were candle ends in some others. Army gear lay between the tables. A few trim-looking officers sat to the rear at cleared tables, deep in talk. Clean-shaven, they looked as if they were waiting for a commuter train. Two or three young hotel employees were sweeping up the debris. A solitary clerk sat at the desk—his eyes fixed, as if in a stupor.

As I went to the desk, the clerk's eyes came into focus. He muttered some words about the German officers going out through the door all yesterday morning, and the American officers spilling in during the rest of the day. The clerk assured me that confusion was at present the norm, but he also assured me everything would be sorted out. A room check was already under way. We would soon know where to find all the new guests who had poured in to the sound of gunfire. In the meantime he remained polite—perhaps I would like a cup of coffee?

Of course the Scribe had no real coffee, but they could supply boiling water and cups and saucers, and we could drink our Army powdered brew. I sipped the hot drink, and soon sank into pleasant inertia. I was sinking into sleep when a firm hand grasped my shoulder. I looked into the smiling face above me. A bushy mustache, gray eyes. They belonged to Alex Uhl, foreign editor of *PM* in New York. Alex was in a correspondent's uniform.

"I figured," he said, "we'd meet up sooner or later if you weren't off somewhere in the Pacific."

We gave each other an affectionate hug in the Spanish style. (He had been a correspondent in Spain during the Civil War in the 1930s.) Uhl told me how he became tired of armchairing the war, day after day, and convinced *PM*'s editors that he could be more useful as a correspondent. He had gone first to Africa, then he had come up the middle of France with the Seventh Army. He ceremoniously took a German revolver from his bag.

"Here's a souvenir. I'm not supposed to be armed."

Since we were both pacifists, we congratulated each other on our conversion into quasi-combatants.

Uhl was a mild, courteous newsman, genial and warmhearted. At *PM*, he used to lean against a wall or a door, his body always describing a lazy curve, his inquiring smile framed by his mustache. He said he would be in and around Paris for a while, probably at this hotel.

The lobby was filling with officers and civilians from the OWI and General Donovan's Office of Strategic Services. I decided to get out of the hubbub, and into the street again. The lobby clock read 7 a.m.

* * * * *

I stood on the broad pavement of the Boulevard des Capucines, and looked into the tall trees. My eyes transformed the image into a painting I had once seen by Camille Pissarro, who gave to his urban pictures a unifying effect of light, reflected in hundreds of little pigment brush strokes. In Pissarro's time, the street was filled with carriages and other horse-drawn vehicles. In my early years in Paris it had been clogged with taxis. Today, in a city without fuel, the Boulevard seemed like the main street of a country town. No exhaust, no noise. I might have been back on Portage Avenue, in Winnipeg. I filled my lungs with the newborn world's fresh air.

I crossed the rue Auber. Standing at the corner was Corporal Augier, our cross-country jeep driver. I had last seen him in Rambouillet.

He introduced me to a man hovering next to him—a heavy-set, expensively dressed man.

"This," said the corporal, "is Mr. . . ." He fished for the man's name. "Huber," the man said, cautiously opening his lips a little, and proffering a clammy hand. He had a foreign accent.

"He's from Budapest," said Augier, "and he was telling me what an awful time he had with the Germans."

Augier added he was going to Huber's flat to have breakfast. Huber hesitantly invited me along. I took in the man's jaunty hat, his light topcoat, his shining black shoes. He had shifty dark eyes and was too prosperous-looking to have had an "awful" time with the Germans. He might indeed be a civilian agent of the Gestapo. Augier, naive and trusting, swallowed Huber's stories, untouched by the suspicions I entertained as a consequence of my military intelligence training. Why should this Huber be offering breakfast and hospitality? No Frenchman would have done this—it wasn't the French style. Huber might be a refugee, but he seemed more like a collaborator. Having lost German support, he was probably seeking at this early hour to ingratiate himself with some Americans. Huber's flat was just a few steps away. I went rather unwillingly, though I was curious. Was he a German decoy trying to "use" Americans?

His fourth-floor apartment was small and dark. The living room was overstuffed with expensive furniture and art. His plump wife and two adolescent daughters were tumbled out of their beds to receive us in fluffy peignoirs. The girls were about fifteen and seventeen; the mother, who smiled as if to please her husband, seemed in her early forties. My suspicion didn't diminish when she spread a white linen tablecloth with butter and cream, some starved-looking croissants, and stale sweet rolls. She apologized for their staleness. I could smell coffee. It was not *café national.*

I was too much aware of what Paris had undergone to find Huber believable. It went against the grain to break bread here. I declined the food but sipped the coffee. Meanwhile, Augier drank cup after cup, and munched the desiccated pastries. Huber sensed my aloofness. When I said I had to go, he made no effort to detain me. I left Augier flirtatiously telling the awkward adolescents anecdotes about our arrival in Paris. As I walked down the four flights, I remembered Beaufort's warning. Would Huber someday pretend he was in the Resistance?

* * * * *

The Café de la Paix was emerging from its improvised fortifications. Chairs and tables were now regimentally lined up. Some people were sitting on the *terrasse,* with the usual sense of idleness so attractive in Europe. What caught my attention, however, was that the newspaper kiosk in front of the café was open for business. This seemed as incredible as finding the phones working in embattled Paris. I approached the vendor but saw no newspapers. Instead he produced for me ten one-page sheets printed on letter-size paper, with headlines announcing that Paris was free, that de Gaulle had arrived along with the Americans.

"There you have it," the vendor said, "the press of the underground —now above ground, quite legal."

I was looking at mini-editions of the long-familiar conservative and traditionalist *Figaro*, the socialist *Populaire*, the communist *Humanité*, and a flock of new journals with fighting names—*Franc-Tireur, France Libre, Le Parisien Libéré, Résistance, Défense de la France, Front National*. What they stood for was summed up by a neatly-arranged and well-printed little sheet called *Combat*, with an editorial in its first column, brief and forward-looking, by the then relatively unknown Albert Camus. I asked for *Le Temps*. The vendor said that journals which had kept publishing during the occupation would not dare to be seen now. Only later did *Le Temps* appear in its old format—but under new management, and with the new name *Le Monde*.

I took my little collection of news sheets to a table. The waiter was sorry, but it would take a while before they could reopen their bar, and find food worthy of a menu. He poured out a glass of wine; it was sour. I allowed it to stand, and caught up on the news. Displaying the power and virtuosity of the French language, with crispness and succinctness these informative sheets told of the events of the previous twenty-four hours. The tone was self-congratulatory, which was understandable. The liberation and resistance groups had carried out a successful insurrection against the enemy, and relieved the Allies of the burden of a siege. There was a profound feeling that the city—for the moment unified—had experienced the truest meaning of the French word *revanche*—return, revenge, a turning of the tables—after the long winter's night of the Nazi occupation.

Threaded through these accounts were the movements of General de Gaulle after his arrival in the city. The Free French leader had driven through sniper fire to the seat of government and to his old office in the Ministry of War. He had announced this would be the headquarters of his provisional government, carefully avoiding any suggestion that he might move into the Élysée, the residence of the Presidents of France.

At the same time, he had scrupulously avoided formalities with the resistance leaders and other organizations.

What de Gaulle said from the balcony of the City Hall to the wildly cheering crowd was filled with powerful emotion:

"Paris, Paris insulted, Paris broken, Paris martyred, but Paris liberated, liberated by itself, liberated by its people, with the help of all France."

The sun was shining brightly as I started back for the Scribe. The boulevard was filled with people. If Paris lacked fuel for its cars, there was no shortage of bicycles. Young girls sailed along in improvised costumes of their years of penury—their wide skirts ballooning. Women stopped me and planted moist lipstick kisses on my cheeks. Men shook my hand or patted me and admired my uniform. It was Saturday, the 26th of August, 1944.

DE GAULLE TRIUMPHANT

Freshly shaved and looking as if he had just left his tailor, our captain greeted us in his comfortable room in the Hôtel Scribe with the broad smile of youth and victory. He announced that General de Gaulle would be at the Arc de Triomphe at three o'clock to re-light the eternal flame of France's Unknown Soldier. This would be his first formal appearance before the people of Paris. The radio was telling the Parisians to celebrate—victory weather was promised, the beauty of a late summer's day. Our mission would be to handle the recording of the ceremony. The platter would then be flown by a Royal Air Force plane to London, and broadcast by the BBC to the entire world.

Augier had parked our jeep under some trees on the Boulevard des Capucines. I promised to stay with it, as he rushed away to call on a girl he had met the previous evening. The vehicle and I became an instant object of curiosity to strollers, idle in a shut-down city where great events were taking place. Some went through the now familiar touching of the vehicle and then my uniform—feeling the buttons, rubbing thumb and forefinger over my lapels. They tapped my light helmet and took note of my M-3 weapon, which lay beside me. Young girls bent into the jeep to hug me, enveloping me in their fragrance. It was a moving experience, and also a painful one. Besides the smiles and kisses, there were tears. A young girl with gentle blue-gray eyes asked whether I'd mind giving her my autograph. I assured her I wasn't a movie star, but simply what we called in America "General Issue." She replied that since I was the first American she had ever set eyes on, my autograph would have special meaning for her. Rummaging in her bag, she produced a 100-franc note for my signature. I said I hesitated to sign currency that had been issued by the Vichy government. She insisted this made my autograph all the more valuable.

Others followed her example. With the emptying of pockets came tattered photographs.

"This is my son. He's a prisoner in Germany."

"My boy was in the Resistance. The Gestapo shot him."

"My husband—they deported him to Germany."
A picture of a youth in the uniform of the first war.
"He was killed in 1916."
Attempting to be upbeat, I said this would be the last war. Germany wouldn't try again.

No one agreed.

One young man said he had gone to the outskirts of the city and seen the Americans arriving. He found them "very democratic"—generous with cigarettes and chocolate bars, and full of fun. Above all, Americans didn't strut like the Germans. I wasn't sure I liked being measured by a Nazi yardstick, but I thanked him and said he mustn't glorify us too much.

"Oh yes, you are full of magic: your *matériel,* your clothes, your vehicles. How could the U.S. produce so much so quickly?"

A pale-faced youth leaned into the jeep, and in a soft voice began to croon, "Yez zir zat's my bébé." He got every word right but couldn't speak English. He had learned a lot of songs, letter-perfect, without knowing their meaning, in long nights of listening to the American short-wave.

* * * * *

We drove that famous Saturday, August 26, 1944, up the Champs-Élysées. The Elysian Fields—a name we don't often translate to ourselves. It invokes the myths of Greece and Rome as well as another era in France, when classical allusion was more common than it is today: those fields to which national heroes withdrew when their time on earth was over.

On Day One of the liberation of Paris, the city was to honor a new hero. Crowds massed along the avenue, gathered for a ritual which few of them could actually see. They could however endlessly shout, "*Vive la France! Vive de Gaulle!*"

During our trip to the Arc, I was conscious of thousands of pairs of eyes peering down from the slanted rooftops, where people were ranged in rows like bees in a honeycomb, or an assemblage of birds. How they kept themselves from slipping down those roofs I couldn't imagine, but they seemed firmly perched. People filled every balcony that hung above the avenue. All had come in hope of some glimpse of the now famous leader. Though he hadn't fought battles like most of the other generals in history, he had clung tenaciously to the idea that France in defeat had to fight on. Now, obviously at great risk, he would show himself as the prime liberator of his compatriots.

I found myself wondering at de Gaulle's exposing himself to a crowd that inevitably had in its midst certain enemies—the snipers we encountered at our entry, the followers of traitorous Vichy, Germans in civilian dress, and the mentally disturbed victims of war's deceits and hardships. Wouldn't the courageous general have done better to wait, to give Paris time to return to a certain order and stability? And then it seemed to me inevitable that a man cast in the heroic mold would quite naturally seize every right moment.

As we approached the Arc, which seemed to be moving toward us, I was struck anew by the singular perfection of its proportions. It made the ancient arches of Rome, or the little arch raised to George Washington in the New York square at the bottom of Fifth Avenue, seem like miniatures. I remembered how the Arc commanded the avenues that radiate outward, as if it were the hub of a wheel. The French had another image in mind when they named the spot "Place de l'Étoile." This star, in its illumination, converts its radiations into avenues. Although the name Étoile remains attached to it by memory, in later years it would be renamed "Place Charles-de-Gaulle."

What comes back to me suddenly is seeing, among all the flags and bunting, a huge banner stretched across the buildings of an entire block. The words I read were formed in big black letters. They were in the American language, and intended for American as well as French eyes. With a directness that exalted U.S. free enterprise, the sign said—

CONGRATULATIONS ON A JOB WELL DONE,
HART SHAFFNER AND MARX CLOTHES

This was the voice of business-in-the-field, as American as "Happy Birthday to You." In the journey from Normandy to Paris and beyond, American blood had apparently been gloriously shed on behalf of the U.S. garment industry. This was funny. It was also depressing.

A week or two later one of the French newspapers—I think it was *Le Figaro*—took note of the sign. After complimenting Hart Shaffner and Marx on their resourcefulness, the paper wondered how the message might have been conveyed in French. Perhaps *Bravo les Gars!*—Hurrah for the Boys!—signed by Félix Potin—the great wholesale and retail food supplier to a capital at that moment without food.

* * * * *

The view of the Champs-Élysées from the Arc de Triomphe suggested triumph in its fullest sense, a historic Roman holiday. Psychwar's spot for the recording was only a few paces from de Gaulle. I was about six feet from the tomb of the Unknown Soldier when Alex Uhl joined me. I whispered to him that I didn't see many correspondents. He replied American newsmen considered this sort of celebration to be small potatoes. At the rear of the Arc, in the appropriately named Avenue de la Grande Armée, a regiment was drawn up as an honor guard. I could take in the circle of avenues the Arc knotted together, their names honoring the winners of battles defending France from attempts by other European nations to deconstruct the revolution of 1789. Seeing the crowds gathered in these avenues, quite as large as those on the Champs-Élysées, was startling. I didn't know the measurements of the Arc at the time—it stands 162 feet high and 137 wide—but I felt the splendor of its command over the generous space given it. The romantic sculptures of the facade displayed old moments of history. My eye fell on the names of battles, and picked up Napoleon's presence at Smolensk and Borodino in Russia. An enormous tricolor banner hung in the center of the archway, from ceiling to pavement. When I looked up at the Romanesque curves, it was as if I were in a marvelous outdoor cathedral. Mass, weight, memory, power. And glory—*gloire.*

The general suddenly appeared, erect, unsmiling, surrounded by his officers, a small tight group. He was taller than I had thought. He shook hands with various political figures. Showing a certain tension in his rigid carriage, he slowly and attentively inspected the honor guard, composed of the men who had made the incredible march with Leclerc across the Sahara, before their journey from the south of France to Paris. A police band was playing. Thundering down the avenue, like great waves of an ocean, I could hear the repeated cries, "*Vive la France! Vive de Gaulle!*" De Gaulle was very still before the stone—the altar—of the Unknown Soldier, who since 1918 has symbolized the uncountable sacrifices of human life, the mystery and anonymity, the mourning of France and the world. De Gaulle was given roses and gladioli shaped into the Cross of Lorraine. Very slowly and gently, he placed the cross on the altar. Then, deliberately, he relit the flame, renewing in that moment the life of the French Republic.

The *Marseillaise* roared from miles around. I saw de Gaulle bite his lip. A figure of noble dignity, he was doubtless holding back certain emotions. As the *Marseillaise* died away, a solemn voice came from the loudspeakers: General de Gaulle said he was confiding his security to the people of Paris. He appealed for their cooperation, and help for the heroic police and the FFI, "weary of their five days of battle." Then, suddenly, de Gaulle stepped forward. The tanks of the honor guard moved from the rear of the Arc to its front. A few yards behind these vehicles, de Gaulle spread his long arms wide in a beckoning gesture, and showed himself in his singular height to the assembled thousands. His generals and the Free French advisers fell in on either side to form a long single line, stretching from one side of the Champs-Élysées to the other. De Gaulle recognized that the intimate ceremony at the Arc had been seen by only a small part of the crowd. He would now brave possible assassins by walking down the historic avenue. The action seemed spontaneous and bold—a fearless gift to the people who had given him their loyal act of presence.

By this time we were back in our jeep. Augier placed our vehicle a few yards behind the single line of march, next to other Army vehicles. We were however immediately separated from the line by a surging crowd that broke through police lines, and undertook to march with and around the general.

In a few seconds we were surrounded. Half a dozen young people clambered onto every available surface of the jeep. Overburdened, we rolled slowly down the Champs-Élysées, within the surging mass. De Gaulle and the Parisians were creating their own parade. I can no longer remember how long it took us to make our way down the avenue. The distance between us and the general grew. The young people on our jeep were lively and amusing—two or three young women, and as many young men. One girl had her arms around me all the way, planting lipstick kisses on my cheeks. The young were filled with (I suppose I must say it in French) *élan*: transport or rapture.

In the distance de Gaulle moved slowly, spreading his arms again and again as an embrace—of the people, of France—all the way to the

Place de la Concorde. An open limousine awaited him, and he rode off to Notre Dame for a celebratory Mass, down a narrow corridor left him by the engulfing multitude. With the continued feeling of being at the very center of an historic moment, we eventually reached the traffic corridor kept open by police.

At that moment there occurred what everyone had feared. Snipers opened fire, shooting from vantage points among the buildings and from rooftops up the rue Royale, rue de Rivoli, and adjoining streets. If they hoped to create a panic, they did not succeed. Although screams of terror were heard, the Parisians knew what to do. In the square, people simply threw themselves on the pavement and around the fountains. Recognizing that our jeep could be an easy target, Augier put on a burst of speed, which made our passengers drop off as we shot forward.

We turned into the deserted and still narrower rue Saint-Florentin, which adjoined the Naval Ministry. The buildings seemed to press in on either side, as if we were in a tunnel. Augier stopped the jeep halfway down, and we threw ourselves on the ground. The gunfire seemed to be coming from both ends of the street. A machine gun chattered non-stop; intermittent sniper shots cracked around us. The guttural boom of a distinctly German gun rose from somewhere near the Church of the Madeleine.

The shooting was erratic. At no time did I have the feeling that any shots were directly aimed at anyone. We were simply in a circle of gunfire—designed to spread alarm, to make known the enemy presence. Pedestrians were making their way toward us, staying close to the walls of the buildings. Some were crawling. A man hedged up close to me. Pointing to the top of the building across the way he said, "*Voilà, voilà, voilà,* I see the bastard . . . !" I saw no one, yet in my need to release my pent-up fear and excitement, I pointed my weapon at the area indicated and pulled the trigger. Fired for its first time outside of target practice, my gun let off a couple of shots.

We seemed to spend a quarter of an hour lying in that street, though it may have been five minutes. We exchanged brief remarks about whether to go on or remain. Our captain, pale and at first silent, scanned the buildings, his weapon ready. Finally he called out we might as well make a break for the Scribe. We climbed into the vehicle and took off with a roar. We were an easy target—I expected a rain of bullets. We swung into the boulevard and zoomed along the few remaining deserted blocks. Suddenly we were at the Hôtel Scribe. My next memory was of extraordinary thirst, as if all the moisture had been drained from my body. The captain and Augier also went to the bar. The captain ordered splits of champagne.

* * * * *

I don't remember much about the interval between our drinking champagne, and my finding myself toward 8 p.m. in a long, narrow room on the third floor of a well-kept establishment in the rue du Faubourg-Saint-Honoré, not far from the rue Royale. Certain enlisted men were being accommodated for a couple of nights in this hotel. Augier had gone off to a tryst with his newfound girlfriend Albane. He invited me to join him. Albane had a friend named Gilberte; we could make a foursome. But the long day, the tension, the champagne, had quite flattened me. In the twilight of my room, I peeled off my clothes. With a strange domesticity I decided to wash my underwear and shirt, even if there was only cold water. I then crawled into a cold bath. The bathroom window showed the familiar rooftops of Paris and a stretch of darkened sky. I felt clean again, and relaxed, as the day's glories gave way to a sense of complete exhaustion.

As I lay in the soapy water, I was roused by sniper fire a few houses down the way. Apparently a lone rifleman was amusing himself. I heard a *ping*—and then silence. A minute or two later, another. In spite of this, I rubbed myself down and crawled into bed between clean sheets. Fatigue possessed me. I thought of Augier and Albane, but had to confess that my sexual desire was at a low ebb. I told myself that I mustn't try to keep pace with the younger men; I was about to be thirty-seven.

In that hypnagogic state between dozing and wakefulness, my mind rambled through the past twenty-four hours—from the Hungarian collaborator, to the people on the boulevard, to the ceremony at the Arc. I kept returning most to the street sniping, when I felt as if any moment could be my last. I fantasized myself a lifeless bundle, lying on a Paris sidewalk near our jeep in the rue Saint-Florentin. In the blurred cinema of my thoughts I wondered at my present calm and the quiet, the serenity of lying now, my body cleansed, alone—drifting deeper and deeper into sleep.

And suddenly I was awake. I was hearing the familiar drone of German planes. My mind jumped to the first evening in Rennes, when the enemy had bombed the city it had abandoned earlier in the day. Clearly this now was happening to Paris. I heard no anti-aircraft fire. Paris had been comparatively unbombed throughout the war. Through the window I now saw a great wall of yellow sky. The bombs had set a tremendous fire, which had lit up the entire city. Roofs in the foreground stood out deep black. I would learn later that the Germans had destroyed some five hundred houses and the great wine warehouses of Paris—the *Halles aux Vins*. The alcohol had acted as a torch. Fifty persons were killed and five hundred injured. Though some American soldiers later fell victim to snipers in lonely streets, these were among the last casualties of the liberation of Paris.

I pulled on some clothes, having no wish to be on a fifth floor if the planes should return. In the street I found a few other enlisted men, who like myself preferred to be out of doors during an air raid. Pretty soon the all-clear sounded. After a bit, I went back upstairs and once again crawled into bed. Finally, I slept.

MUSINGS AND MEMORIES

I awoke that Sunday—August 27, 1944—in a phantasmagoria of history: a sense of floating crowds, masses on rooftops, martial music, stuttering machine guns, and the tricolor rustling under the Arc. Overnight, these images melted into the peach-colored flame I saw before I slept. Stretched out in my bed, warm and relaxed, my eyes followed little beads of sunlight along the ceiling. Bathed in stillness, for a moment I felt like a civilian again, in a tourist hotel.

It was good to be back in Paris, the home of my youth. I had adopted it years ago, in the 20s. When I left it in 1932, I had wondered whether I would ever see it again. Four years later I returned, during the turmoil of civil wars and the coming world war. Now crazy fate had brought me back into a surviving city, most of it physically untouched by the war. Paris, the impersonal, glittering, feminine city which belongs to everyone and to no one, with its imprint from the days of Baron Haussmann, the town-planner: those expanded boulevards and wide spaces for marching men that contrast with the density of other cities. It is the great center-city that we carry away in memory—a honeycomb city, a trap for the lonely like all cities, gregarious yet impersonal.

My senses renewed themselves, and with them came memories of freshly-baked bread, perfumes, urine, and tobacco. Granted, most of these smells were not available now. The city was without bread; the perfumes were doubtless still in the shops, but at fantastic prices; the tobacco was gone, though the Americans were bringing it back. The *pissoirs,* however, remained. These at least were not being denied the French males.

I had just turned twenty-one when I saw Paris for the first time in 1928. It was a bright, warm, and glowing autumn day. The leaves were turning. The buildings, old and gray, blended their shabbiness with bright awnings and a tender blue sky. I looked up and down the streets and avenues from my taxi. I had known Saskatoon and Winnipeg and Montreal. I had just seen London. But the French panorama created an inner murmur of delight during that long ride from the Gare Saint-

Lazare to the Maison Canadienne in the 14th *arrondissement,* where I would live for the next three years. I had never seen so much exterior life in any city. This was the great, wide, peopled world—and I was in it. I have never known more happiness than during that first ride across Paris. I experienced at once a kind of intimacy that belongs now to nostalgia and a groping for words. Above all, a sense of freedom.

I studied—not strenuously but with some attention—at the Sorbonne, one of thousands of students who came from around the world. Why to France, why to Paris? Because the French themselves compromise neither language, logic, nor taste, their city seems to offer the less spontaneous foreigner an extraordinary feeling of possibility. I lived during those years among this distancing people, learning to talk their language and take them as they were—their naturalness, their love of words, their wit, their "arrangements" of morality and manners.

There were also their rages, their insularity, their distrusts, their greed. There were French in whom the violence of the French Revolution still ran wild. One would see this in their erratic ways of dealing with collaborators, their impromptu executions or head-shavings. Certain elements were still profoundly bigoted and nasty—one remembers that it was often French neighbors who revealed to the Nazis the whereabouts of hidden Jews. It was my good fortune, though, since I moved among the educated *"élite"*—a perfectly good word in French, nothing pejorative about it—to see the French at their most civilized. No one asked me about my being Jewish. I was an outsider who was made welcome as a Canadian-American.

I had returned to Paris during the mid-thirties. I worked for a French news agency during the period of the Popular Front of Léon Blum, when the working classes showed a brief militancy toward advancing fascism in their northern and southern neighbors. Nightly the trains at the Gare de Lyon carried volunteers to fight for democracy against Franco in Spain. Battle lines were also being drawn that later weakened France against its most serious enemy, led by a paranoid hysteric with a silly bristling mustache under his nose: the greatest modern illustration of how contagious hysteria can be when it occurs in high places, and is focused by a controlling medium. I remembered that period vividly, a twelvemonth of pain and disillusion. Paris was no longer my dream country, but a land of fear and cruel division.

And now I was once more returned to it; to be, even if briefly, a spectator and reader of its further chapters. I studied the familiar rooftops, and looked down into the rue du Faubourg-Saint-Honoré. Gustave Flaubert had lived in its upper reaches during certain winters. In his flat his little *cénacle* met on Sundays, occasions chronicled by Henry James, an American who had been escorted there by a Russian, Ivan Turgenev. In the higher reaches of Saint-Honoré was the Salle Pleyel, the favorite haunt of my student days. I had heard Stravinsky conduct his newest works there, and old Richard Strauss play his oldest tone poems. I had seen Manuel de Falla, Ernest Ansermet, and Maurice Ravel conduct, and others, including members of the French "Group of Six." I had floated in an aesthetic ocean, and almost drowned myself beyond reality in its torrents. The arts nourished me; they were also my anodyne against loneliness.

* * * * *

I surveyed my shirts and battle fatigues, hanging stiffly in the dry air. It was Day One of the liberation, and I told myself I should report to the Hôtel Scribe. A rare day—no traffic in that tremendous square, the Place de la Concorde. On the Tuileries side I found a series of little bouquets, neatly placed, with cards giving the names of the young who two days earlier had been killed fighting the Germans. (I always revisit this spot in Paris, where a small commemorative stone has been set low into the wall near the sidewalk.) As on the previous day, I found a kiosk selling the notepaper-sized newspapers, and bought one of each. Their headlines celebrated de Gaulle and the day of *gloire*. They told of trouble at Notre Dame before the victory mass was sung. Shots had been fired within the high Gothic arches and stained glass. As before, de Gaulle had remained cool—and devout.

I had read my way through half a dozen sheets, when, beaming with great self-satisfaction, Corporal Augier plumped into the chair beside me. He began to tell me his night's adventures and scolded me for not making up a foursome. He had found an OWI man to take my place. That man was now "fixed up" with the lively Gilberte. And Augier had Albane. He described her tidy expensive little apartment in the Champs-Élysées, her faithful maid, her dog named Rabbit. She was the mistress of Marcel, a black market racketeer who ran a prosperous restaurant. He and Albane had given Augier a fine dinner—caviar and *foie gras, rosbif* and champagne, and even a salad. Augier and Albane then adjourned to her little place, where they made love. In her eagerness, however, she miscalculated her timing. The boyfriend walked in on the lovers. He pulled a revolver on Augier. Albane told him not to be a fool. Shooting an American soldier would put an end to his illegal food deals. Finally, Marcel pocketed his revolver.

Augier was beginning to repeat his embroidered tale when Captain Auberjonois joined us. We could take the day off, but I was to go next morning to be translator for an American captain named Miller, who was liaison to the Leclerc Division. I wondered why a liaison officer needed a translator. Our captain speculated that the officer probably knew only academic French. The captain said we would be moving in a day or so to other quarters. Everything, he assured us, would fall into place.

CARNIVAL WITHOUT MASKS

In Paris that Sunday, French of all ages filled the boulevards. The rue Royale became a promenade, where the young of Paris were meeting the young of America. Late in the afternoon, I found a group of GIs trying to talk to half-a-dozen young girls, who seemed of high school age. There was one I noticed immediately. She had bobbed black hair, wore a neat, rather worn jacket and skirt. She had considerable vivacity, regular features, and little make-up. She spoke a fractured English consisting almost entirely of nouns. The girls with her had no English at all. The soldiers, who also seemed just out of high school, had no French.

"Can I help?" I asked in French. The girls, laughing, said they needed a lot of help, but the GIs saw me as an older man, trying to interfere. I took the hint.

"Have fun," I said. I waved and walked away.

The carnival—if we may call it that—was a mix of merriment and sobriety. The mood was one of sudden, unexpected freedom, and many felt a desire to talk openly after long confinement and suppressed emotions. But there was nothing riotous about the crowds. The foreign soldiers, and especially the Americans, found themselves at the center of clusters of people. The sexual hunger of the young soldiers was manifest on all sides, and many streetwalkers with beckoning eyes and inviting bodies were available to help them out. To many the war seemed over—at least for the moment. But the final hour was yet to come. From time to time, shots from the rooftops or from certain windows reminded us of lingering enemies.

A smartly-dressed young woman placed her hand tenderly on mine. I looked into her shining eyes, and a visage rouged and lipsticked. I said I wasn't really in the mood for lovemaking. Besides, I shrugged, I was broke.

"An American soldier broke?" Her wide mouth burst into genuine laughter. "Put your hand in your pocket," she said, "I'll bet you come up with a hundred francs. You can have any girl in the street at a bargain price. We give discounts to Americans."

I shook my head, patted her on the shoulder. "Not today," I said.

"How about giving me an English lesson? I want these boys to tell me their ages."

I taught her how to say "How old are you?" She repeated it with a charming French accent. I asked why the age of the soldiers mattered. She said she had no wish to get into bed with schoolboys.

A second girl with fiercer make-up joined us.

"They're a lot of babies. Imagine! They offer to pay in cigarettes and candy."

I wished them a happy day, and walked on.

A block or two farther up the boulevard, a streetwalker who overheard me speaking French asked me to interpret.

"*Dites-lui qu'il est trop jeune pour comprendre les femmes.*"

The young Americans she was with did indeed look wet behind the ears. I translated this bluntly.

"You guys are too young to understand how women feel."

The GI exploded.

"She's a bitch. Tell her to go to hell."

Many soldiers did talk as if all Frenchwomen on the streets were whores. I encountered one batch of men whose manners and approach offended a number of French girls. These girls vehemently asked me to explain that they were not for sale. I did what I could to disabuse the GIs of their ideas, perhaps the lingering traces of veterans' talk going back to the enraptured American soldiers in Paris at the end of the first war.

As I approached the Café de la Paix, a woman of about thirty stopped me. She was attractive, even chic, but her eyes were veiled. She took hold of my hand, and remarked I appeared older than most of the soldiers around us. Where had I learned my French? She was wistful and sad. She wanted to cling to me, though, and she saw my reluctance.

Suddenly she said—

"*Vous savez, j'ai fait des bêtises.*"

I wondered at this confession. Why was she telling me she had done stupid things? Later I speculated that she probably was saying "I slept with some Germans. Don't hold it against me." All I could answer was that we all did stupid things sooner or later. Still, I was put off. She wanted sympathy I couldn't give. I wished her well.

Later that day, I came on a soldier with a sad-faced woman of a certain age and her husband. The man ran a bistro nearby, and invited us for a drink. After a bit he proposed we stay for supper. His wife said that it was refreshing to talk with Americans like us—like being suddenly taken out of a prison. She was half-Jewish, and had been in a cell at Fresnes, one of the depots from which French Jews were shipped to Nazi camps. The woman seemed lost in a fantasy; her husband tried to bridge the silences by talking of trivial things. He described the black market; he talked of the way you had to suppress your rage in the German presence. The candlelight revealed shadows and wrinkles in their faces, above which their eyes showed stress and anxiety. She made no allusion to her experiences with the Germans, and we tried to keep away from that subject, yet its deeper drama remained one of the mysteries of that day, when Paris drew its first breath of freedom after four years of bondage. Out of the silences of the occupation, all sorts of legends emerged, but nothing ever seemed complete.

CAPTAIN MILLER AND THE PLACE DE LA BOURSE

On Monday I went in search of the Captain Miller who had asked for a French interpreter. At the American Information offices in the Boulevard des Capucines I found chaos. GIs were moving filing cabinets, stacks of documents, and books into the offices. I asked for Captain Miller, but no one knew anything about him. Finally, a short dapper man with black-rimmed glasses and a thick graying mustache introduced himself as Lewis Galantière. I knew the name. I had read his translations of Stendhal, and his reviews of French authors in the *Times*. Galantière was cheerful and talkative. A civilian in the Office of War Information, he was full of stories about the 1914–1918 war. I asked for Captain Miller. Galantière said he would lead me to him. Galantière also gave me Miller's first name: Perry.

Though I recalled hearing the name at Harvard in the late 1930s, when I had a Guggenheim fellowship and was seeing for the first time the archives of the James family, I knew nothing about Perry Miller, the Harvard professor and America's foremost authority on Puritanism, at that time. My years in journalism had shut me off from many academic areas. Presently though, I was saluting him. He turned from studying the baroque Paris Opéra through his large plate glass office window, ignored my salute, and offered a handshake instead. Tall, vigorous, alert, with handsome features, his manner belonged to the open spaces of America. He shook Galantière's hand, thanked him, then said to me in a whisper, "Let's get out of this place."

We sauntered down the boulevard. I waited for him to tell me about the job I was to do as an interpreter. He didn't mention it. He asked me where I'd learned my French, and I told him in Saskatchewan, then in Montreal, and finally in Paris. He said he came from the midwest too. He wanted to know about my studies in Paris, and I told him that in the late 1920s, I had decided to unite American studies with French. The University of Paris then had a professor of American language and literature. Miller said he had heard about him, and that the professor had once studied at Harvard. He even knew his name—Charles Cestre.

Miller didn't talk much about himself, and didn't ask many questions. Although he was informal and outgoing, I insisted on being the sergeant waiting for orders from a captain. The captain asked how I had entered Paris. I told him about our procession with de Gaulle at its head, and the night at the Préfecture. He then talked about the snipers that had pinned him and some of the Leclerc men down in front of the French Foreign Office on the Quai d'Orsay. With considerable pleasure, he described how they took shelter along the Seine wall. He saw a Nazi appear at one of the windows and then withdraw. He took aim at the window and waited on the chance the target would return; the moment the figure reappeared, he pulled the trigger. The Nazi seemed to topple backward. Miller hoped he had "gotten his German."

The Avenue de l'Opéra was deserted during our stroll. We inspected the Théâtre Français, seat of the French classic stage, with its bullet-chipped facade. We walked into the Palais Royal, where I used to go in the days when I was reading at the Bibliothèque Nationale nearby. I reminisced cautiously. Miller was relaxed, and seemed very comfortable. We surveyed the Louvre facade at the end of the avenue, and then entered the rue Saint-Honoré, which was equally deserted. At one building we stopped because it was a fine specimen of architecture. The door was open, and we entered. We paused in front of a large, darkened pool of blood, spread across two or three squares of marble, the residue of some sort of battle. It made me feel queasy, and I noted that Miller was equally uncomfortable. We turned away, into the street.

I recall that I spoke of having felt trapped in journalism during the depression. He responded that Harvard could also be a trap. He himself dropped out of college at eighteen, and spent two or three years roaming in New England and the American west, then going with the merchant marine to the Belgian Congo, on a Conradian adventure. Then he returned to take a doctorate.

It seemed to me in 1944, and in later years when we met in New York or Cambridge, that the army had been for Perry Miller a renewal of his early vagabondage, and that he preferred this kind of life to teaching. I wondered whether ultimately we didn't have in common a feeling that we had begun life not in books, but in the world of human lives. Perry Miller had ultimately been absorbed into the sermons and tracts of the old divines and preachers. Out of this material he extracted his celebrated book on "the New England mind," just as I would in later years extract lives, in my forays into biography.

Throughout, Miller acted as if we were old friends out for a stroll in the heart of the newly liberated city. He made no mention of interpreting and translating from the French. In future years I never mentioned this to him. Something kept me from bringing it up. I seemed to want to spare him explanations, whatever they would have been. I had some private theories, but none seemed worth pursuing. Was it possible that the reasons for his needing an interpreter ceased to matter? Had I been summoned simply to serve as a companion against certain insecurities hidden deep within this outgoing and gracious man? The questions became irrelevant. We remained friends. I gave him pleasure later when I reviewed *The Raven and the Whale,* his neglected book on Poe and Melville. He in turn reviewed my later works on James with warmth and charm in the *Christian Science Monitor.* When finding myself in crowded Cambridge without a place to stay, there were times he put me up in his home. Both he and his wife proved very hospitable. These memories belong to the 1950s. I did not see him in the early sixties, when he grew stout, drank too much, and died prematurely at 58.

* * * * *

When Perry Miller left me, I felt a certain letdown. I had come to do work which hadn't materialized; it had been a privilege, however, to spend an hour strolling with so civilized a person. I decided I might as well take advantage of my situation, and enjoy a few more hours of relief from Army duty. It was pleasant to be at loose ends in the heart of Paris.

A short walk away was the old Agence Havas, where I had worked during 1936 and into 1937. The Agence was one of Europe's pioneer news agencies. Monsieur Havas, an enterprising Hungarian, had been in the eighteenth century among the earliest users of carrier pigeons; later, they supplied news dispatches during the Napoleonic Wars. The Agence evolved into a well-known European institution, and ultimately was divided into a news section and the Havas advertising agency. It often served as a mouthpiece for the French Foreign Ministry, and was probably subsidized. I had obtained my job originally in the New York Havas bureau in 1934. It had been a hack job, but in the world economic depression I was happy to be paid $50 a week after living from hand to mouth in Montreal. We spent our working hours translating French cable-ese into readable American news—no easy task, for French news is written in a more editorial style, and the French had yet to learn how to make foreign affairs into exciting (if rather meaningless) American headlines.

The attempt of Havas to sell its news in New York was a poorly planned initiative. The cable-ese arrived in code; by the time it was deciphered and converted into U.S. journalese, the news was often old—and cold. The American desk in Paris also had no sense of what New York newspapers wanted. We worked five hours earlier than Paris, which meant I had to reach the office on Madison Avenue between 5 a.m. and 6. I worked at these uncomfortable hours for two years, when I suddenly found myself dispatched to Paris to improve the American desk's selection of news. In the spring of 1936, then, four years since I had said farewell to my student days, I was lifted out of my Manhattan cul-de-sac into better working hours, more pay, and the pleasure of being back in the capital of France.

The truth was that the European pot was boiling, and Havas badly needed changes if it was to make any headway in the U.S. A great deal was happening. The Spanish Civil War had reached its doleful end. Mussolini's Ethiopian war was winding up. Hitler had invaded the Rhineland, his first blitz to erase the Treaty of Versailles. And Britain was having a constitutional crisis, Edward VIII having manifested a desire to make the divorced American Mrs. Simpson his Queen. The latter news story was beyond French understanding. A puritan and mindless king wanted to marry his mistress and enthrone her! To the French this seemed a great folly.

At Havas I had been viewed with good-natured amusement by the younger newsmen, who were eager to learn American journalistic "technology," and with some alarm by the old-timers, who felt Americans shouldn't be given jobs in a French office where careers had to be made, and foreign labor was uncalled for. In due course, they accepted the idea that I was distinctly a temporary phenomenon.

As I approached the Bourse—the French Stock Exchange—I recalled the strange cries, as of hurt animals, that used to issue from the large building. You could hear them blocks away. The exchange was understandably silent now, and probably would be until this French equivalent of Wall Street adjusted itself to the newest march of history.

A large banner floating in the breeze told me that the Havas building was now the Agence France-Presse. The change of name was no surprise. The Havas Agency would be tainted by having served the Vichy regime during the occupation. Since the elevators weren't running, I climbed two steep flights to the editorial room, and came at once on the familiar row of desks and copy boys distributing mimeographed sheets. The place was as musty and ill-ventilated as ever. Nothing seemed changed.

I asked to see Monsieur Perrin, the editor-in-chief. Meanwhile I glanced at the street side of the room where he used to stand, ruddy-cheeked, his hands perpetually stuffing Algerian tobacco into his short pipe, but he was nowhere in sight. I looked forward to his plump cheerfulness and his boyish curly red hair. He used to greet me every day with *"Voici l'oeil de New York!"*—"Here he comes—the eye of New York!" Nothing escaped him. He read every word on those mimeographed pages that fell endlessly into waiting baskets.

Perrin had a charming way of gently letting me know how much he disapproved of the American simplification of news. The headline-bulletins I dispatched, he used to say, reduced complex stories to meaningless sensationalism. When I sent a story saying "France today told the U.S.A.—" he demurred: "Why, Monsieur Edel, do you make France speak that way? It wasn't France that told the U.S.A.; it was a spokesman in the Quai d'Orsay who hinted to the press that such and such a policy was being contemplated. That spokesman was by no means 'France'; he was a bureaucrat making soundings for French foreign policy." I tried to explain that Americans liked to have news shouted at them in three or four lines, and didn't have time to be told the mechanism by which the news was imparted.

One day, when I talked to him about the Spanish Civil War and said, "When peace will return . . . ," he looked at me with incredible sadness.

"Ah, Monsieur Edel, there will be no peace."

As I was dwelling on these memories, a man I remembered as one of Perrin's assistants came toward me. "Where is Perrin?" I asked, as we exchanged greetings.

"Monsieur Edel, I regret to tell you that Monsieur Perrin died in a German concentration camp a few weeks ago."

He had refused to surrender his journalistic integrity to Vichy and the Nazis. He would not preside over the dissemination of German lies.

The Gestapo came for him very early. He spent a long time in the camp. If only he had endured a little longer.

We shifted from this painful news to talk of other Havas newsmen I had known. I asked about Maurice Schumann, who had often written features for our Canadian clients. Was he really now very high in Gaullist circles? I had caught a glimpse of him at the Arc de Triomphe ceremony. Known in France through his lively BBC broadcasts, he had become one of de Gaulle's cabinet ministers. We talked also of the younger men, all scattered. Some had gone abroad to be with the Free French. Others had remained in their bureaus in the European capitals. A few had died early, when the Nazis invaded France. I was reminded of the many ways in which wars destroy lives beyond the battlefields.

* * * * *

We did not remain very long in the Hôtel Castiglione. Reveille was restored the very next morning. We were rushed from our warm beds at 6 a.m. into an adjoining chilly mews. After the roll call, we performed calisthenics on the cobblestones of another age. Our officer, a young captain, moralized briefly. We had had, he said, a sort of holiday after the liberation. Now we faced anew our duties and responsibilities. The war was far from over. We were in a city of numerous distractions, temptations, and even dangers. We must keep ourselves fit, and remember that those of us who were in Paris as specialists were first and foremost soldiers. Our roll calls would be maintained: there would be bed checks at night. He cautioned us against wandering into lonely streets after dark. Snipers would be active for some time to come. Their quarry was the American soldier. He then announced that we were to move into the Hôtel Perey, a solid chunk of brick which in peacetime was probably a hotel for traveling salesmen, and for lovers who needed a bed for the night.

Augier missed roll call. He turned up an hour later at the Castiglione, where I was preparing for the move from modest comfort into tawdriness. He had had another happy night with Albane. When he heard about reveille, he dashed off to explain his absence. Then he returned with his duffel, and suggested we hurry over to the Perey to obtain a good room.

We staked a claim to a small but reasonably decent chamber with a dirty window looking on neighboring rooftops. I knew that I would have it mostly to myself, so long as Augier's romance with Albane lasted. For a moment, as I surveyed our tiny domain, I once again had an acute longing for the Normandy cow pasture, where close to the earth in my sleeping bag I had found genuine comfort. Then I reminded myself that the cow pasture would hardly be comfortable during the coming winter. We talked enviously of our captain, and the luxury of the Hôtel Scribe. Augier said I shouldn't envy the officers. I should envy him, and the percale sheets in Albane's Champs-Élysées apartment. I confessed I did envy him, but didn't want to be enslaved by *amour*.

Lunch in the ground floor field kitchen consisted of soup, bread, spam, and some canned fruit. We carried our clanking gear along a service corridor into the cobbled yard, where the traditional disposal cans were placed. What wasn't traditional, from that day and on into the winter, was the line of men and women, and sometimes children, each an emissary of a starving household, holding pots or dishes out to us, soliciting leftovers. Into these we pushed whatever we had left over—oatmeal, pancakes, bits of stew and steak. And always coffee, for which the Parisians brought special containers. Much of the line was composed not of the impoverished, but simply bourgeois victims of war who couldn't pay the extortionate prices of the black marketeers. We got to know most of the people in line, joked with them, brought them extra bits and refills of coffee. In this way we helped feed a tiny segment of a once fashionable neighborhood.

LIANE AND HER COMPANIONS

In the past, I had always lived on the romantic Left Bank of the Seine. Now in the quaint and gloomy little Cité du Retiro, I was in the very heart of the Right Bank. Here stands the Louvre, the great private hôtels, the splendid parks, the Arc de Triomphe and *grands boulevards,* the spacious and affluent sections, the seat of government, and the imposing churches. I found my first days in the *rive droite* enchanting. From my tucked-in corner, I stepped with ease into a metropolis. Each evening during these days of liberation people gathered, prolonging the carnival spirit. Strangers embraced as if they were old friends.

As had been predicted, everyone now seemed to have been in the Resistance, although there actually had been a great acquiescence by many. What can a city do, when an enemy plants its machine-guns in the streets while claiming it is your friend? The impulsive firebrands were shot or carried off by the Gestapo. The timid lived in silence, and tried to act as if they were invisible. Now suddenly, after four long years, the silences were being broken. People could say, without fear, anything that came into their heads. They were back in the world of *Liberté, Égalité, Fraternité*. But political views were always at variance in France, and everyone knew the tranquillity couldn't last. The city needed food. The electricity was shut down, the metro couldn't run. The blackout was real, as it had been during the Nazi presence. Paris had only moonlight, candles, and some weak bulbs.

I set out one evening for my regular fraternization with the people in the streets. I usually wandered up the rue Royale to the Church of the Madeleine, and then sauntered in the boulevards, or sat at the Café de la Paix. Though snipers continued their nightly random shooting, in the crowds one felt safe—protected by the general gregariousness. My notes of the evening are dated September 4, 1944. The moment comes back to me in its crepuscular setting—the sky cloudless, the sun setting.

Suddenly a young girl planted herself in front of me. With a gesture of triumph, she exclaimed she had found me at last! I was looking into a pair of searching dark eyes, a beaming young face. Nothing in her manner defined her as a prostitute in search of a customer. She was shabbily dressed in a faded blue blouse and a wrinkled skirt. Yet she seemed agile and full of energy. She was with another girl a couple of years older, dressed more trimly in the boulevard way.

There was something familiar about the younger girl. I told myself she was probably just another schoolgirl who wanted to talk with an American soldier. She surprised me by saying she'd been looking for me every evening during the past week. I struggled to place her. She gently touched my shoulder, and said that she could help me out. Didn't I remember, outside the Hôtel Corneille, how I had offered to translate for a group of girls and some American soldiers? Yes, I replied, recalling that she spoke a fractured English consisting entirely of nouns.

"You were ready to help us," she said, "and then you disappeared."

I could satisfy her about this. The young soldiers thought I was interfering with their pick up, and so I'd backed away. I was a sergeant, and didn't want to make the soldiers feel I was pulling rank. The girl said I had left them stranded with "a bunch of infants" who wanted to bed them. She and the other girls weren't looking for sex. They wanted serious conversation, and I looked very serious. I suggested that if they wished to continue the conversation, we might try to get a table in the Café Weber.

Sitting between my new acquaintances, I asked their names. The talkative one was Liane. The other's name was Annic. She wore a modest brown dress, a thin white sweater, and stockings that showed off her slender legs. She used little make-up, and looked at me with calm but inquiring eyes. She seemed less impulsive, less spontaneous than Liane. They sat quietly, expecting me to start saying "intellectual" things. I was highly amused. I told the girls my first name, and remarked that it sounded almost like Liane's. Liane said that was a very intellectual observation. Intellectuals are always involved with words. The French nation, she said, took pride in its intellectuals, but made no fuss about them. In fact, it usually spoke of its "*élite intellectuelle*"—meaning people who offer ideas, explore problems, and propose solutions. Rousseau proclaimed that all persons were born equal, but in actuality people attained different degrees of equality.

This display of conversational agility prodded me into saying that in America, a culture made up of people originally from Puritan England and other parts of Europe, material gain was more valued than learning and culture. Professors were mostly considered impractical and absent-minded. Intellectuals were usually designated as highbrows. This implied a certain contempt. The girls thought this very funny, and made me spell "highbrow." In addition, the word *"élite"* was considered in America a bad word, even a dirty word. It implied class distinctions, as in Britain—people who consider themselves superior to their fellow citizens.

Liane went on to ask what kind of doctors we had in the U.S., and who the most important poets and writers were. She said she knew nothing about the U.S.A., or very little. She had grown up in Central Europe before coming to France, and had never had a chance to listen to American broadcasts, through they had picked up some pop songs. Annic wanted to know when they would get to see *Gone With the Wind.* I couldn't say when American films would start coming to France, but I was sure Hollywood wouldn't delay very long once the war was over.

I told the girls I was flattered to have been selected as an informant to a young generation of schoolgirls like themselves. Schoolgirls? At this they laughed. Did I think they were schoolgirls? No such luck, they said. The war had cut them off from schools. Liane was a ballet dancer; she had been from childhood. I realized why I had thought she walked gracefully. Annic said she was probably what Americans call a "social worker." She had spent many months helping Jewish victims—especially children—escape from Nazi roundups. Liane said that it would be delightful to have been the kind of schoolgirls I imagined. "But," she said—and her voice became dry and filled with sorrow—"I'm Jewish. Annic is half-Jewish. We can laugh now because we're probably at last free. I say probably because Jews can never be positive about their fate."

I watched the waiters draw blackout curtains across the café front, as we sat for a few moments in silence. The physical blackness conveyed a moral blackness. Finally, I broke the silence by saying that I too was Jewish, and that it made me wonder that they hadn't discerned this. Words began pouring out. Annic said that her Jewish mother died before the war. Her Protestant father was a soldier in the defeated French army. She passed as a Protestant. Liane spoke as if she wished to erase history, the history of her coming-of-age. She escaped a roundup of Jews one day in 1942. She was with friends in another part of Paris. She came back to the family apartment, and found it empty. Her mother and brother had been taken, her father having been deported some time earlier. She said she could talk of this only "with a feeling of ice in my heart." She described how she had only one thought once she emerged from her grief and her sense of being suddenly alone in the world. "Survive, survive, you must survive!" She was ready to move heaven and earth to avoid the fate of her parents.

In the autumn of 1944, American Jews had not yet used the word "Holocaust"—an old Greek word, meaning ritual offerings that are wholly consumed by flame. We had yet to learn of Hitler's final solution. What was known was that the Nazis were committed to perpetrating anti-Jewish acts, and to the killing of "non-Aryans." Many people presumed that Jews were being taken east as slave labor. I told the girls I had met many refugees in New York, and they sometimes talked of Hitler's belief that the Jews and various other races should be exterminated. I remember Liane spoke as if some day she might again see her parents. It wasn't until the following spring, when our troops pushed through Germany into Poland, that the full horror of Auschwitz and the other camps was discovered.

During the remainder of that evening at the Café Weber, Liane described, more eloquently than I can now record, her sense of finding herself bereft of family, alone and hunted. She had to become, she said, "a forgery"—to pin her survival on false papers and a re-invented self, to keep from falling into the hands of the Vichy *Milice,* which enforced the Nazi racial laws in France. Her father had been moving his family across Europe in flight from the Nazis. They had been in Yugoslavia, in Czechoslovakia, in Vienna. I'm not sure of the sequence. They had ended in France, feeling themselves in a safe harbor. When her family disappeared, Liane was sixteen. She went first to the unoccupied zone of France, dancing in the Marseilles opera and in nightclubs along the Riviera. She moved in a world of fear. The danger of being reported by French informers seeking to ingratiate themselves with the Nazis was constant. She did make an effort to reach Spain—a long walk in the night after crossing the border to a lake, where a boat was supposed to be waiting for her. The boat wasn't there. She made her way to a second place, where there was supposed to be a car. It too didn't materialize. She made her way back to the French Riviera.

When Hitler took over all of France, she decided to return "and get lost" in Paris. She encountered Annic in an underground boarding house run by a Jewish couple, who were constantly mindful of their pensioners. Everyone was provided with forged papers and ration cards. Annic had left her father at fourteen, when he remarried. Near Blois, she had acted in a children's theatre, and nourished hopes of a stage career. At Lyon, she had participated in a scheme to disperse about a hundred Jewish children to the countryside, where they obtained reliable asylum of the kind I had seen at Montigny. In Paris, she had taken care of a series of young women hiding in closets or concealed bedrooms. She claimed she was an artist in the forging trade. She used rubber stamps stolen from préfectures, obtaining the proper inks and pens easily in Parisian stores. Warned that she was on the Gestapo hit list, she fled to Fontainebleau, where she led a quiet life until the street fighting began in Paris. Then she returned to carry the white flags with their Red Crosses, and to rescue wounded resistance fighters. She had since developed a case of nerves. She had nightmares about Auschwitz and other infamous camps. There was no lack of them.

Liane would learn that winter that her father had died at Auschwitz. She never learned while I knew her the fate of her mother and brother. Such were the bare details of the lives these girls led in the months before the Allied landings in Normandy.

* * * * *

After our first meetings, I would find them in later afternoons in a little café in the rue Boissy-d'Anglas, near the entrance to the Cité du Retiro. They would lounge there, on the chance of my turning up for a talk. I had become a kind of guru to them—an American guru. They talked of their new freedom. Sometimes Liane would offer ironic observations, such as the day on which she went to the employment office for dancers, and found that she had to certify that she had never collaborated with the Nazis. "The tune has changed," she said, "I used to have to certify I was an Aryan."

I met the Viennese Kay, whom Annic protected during what the girls called the silent years. Lithe Kay spent weeks in a tiny room in a seventh-floor flat at the other end of Paris. Annic brought her food, books, and encouragement. Later, they showed me this jail-cell, which had one compensation: you could see the Parisian rooftops through a window. There was no way for sudden flight. The books Kay read were still there—French poetry from Baudelaire to Éluard, and a number of Annic's books on the theatre. Willowy and alert, Kay always wore a fuzzy dark blue ski outfit—probably the only warm bit of clothing she owned. Her tousled reddish hair surmounted a pair of blue-gray eyes, friendly and mischievous. There was also a plump girl named Inge, daughter of the couple that had run the boarding house for Jews. That couple had been swept away. Then Inge too had to hide.

Much to their amusement, I used to refer to this little group as "my little nest of female intellectuals." Sometimes, as I listened to their laughter and heard their stories, I had to tell myself that these young women had recollections an outsider could never grasp, no matter how well they described them—memories of another life in old European cities, earlier homes, faces, and rooms with brothers and sisters. Then came their fugitive lives. I found myself thinking more about my own Jewish-American life, from which in my younger days especially I had wanted to escape.

It would have been a pleasure to get to know them more intimately, but I accepted the role they assigned to me. I was an explainer, an informant, a wartime friend. I dispensed information, advice, and the dainties I received in friendly parcels from America. It would be best if I did not step outside my assigned role as surrogate parent. I was twice their age, and they were loaded with too much tragedy.

Liane was clearly the leader. An ambitious and determined young woman who had been delivered to a nightmare, she had read very little, and kept asking me for books, especially American ones. The girls were particularly hungry for stories of freer lives and trans-Atlantic manners. The war had made them in some ways backward children, and they wanted to catch up. They openly talked of being the "lucky ones," and felt a blend of gratitude and guilt. Why had they been spared? Why had others gone into the abyss? That was the way things happened, I insisted. It was all a great human game of dice.

Liane often soliloquized on the subject of religion. Whatever faith she had was gone. How could anyone accept a God who allowed Nazi crimes to happen, not only those against Jews but against all humanity? Who countenanced such a long war and so many other wars, even those in the Bible? How could He accept the crimes committed against children—against human innocence? With a shrug of her graceful shoulders, she added, "A God who makes allowance for devils is unthinkable!" In spite of these crimes, she could feel no hatred against human beings. When she had seen the German dead and wounded on the day of liberation—her first encounter with violent death—she had experienced only a sense of pity. She was shocked when she saw French citizens spitting on the German wounded.

On her way to the Porte d'Orléans for de Gaulle's arrival in Paris, Liane was briefly arrested by the FFI. They hesitated over her papers, which recorded her as born in Vienna. She told the Gaullist soldiers that after four years of Hitler, and the deportation of her parents, they had no right to treat her with suspicion. They eventually apologized, explaining that they were charged with de Gaulle's security and could take no chances, even with an innocent-looking girl.

* * * * *

I still have some notes from the first evening Liane invited me to her tiny room in Montmartre—about ten by ten, almost like a prison cell. It was situated at 74 rue Joseph-de-Maistre. I remember pausing at that name, some dim recollection that he fled the French Revolution and went to live in Moscow, preferring the tyranny of the Tsar. I did remark to Liane that it was strange her home was in a street bearing the name of a rather sinister figure. She rejoined that this was the safest kind of shelter. One must always recognize the presence of evil.

Liane introduced me to her concierge, a wizened old lady who scrutinized me with microscopic eyes. She knew, Liane said, how to be deaf and vague when the Gestapo prowled. Other concierges were police spies. Liane's room was one flight up. There was a small washstand at the entrance. You had to go down the hall to the toilet. Liane had scattered brightly-colored cushions along the narrow sofa that served as her bed. Above the sofa was an old-fashioned wire mesh, in which she had placed a few surviving family snapshots—her older brother, her mother, and her beloved father. Some were of herself as a baby, and on her toes as a child ballerina. The mother looked worn and frightened, always on the edge of each snapshot, as if she wanted to escape.

There were a couple of chairs, and a tiny table near a very small window. On it, a single candle. I settled into a rickety chair. Annic sat on the couch. A few minutes later I heard a peculiar whistle: two or three notes, and a warble. Liane's visitors always signaled: surprise was dangerous. The friend knocked, a single short tap and then a sequence of them, as if this was the office of a secret society or a spy agency. It was the slim-waisted Kay, her reddish hair piled high on her head. On other occasions there were new faces. Young men whistled, warbled, and tapped their way in.

When my birthday came round, I invited Liane to help me celebrate it. I wanted to see whether I could have a date with her alone. When the time came, however, Liane had Annic with her as usual.

I had planned to take them to a concert—that, I thought, would be nice and even highbrow. But the event was canceled, and when we got to a movie house showing newsreels of the battle for Paris, we found a line winding around two blocks. Liane then suggested we go to her place. I picked up some tinned food, biscuits, and wine at the Hôtel Perey. They had some apple sauce, the only food in the house. We ate the corned beef, stew, and biscuits I brought. The girls solemnly toasted the beginning of my thirty-eighth year.

On another evening, Liane had over half-a-dozen young men from a group called "*les Compagnons,*" which sang stylized versions of old French songs like "*Frère Jacques*" or "*Au Clair de la Lune.*" (I would later hear the entire company in concert in Paris, and on one occasion after the war, in New York.) We cleared enough space for their movements, which cast grotesque shadows on the wall. The large shadows in the candlelight reminded me that they were children of disaster. Few were Jewish; all had served in the Resistance. They talked freely, and exulted in their sense of freedom. Still, I felt that their inner worlds were clouded and troubled, as if in turning a corner they might still find themselves looking at a Nazi pistol or machine gun. Small wonder, then, that the *Compagnons de Musique* offered nostalgic songs with distortions of voice and manner, and with ghostly shadows.

We asked Liane to dance for us. When she said there wasn't enough room, everyone drew against the walls. Reluctantly, she agreed to take a few steps. She used a recording of the Tannhauser Overture. She was wearing her leotard, and threw a shawl over her shoulders. It was easy to appreciate her grace of movement and the depth of emotion. On that limited stage, her dance became a mix of mime and body posture, with much spinning in one place on her toes. She too cast a strange shadow, an uncalculated caricature of her belief in her art. What we saw did suggest that she had a distinct talent, and that fate had deprived her of an opportunity to expand and test herself. Later that evening, I went back to the sofa and studied her father's face in the little snapshot. His penetrating troubled eyes looked directly at the camera. A small, neatly-dressed man, his beard was carefully trimmed, and there was a suggestion of elegance in his stance. I thought of his years of wandering from country to country, so that the family never could put down roots. Liane came over. I told her I was deeply moved by the sadness and worry I read in her father's face. Liane assured me he wasn't always so serious or anxious. He talked brilliantly about world affairs, and lived in high hopes that they would make their way, even to America if necessary. And then she added, after a pause, "You know you remind me of him."

This was my last visit to her little room, but in the coming months I did receive a handful of letters from her. A note that reached me in Strasbourg announced, "I work and am having a very nice success" as *première danseuse* at the Théâtre Sébastopol in Lille. Some time later, another letter began in English, "I received your letter with a great plaisir. It is very nice from you to remain your little dancing girl, and your great friend," but soon lapsed into French, "even though it will be less funny than my English, which is certainly a bit comical." Still at the Sébastopol, she found herself yearning for her room "among my dear friends because I've had enough of Lille and the Lillois. Even my nice success saddens me because I enjoy it here in solitude."

She would turn up that spring in Paris for a long weekend to celebrate the victory in Europe. Hitler was dead; his Chancellery in Berlin was in ruins. I invited all the girls to a dance held during the universal delirium of that week in an old warehouse—our improvised barracks after I returned from the Alsatian front. We danced far into the night. Liane was a delightful partner. I remember how at a given moment she broke away—I wasn't able perhaps to give her the proper sense of floating on air—and began to do pirouettes. The other dancers stopped to watch her. Her exhibitionistic side was now on display, a burst of light airy spinning. The soldiers and their girl friends clapped and cheered. I left soon after for Germany. Though I would hear from Liane occasionally in later years, this was my last memory of her.

TOP LEFT: Fannie and Simon Edel, Montreal, November 12, 1930.

TOP RIGHT: Leon and Abraham Edel, in pony fur coats, in Rovno, Russia, about 1911–1912; Leon, left, is between 3 and 4, Abraham between 2 and 3.

BOTTOM RIGHT: Leon and Abraham Edel, McGill University graduation, 1927.

BOTTOM LEFT: Leon Edel, in robe second from left; Louis Rapkine, in suit; and other residents of La Maison Canadienne, Paris, 1931.

The liberation of Rennes, August 4, 1944 (all photos by Lawrence Riordan, Psychological Warfare Division, Office of War Information).

TOP: Ceremony in the Place de la Mairie.

BELOW LEFT: Inside the Mairie; Leon Edel sits at the table, far left.

BELOW RIGHT: Louis Huot addresses the press.

TOP LEFT: Camille Lemercier; the photo is inscribed on the back:
   For "Doc" with best wishes—and in memory of our late good friend. Louis [Huot].
TOP RIGHT: Louis Rapkine.
BOTTOM LEFT: Eugene Jolas.
BOTTOM RIGHT: Paul Dombrowski; the inscription reads
   To Leon: From the alter ego, Paul, 14 Apr. 1944.

Leon Edel, Honolulu (photo by Ron Ronck).

PART FOUR
BOULEVARD WINTER

In the rue d'Aguesseau
Behind the Lines
Searching for Sylvia Beach
Edith's Lover in Old Age: Encounters with W. Morton Fullerton
Interiors
From My Notebook
A Parachutist's Story
The Performing Arts
Hospitals
Romances and Show Biz
Réveillon 1944

With Luther Conant, Spring 1945.

IN THE RUE D'AGUESSEAU

Psychological Warfare had installed itself in a series of dusty offices formerly used by the Nazis in the rue d'Aguesseau, about three minutes from the Hôtel Perey. We were the Psychological Warfare Division of Supreme Headquarters, Allied Expeditionary Force (SHAEF). Our mission was to outflank Hitler's propaganda machine. Our method was to use political and propaganda warfare—leaflets in the field and radio broadcasts—to block or counteract the German radio that sought to keep the Germans hypnotized and to frighten the rest of Europe.

Though I was on loan from the Twelfth Army Group to SHAEF, I recognized at once that I would have few immediate duties. I had no desire to be sent to Nancy, where my old unit was settled in as part of General Patton's psychological warfare. The snows came early all along the western front, and Patton might have to spend the winter on the periphery of Germany. Our month in Normandy had been a delight; a winter in Alsace or Lorraine would be a misery. In my first interview with Luther Conant, the civilian head of the Psychwar press section, and someone whom I had worked with before, at *PM*, I therefore offered to write a daily intelligence report on the contents of the French press—those little sheets without advertisements I had been reading with fascination from my first days in Paris. Conant said this sort of work belonged to the chief intelligence officer in the upper ranks of Psychwar, or to the Office of Strategic Services. I reminded him I had worked for the Agence Havas in the mid-thirties. Conant asked me to deliver a sample report during the next few days, and we'd go on from there. For the present, it could serve as a useful in-house resource.

To an uninitiated person, the French newspaper sheets, each about nine by twelve inches and printed on both sides, must have seemed a hodgepodge of fragmentary items. When I read these sheets, I learned that individuals who collaborated with the Nazis were being punished by special tribunals. In various parts of France, courts were conducting summary proceedings. Firing squads were busy. Little paragraphs—

usually three lines in minute print—reported that specific collaborators had been executed. Some well-known figures committed suicide. Others disappeared. Still others faced treason trials. More vital space was given to food rationing, and news of what supplies were arriving from America as well as from the provinces. The closings of black market restaurants were also headlined. I remember one item about an unnamed GI convicted by a U.S. Army court martial to life imprisonment for selling twenty gallons of gas on the black market. Army public relations kept such items under wraps, so as not to disturb Army morale, but occasionally the items found their way into the French newspapers.

My main purpose was to appraise the political shading of each paper. The conservative *Figaro,* which had refused to publish under the Germans, was among the first to emerge. It covered the news in its old-fashioned way, with small, often witty editorial commentaries set in italics. *Combat,* a new leftist journal representing an important segment of the Resistance, had its crisp daily editorial by Albert Camus. Freedom of the press—among the original Rights of Man proclaimed by the French Revolution—was being re-established. The only freedom disallowed was freedom for those judged to be traitors. There was also French Army censorship, similar to ours. No news was published that might help the enemy.

My daily intelligence analysis was received with distinct surprise and approval. Within a few days, I was told I was producing a kind of reader's digest of the press for the many officers and other personnel who couldn't read French, yet wanted to know what was in the papers. Word came from on high that a complete summary would be appreciated. The intelligence agencies, including the OSS, signaled that I was filling a gap in their own work. They liked my format and political analysis. From my Havas days, I had at my fingertips the political nuances that are typically a mystery to Americans. The French Radical Socialists, for example, weren't as radical as the socialists, or the left liberals like Camus, who were cautious about Russian communism, or certainly the hard line communists themselves, whom I knew well from their newspaper *Humanité.* This entire spectrum was further subdivided by the new resistance groups, and not least by those newspapers reflecting the politics and administration of Charles de Gaulle.

Soon Conant arranged for wider distribution. One morning a baby lieutenant entered my office, and announced self-importantly that he had been assigned to deliver the report every day by 3 p.m. for mimeographing. I asked whether this job would interfere with his other duties. He was naive enough to announce it was his main responsibility.

BEHIND THE LINES

My Parisian geography that autumn consisted of the boulevards leading to the Place de l'Opéra, and a few fixed points within them. Once winter set in, my main quest was for warmth. At the far end of the day, I would risk a few minutes in my overcoat at my little writing table, recording with numbed fingers the notes from which I derive much of this narrative. Augier was absent, doubtless in soft warm sheets somewhere in the Champs-Élysées. In the boulevards, bistros, cafés, and *boîtes de nuit*—"boxes of the night," i.e. cabarets—I found some warmth in drink and fellowship, largely military. *Vin ordinaire* was warmed up for the habitués.

My wanderings took me from the Hôtel Perey to the Café Weber, from the Weber to the Scribe, and from the Scribe to the newly opened Rainbow Corner, which the Red Cross set up in what had been a lounge for Nazi soldiers at the Café de la Paix. German murals were still in place: scenes showing Salzburg and Munich, or a German farmer at his plow, or a bit of Nazi humor—a wife leading a besotted husband out of a Ratskeller. In these spots I found female company—Red Cross workers, or the new WACs, who had not yet been integrated, as they are today, into the fighting forces.

One distinct spot of warmth was our mess in the Hôtel Perey, where we breakfasted in the comfort of the kitchen stoves. The shivering line of Parisians waiting for scraps contributed to a vague sense of guilt. Our discomforts came from Paris's winter temperatures, indoors and out, but these seemed trifling compared to the hunger which I saw in the eyes of young and old as they received our leavings. The history of our food supplies was complicated. For a few days our meals acquired a sameness: hot dogs and spam and some canned fruits. Then our mess officer disappeared. He was court martialed for selling our stocks of food, apparently in anticipation of further supplies, to the black market. Cigarette peddling seemed exempt from punishment. We were generously supplied from the PX; the French invariably asked for them—as gifts, or tips, or barter. On occasion I paid booksellers with them. Three or four packs were sufficient to obtain valuable books.

During those early winter days, it took very little time for the "brain trust" of psychwar to find each other. There were GIs from OSS and from military intelligence. I remember one in particular, an aide to our head of intelligence, whom we called the "junior brain" because he was in his early twenties. (Several of us, including myself, were "senior" brains.) His name was Morris Janowitz, and he could brilliantly interpret the army communiqués. He also was an expert on the morale of the Wehrmacht, which he said we mustn't underestimate, although the top German brass knew how befuddled Hitler himself was. A bright rear-echelon corporal—he would later become an officer—he weighed his words and laughed very little. He disappeared for a couple of weeks on an information trip to the front. When he returned, I asked him whether he thought the Allies could soon end the war. We mustn't expect, he said, a sudden victory. I pushed him to say what was the hold-up, since we were now the attacking forces. His answer was short and pointed:

"Because our men don't want to die."

We were not a fanatical army, and we weren't fighting for our own soil. The British and French, the Belgians and the Dutch, and the other armies fighting from exile, had much stronger motivations than we had—all kinds of ties to the land, family, clan, and race. Nor did we have the dedication of the Russian soldiers, who in their tyrannous land fought street by street or across the steppes against Hitler, as their ancestors had fought Napoleon. Whether Californians or Texans, Nebraskans or New Yorkers, our soldiers asked themselves what they were fighting for. When confronted by such questions, the children of the uninvaded U.S. usually thought of the Pacific. Japan had attacked us when it bombed Pearl Harbor. The American boys in Europe—I saw them all around me—were sons of the great consuming American public. No amount of cigarettes, ice cream, or candy, however, could compensate for the soldiers' deep resistance to laying down their lives on foreign soil, no matter how much they were reminded that they fought for the American flag.

Our diplomacy tended to be equally naked and imperative. The British were different. For instance, very shortly after the liberation I attended an Anglo-French evening at the French national theater.

Charles Laughton flew in to do a scene from Molière in French, overacting powerfully and effectively as usual. I remember that Graham Greene talked briefly, and W. H. Auden read some poems. Then, a few days later, a British delegation arrived in Paris for trade discussions with de Gaulle. For the British, culture was an introduction to business, while our officials tended to want to get down to business without any delays, protocol, or amenities.

During the evenings, when we sought escape from loneliness and found ourselves in the small cabarets, we were in the midst of a perpetual conversation, a continuous drinking party, a congress of storytelling. Most of the soldiers I met were depressed. They hated the long periods of idleness. They were homesick. They disliked their officers. Drink was their solace and their escape, and so were women. Tolstoy wrote that when soldiers congregate, they describe battles as they would have liked them to be, or as they heard them described by others, "making them sound more glorious and quite unlike what they actually were." He adds, "to tell the truth is very difficult and young people are rarely capable of it." If one listened carefully, however, truth crept into the interstices of the boasting. One soldier described how on guard duty in a battle zone he stepped in the dark on dismembered corpses. Macho tales, histories of practical jokes, and Rabelaisian adventures alongside complaints of dirt and discomfort were the favorite anecdotes, though. There was also a natural envy of officer privileges—of their comfortable and often luxurious housing and dining, for instance, when compared with the warehouses or shoddy hotels provided for enlisted men.

In my boulevard encounters I was struck by the struggle of the WACS. I remember drinking coffee with a WAC in the Rainbow Corner, and her sitting half-asleep, worn out by seven work days in a row. I also came on a Red Cross girl, who served coffee with tears rolling down her cheeks. She showed perseverance, carrying on although she had just learned her brother had been killed in action. When I tried to find words of comfort, she kept asking, "Why are we fighting the Germans?"

SEARCHING FOR SYLVIA BEACH

I went in search of Sylvia Beach in mid-September, when my routines in the rue d'Aguesseau provided free hours for roaming in a reawakening Paris. I had known Sylvia in the 1920s and 1930s, during the time of her greatest success. I had received little news of her since then, and wondered what had become of her English book shop and lending library, "Shakespeare and Company," in the Latin Quarter. Sylvia was a rooted expatriate. After 1918, she left her clergyman father's home in Princeton and settled in France. She had a deep attachment for her fellow shopkeeper Adrienne Monnier. Adrienne's shop, across the street in the rue de l'Odéon, was the model for Sylvia's own. Both of these remarkable ladies were votaries of the modern from the start, and it had been James Joyce's avant-gardism that thrilled Sylvia into publishing *Ulysses*. In the United States, it was banned; the Nazis, it seemed, were not the only enemies of books.

The two young women were original, amusing, professional, and alert to the literary and artistic winds that blew in the 1920s. Famous writers—French, English, and also American—came to both shops. The light-eyed Sylvia, with her mannish stride and feminine reticence, dressed trimly and often boyishly. She had a winning smile and a musical voice. Adrienne was soft, pink-cheeked, and invariably dressed in full gray skirts and waistcoats, worn over a white blouse. She looked as if she had just stepped out of a Flemish painting. She combed her hair back tight, and offered a kind of historical dignity to the rue de l'Odéon, both in stance and costume, that contrasted with Sylvia's hearty Americanism. In Adrienne's bookshop, you might find yourself browsing next to Gide and Valéry, or lesser lights like Artaud or Maurois. In Sylvia's shop, you met the latest American writers—Hemingway and Fitzgerald, Thornton Wilder or William Carlos Williams, Ezra Pound, and on occasion, T. S. Eliot and Joyce. The shops were complementary, and represented the high culture of both sides of the English Channel, as well as both sides of the Atlantic.

The best place to start searching for Sylvia, and perhaps Adrienne, would obviously be where I had last seen them. The rue de l'Odéon was a neat, quiet street that Simone de Beauvoir once described as having the air of a suburban thoroughfare. I went there upon arriving in Paris during the autumn of 1928. I was eager to buy a copy of *Ulysses,* then considered a rarity. (My discovery of Joyce antedated my interest in Henry James.) When I first saw it, No. 12 rue de l'Odéon seemed a homelike shop, with its crowded shelves, the little stove parked in its fireplace, and the wall above covered with photos of the masters of Anglo-American modernity, along with a few former masters such as Walt Whitman and Edgar Allan Poe. One of the most interesting photos was of Ezra Pound, slouching in an armchair. Ford Madox Ford was stiff and formal, about to wheeze a sentence. And to their right, James Joyce, holding himself somewhat aloof, as if he tolerated their company but didn't want to be too near them. It was a magical moment for me to find myself in this literary shrine, and to have a smiling Sylvia place in my hands, for several hundred francs, a blue-wrapped *Ulysses*—the shade of blue of the Greek flag, she explained. I wondered then whether I would ever get to set eyes on Joyce.

From my first meeting with Sylvia had grown an acquaintanceship. She was always welcoming, in her semi-formal way, and ready to pass on the latest gossip about Joyce, discreetly filtered for general consumption. When she learned of my pursuit of Henry James—I had written an MA thesis on him at McGill, and was writing my Sorbonne dissertation on him as well—she sent me to see W. Morton Fullerton, who was then writing articles on American politics for the *Figaro.* Sometimes when Sylvia had a celebrity in the shop, she would introduce me as a Canadian Jamesian. One day she presented a young-looking, prematurely plump Cyril Connolly—long before he acquired his reputation as editor of *Horizon.* The name of Henry James was a sufficient introduction. He borrowed a sheet of paper from Sylvia, and leaning against a bit of free space on the photo-covered wall, scribbled a letter of introduction to Logan Pearsall Smith, an American expatriate writer, and a former acquaintance of James. "Logan will want to talk with you," he said. I carried the letter to London the next time I crossed the Channel, and Logan promptly asked me to lunch. He told me a goodly number of Jamesian anecdotes—a few authentic, and the rest the fruit of his lively imagination, including James saying he would "walk barefoot in the snow" to meet Santayana!

I have in particular a vivid memory of the pleasure Sylvia gave me in 1931, when she invited me to a special evening in Adrienne's book shop devoted to a reading of an approximate French translation of Joyce's "Anna Livia Plurabelle," the best known fragment of his "work in progress." A distinguished translation committee had been formed, with Joyce as chairman. Samuel Beckett, whose great reputation was yet to come, undertook the job of creating a first draft. Then there was Philippe Soupault, one of France's younger surrealists, and a poet and novelist; Paul Léon, a Russian-English linguist, who became a secretary and financial manager to Joyce; Alfred Perron, a French scholar who was familiar with Dublin; and Adrienne herself. Eugene Jolas, the tri-lingual editor of *transition,* went over the final version. When I arrived, Adrienne was arranging the text on a music stand. She was to read it after Soupault described the translation process. He told us the committee held fifteen meetings, usually on Thursdays precisely at 2:30 p.m. They sat at a round table, with Joyce in a big armchair, for three hours. It was a phrase by phrase job, with Joyce insisting always that the French language capture the rhythms so important to him.

I arrived for the reading when the shop was half full. A number of distinguished men were inspecting Adrienne's shelves as they waited for the start; I thought I recognized Gide and Valéry. Joyce wasn't visible. The shop was warm and festive. The tables had been shoved back, and half a hundred folding chairs placed in a series of semi-circles. As a Sorbonne student, I suppose I felt as if I was an outsider. I looked for the most inconspicuous place I could find—a little corner, where I took refuge. All the chairs were soon filled, and there was a hush as Adrienne prepared to intone "Anna Livia." Suddenly a tall figure brushed past my knees, and took possession of the one other folding chair in my niche. James Joyce was sitting a few inches from me.

I have told this episode before, in my book *Stuff of Sleep and Dreams,* but I am finding other words now. I had glimpsed Joyce before, on certain occasions at the Paris Opera, when I took part in a claque Sylvia helped Joyce organize to applaud an Irish tenor he admired and envied. Now he seemed larger than life, with his thick glasses, which gave him an owl-like countenance, set into his tall head. He slouched in his narrow chair, his body descending into a kind of question mark, the position he favored for himself. I don't think he saw much of me, given his near-sightedness. He sat distant and aloof. I cast furtive glances at him at certain moments, though I wanted to stare. I still thought of him as my culture hero. Fate had granted me his presence for this hour. Had I been a bit bolder, I might have made a remark or two, to see whether he would respond. But I was over-awed. Any remark on his work would seem to be fatuous, as if I were showing off my having read him. He doubtless would have liked to hear praise. But I remained silent—frightened by his reputation and his passive presence.

The memory of that evening reminds me of an afternoon a few months earlier, when Sylvia was alone in the shop. Her eyes bright, she said she had a surprise for me. From an adjoining room she brought in a shining new record from the Orthological Institute in Cambridge, made by C. K. Ogden and his associates, who experimented with language and verbal novelty. She moved a gramophone to the table and slowly wound it up. "I must show you something else," she said—a series of large sheets that looked like medieval parchments. It was the text of the Anna Livia fragment, enlarged to facilitate Joyce's reading, given his damaged eyesight. I followed the text as she played the disc. His fine tenor voice suddenly filled the shop—

Well, you know or don't you kennet or haven't I told you every telling has a taling and that's the he and the she of it.

The voice was firm and clear, the words clipped, the words like a series of precise musical notes.

Look, look, the dusk is growing!

Joyce read the word "look" with an "oo" sound.

My branches lofty are taking root. And my cold cher's gone ashley.

The voices Joyce imitated were those of washerwomen on the banks of the river. He read on through their counting of the items of clothing being washed, the gossip of the women. The flipping and flapping of the clothes, words that imitate the sounds, and the sounds that convey the voices, continued until we came to the final fading of his voice, as Joyce ended softly and tenderly:

Night! Night! My ho head halls. I feel as heavy as yonder stone. Tell me of John or Shaun? Who were Shem and Shaun the living sons or daughters of? Night now! Tell me, tell me, tell me, elm! Night night! Telmetale of stem or stone. Beside the rivering waters of, hitherandthithering waters of. Night!

I call up these bits of verbal beauty, recollecting in my inner ear the Joycean skill and charm—that charm Sylvia Beach found in Joyce when he first came to her old shop in a nearby street. In later years, I was to scale him down to his human size, recognizing his endless aggressions and audacities, his strange preoccupation with himself, as if he were the sole inhabitant of the universe. I came to think of him as a poet lodged in the perceptions of a journalist, who attached too much importance to what was said about him in the papers. Certainly he was an eccentric genius, and the most rebellious and difficult of all the Anglo-Irish writers—from Wilde to Shaw, and Yeats to George Moore.

Sylvia's own memoirs remind us how much it meant for her to encounter the mysterious Irishman whose *Ulysses* was then being serialized—and banned—in an American journal. We cannot say any longer whether she was in love with him. We know her deepest love was for Adrienne, but certainly she felt a kind of spiritual exaltation at that early meeting in her first shop, for Joyce had great charisma—as if he had devoted his genius to giving himself a special character. And then in his talk he had a way of laughing at himself which amused people, until they realized that this was artful conning—a kind of confession of sins, and a suggestion that they were laughable. In his biography of Joyce, Richard Ellmann makes a great deal of this sense of humor, without realizing how much it was the work of an artful egotist, inventing funny excuses for his pathological shortcomings and his inconveniencing of others. Perhaps Sylvia's admiration was more awe and bewilderment; in due course, though, she discovered the real Joyce, merciless in his belief that the world owed his genius everything.

Once she became his publisher, he demanded much more of her than any author in the whole history of Anglo-Irish literature. She constantly paid him advances for unearned royalties; in fact, she paid him to the verge of bankruptcy. He treated her as if she were a young girl hired to run errands, search in libraries, read his proofs. He always traveled without cash, and sent wires for money for himself and his wife. His son also dropped into the shop, asking for a 1000 franc note or other sums, carrying a quick apologetic note from Joyce. Sometimes the apology was omitted. She had to fetch eyedrops from the clinic where his glaucoma was under constant treatment. Ellmann treated this as if it were a routine author-publisher affair, admitting the personal dimensions only in a footnote: "That Sylvia Beach had much to complain about is substantiated by Joyce's letters to her." He cites a confessional note in which Joyce resorts to self-mockery to obtain forgiveness. "I do not think I have the right to plague and pester you night, noon and morning for money, money, money," he wrote, "You are altogether overworked without my rapping at the door." But he did certainly plague and pester, and he obtained the money. All Paris knew this. Janet Flanner described Sylvia as "a beast of burden struggling beneath the crushing load of a singular author's genius and egotism." The French poet André Spire, at whose home Sylvia first encountered Joyce, spoke of her "at the service of the most demanding, capricious, harassing of authors," while Malcolm Cowley said, "Joyce accepted favors and demanded services as if he were not a person but a sanctified cause."

Everyone wondered why Sylvia never protested. She was usually very direct and clear about her business relations. And yet she allowed Joyce to exploit her time and time again. Joyce himself did note that "All she ever did was to make me a present of the ten best years of her life." In a later time, after Joyce was dead, Sylvia allowed herself to say that Joyce did as much persecuting as being persecuted. In her private correspondence, she described him as "not only a very great writer but also a great businessman, hard as nails." She also called him "the great lovable but merciless man," whose "one-sided business methods" were the least admirable side of his character. "He thinks, like Napoleon, that his fellow beings are only made to serve his ends," she writes, "He'd grind their bones to make his bread." But again she wavered: "After all, the books were Joyce's. A baby belongs to its mother, not to the midwife, doesn't it?" This was a high example of Sylvia's confusions of feeling.

* * * * *

The rue de l'Odéon seemed deserted when I reached it early one afternoon in mid-September, a day of cloud and chill in post-liberation Paris. On the left side I saw Adrienne's bookshop was intact, but closed at that hour. A glance across the street confirmed my worst fear—Shakespeare & Company was gone. The portrait of the Bard that hung at right angles to the shop—as if it were a pub or an inn—was missing. The name over the windows had been painted over with a dull thick gray. The paint was cracked. I stared through the dirty windows into emptiness. The shelves were gone. I entered No. 12, under the familiar archway next to the shop. The concierge did not respond to a ring. Wondering where I could turn next, I heard a rustling sound, and saw, advancing from the rear through the shadows, a woman leading a bicycle.

We shook hands. "It's as if I had an appointment to see you at this very hour," Sylvia Beach remarked. We searched each other's eyes. I would have liked to embrace her, but we had never been as familiar as that. She smiled and exclaimed, "Almost everyone who has come to see me is in uniform." I had last seen her during the late 1930s. Her old tasteful outfits were always pleasing: now she wore heavy clothes, as if inured to cold weather. The light showed me the lines in her face. She was no longer the dark-eyed vigorous young woman of the 1920s, the Diana of the rue de l'Odéon. But wrinkles and a certain increase in weight aside, her eyes still shone. In the pleasant chiming voice I remembered so well, she was telling me that Hemingway had roared into the street on liberation day, screaming her name. He had a few of his French guerrillas with him, and waved an automatic weapon. I laughed and said he must have come from the Ritz, where he claimed to have liberated the bar. She said yes, that was exactly what he said.

I told her how surprised I was at the disappearance of Shakespeare & Company. "Everyone wishes it were open," Sylvia said, but she wasn't sure she felt up to that, after the long period of Nazi occupation. I also wondered how Adrienne's shop had survived. This was a long story, Sylvia said. She would tell me about it if I wished to accompany her. She had some errands on the Right Bank, and if I was free she would wheel her bike. We started off at a leisurely pace. Adrienne had remained open, Sylvia explained, because the Germans had been instructed to leave French shops alone. They tried to be very correct, catering to the French by showing smiling faces and being excessively polite. Adrienne maintained her circle of friends, those who remained in Paris after the fall of France.

Shakespeare & Company was another matter. It was an English and American bookshop, and the Nazis were at war with England. (After Pearl Harbor, they were at war with the United States as well.) As we sauntered toward the Seine, she told me how a German officer arrived at the shop a few days after Paris was conquered, and demanded a copy of Joyce's *Finnegans Wake*. The book had been published in 1939, the year the Germans marched into Poland. It clearly had not been available in the Reich. Sylvia told the officer the copy in her window was the only one she had. She didn't intend to sell it. The German officer became nasty; she refused to yield. He finally threatened to confiscate the entire store, and left in a rage, promising to return. Sylvia came to an immediate decision. She must close her shop. She wanted no further encounters with German officers, no visits from the Gestapo. Adrienne and various friends in the neighborhood went to work at once, carrying Sylvia's stock of books, including the entire lending library and its furniture, to an empty apartment the concierge provided in a higher story of the building. Sylvia's rare papers, manuscripts, and other memorabilia went into Adrienne's flat nearby. A can of gray paint did the rest. When darkness fell, Shakespeare & Company had disappeared.

Sylvia never knew whether the blustering officer returned, but shortly afterwards the Nazis came for her. They apparently had Gestapo signals about her, since she had befriended Walter Benjamin, the German literary critic, when he was in Paris before his last journey to the Spanish border, where in a moment of panic he committed suicide. Sylvia had also helped Françoise Bernheim, a Jewish student whom in defiance of Vichy she had escorted in Paris when Bernheim had to wear the yellow Star of David. Sylvia had also hidden her in her apartment. Françoise later was captured and died at Auschwitz.

I asked Sylvia to tell me about her internment. She shrugged away this period, saying "They kept me for seven months in a drab hotel in Vittel. They left most of us alone. Later Adrienne got me out." Sylvia did however write a vivid account of this time. The Germans rounded up some five hundred American nuns, and some women who had been American war brides in 1918, after the first war. There were a couple of poets, a few young American hookers, some society ladies, and prominent businesswomen like Sylvia. The women took advantage of their rather placid and dumb German guards. Sylvia took charge of the mail, and found other useful chores to overcome the monotony and discomfort of being, as she put it in Joycean language, "in-turned." Red Cross parcels helped sustain the women. When released by Adrienne's adroit use of pressure on French authorities, Sylvia decided to disappear like her bookshop. She went into hiding in the women's student hostel in Boul' Mich, but spent much time with Adrienne in her flat.

We crossed the Pont des Arts and strolled through the grounds of the Louvre, eventually coming out in front of the Théâtre Français. I could see that Sylvia had retained her old gifts of acute observation, and a shrewd and sympathetic pleasure in the arts of living. I found it painful to think of her now as rather adrift in the anarchy of wartime without her old center: the shop that had brought her high adventures in the arts, and been James Joyce's stepping stone to fame. She was like an aging singer in the process of losing her voice; however, she spoke courageously, if with a certain resignation, of her ongoing life. She had learned much about human grief and the waste of war with Adrienne. She had boldly survived the Germans' rule.

We didn't talk much about Joyce during our walk. I had heard long before of their estrangement. We did discuss *Finnegans Wake,* and I mentioned in passing Joyce's death not long after its publication. "He wanted to die," she said. I thought she was probably right. Joyce had much chaos in him. War meant the collapse of his sustaining world, for war undermines egotists and obliterates their creativity. Pausing in the rue Saint-Honoré just before she left me, Sylvia mentioned Charles de Gaulle. She was critical: he was being tough with the Resistance. I responded that the time for resistance seemed over. The next phase would be to have France take part as quickly as possible in the final conquest of Hitler. She mounted her bike. She hoped I would come and see her again; I would see her again, but not in Paris. I told her how much she had meant to me, and she said, "Well, that was another world."

EDITH'S LOVER IN OLD AGE:
ENCOUNTERS WITH W. MORTON FULLERTON

When I entered Paris in late August of 1944, my thoughts were elsewhere than on my old days in the capital. The city seemed benign in its beautiful summer weather, but there were German and French snipers, and we did not know what traps the Nazis had left. During the first few days at Psychological Warfare headquarters in the rue d'Aguesseau, we talked constantly with French journalists who came for explanations of the U.S. Army's doings, now that the city was in Charles de Gaulle's hands. But one day a bright newsman who spoke fluent English mentioned he worked for *Le Figaro,* and my memory suddenly went back to 1929.

"Whatever happened to Morton Fullerton?" I asked, and immediately chided myself. The newsman was too young to know; in fact, he had only recently joined *Figaro.* But he would make inquiries. I assumed Fullerton was long dead. He seemed quite elderly when I talked to him in 1929, and then again in 1930, when I found him as gracious and vague as before. But the young man telephoned me promptly to say Fullerton was alive and active. "He must be a hundred," I said. The reporter replied he was eighty; and added that Fullerton remembered me, and said he'd be glad if I would come to his mid-town rooms at 8 rue du Mont-Thabor, which served as his private office. I was welcome to come any day, at 3 p.m.

I suppose I am one of the very few survivors, perhaps even the last, who can claim to have met both Edith Wharton and her lover, W. Morton Fullerton. I went to see them on separate occasions, unaware that they knew one another. I was living and studying then in Paris. One day in late December 1929, when I was browsing in her little shop, Sylvia Beach, who had taken a lively interest in my project, said she had just met a man who had known Henry James. "One of those Americans," she said with a smile, "who seems to have lived always in Paris." He was readily accessible, for he worked at *Le Figaro,* and had once worked in the London *Times* bureau in Paris. Now in his late years, he was writing occasional French articles on American politics. "He told me he had known James long ago and for many years," said Sylvia, "They had been good friends." Such sources came scarce by that time. I wrote that very day to Fullerton, and received a prompt reply. He would be delighted to talk about Henry James.

Le Figaro's offices were until recently in the very heart of Paris, at the Rond-Point des Champs-Élysées. I approached them with a sense of excitement. Fullerton had a small office in what seemed like a labyrinth, and I was ushered in to find him sitting behind an imposing Empire table. He got up so energetically that the flabby handshake he offered seemed an anti-climax. Graying hair efficiently parted, he looked like a diplomat from the Quai d'Orsay—striped trousers, morning coat, gray necktie, the insignia of the Légion d'Honneur, and a fresh flower in his button hole. A Proustian fashion plate. His eyes wandered a great deal. He had long brown mustaches, carefully waxed, which he stroked with long tapering fingers. He reminded me of "mashers" in old illustrations of Victorian novels. He quoted poetry, as if everything he said needed rhymed support. His florid stylishness made me feel out of place. I didn't know how to deal with this phenomenon. What was more, I hadn't done my homework. I should have at least looked him up in the directories or made discreet inquiries. I took Sylvia at her word, however, and presumed he could be turned on by the mention of Henry James.

Fullerton proceeded cautiously. What sort of book was I writing? I said I wanted to get at the history of James's plays. Gradually Fullerton grew expansive. He recalled this period very well. James had come to Paris during 1893 and 1894. He stayed at the Hôtel Westminster in the rue de la Paix, and interviewed French dramatists, critics, and even a distinguished actress at the Théâtre Français. Fullerton had often accompanied James to the theater. The novelist was insatiable. He went every night. But he suddenly developed a bad case of gout—the first of many attacks he would have—and it kept him indoors. Fullerton ministered to his frustration, bringing him books and Parisian gossip.

"Do you remember any of the plays you saw together?"

My question was naive. Fullerton said he had seen so many that they were now a jumble in his mind. Well-made boulevard pieces. The husband, the wife, the lover—endless combinations and variations. James also liked music halls in London and Paris, and the Folies. The classics were always available to him at the Théâtre Français.

Fullerton dropped a few names, as if I was supposed to know to whom they belonged. My eyes and ears told me James's friend was a romantic sentimentalist and a snob, who derived his identity from a constant quest for place in French society. He had a way of exuding intimacy and charm without inspiring confidence—at least in me. I reminded myself however that he was talking to a very inexperienced young researcher. I was twenty-two.

He did offer one potential fact, a little one. He said he had somewhere a letter from James, containing the novelist's reflections about his failure on the stage. He promised to look it up for me. I told myself it was an idle promise. Fullerton wasn't the sort of man who would bother. I think he read my mind, for he assured me the letter *did* exist. However, he didn't know at the moment where to look for it. It was buried in five decades of papers. That was pretty much the substance of our first meeting. Affable throughout, he escorted me politely to the door with another soft handshake.

Many months later, when I was nearing the end of my book, I wrote to jog Fullerton's memory. Had he ever found the letter? He wrote back that my inquiry embarrassed him. He couldn't help me at this moment: his papers were in worse disorder than ever. He assured me that the letter wasn't a fiction, it existed. I went to press without it, telling myself one never finds in one's searches the last word about anything. The book appeared in 1932. I sent Fullerton a copy. His reply, very prompt, was in his truest form—

"Do you know my quick and first reaction on contemplating the impressive wide-margined pages of the two volumes you have devoted to the greatest of our American artists in prose? It was pathetically this: I must be off to show them to James!"

And then a half a dozen lines of poetry—

Oh sweet communion of the vanished days
When his large eyes looked calmly into mine
But gone he is, and I am left alone.
And pleasant places, knowing him of yore
Seem strange without him, for their charm is flown.
And yet they speak of him as not before.

He truly was *un homme de coeur*. I can't imagine anyone else offering such verses; they were the lucubration of a fashion plate like Fullerton.

These lines appeared on *Figaro* stationery—a capital F with a quill pen run through it. The date was February 11, 1932.

*****

As I climbed to the sixth floor of Number 8 in 1944, I told myself that Fullerton at eighty must be a hearty individual. I had asked the concierge how so old a man managed the ascent. She assured me he was spry enough. "He does it every day," she said. Her smile showed a fondness for the old gentleman. Puffing a bit at the top, I saw one door open in the curved corridor. I peered in to make sure I was at the right entrance. A little old man sat at a small desk in the corner of a large cluttered room.

There were books on floor and table, and shelves piled high with the funereal black library boxes usually designed for documents. I said "Mr. Fullerton?" He responded in French, but didn't get up. I walked over to him. His hand was wispy, cold, a mere touch of a handshake. We exchanged courteous remarks in French. He said he had lately come on my long-ago book about the James plays, and wondered what had become of me. I told him I had often wondered about him.

My glance took in a wreck of the old fashion plate. The fine aristocratic mustaches were now drooping irregularly. His clothes were shabby. His eyes were rheumy. His gray hair was in disorder. At moments he drooled like an infant. He had the look of a dried plant. With the picture of the old Morton Fullerton in my mind, I had difficulty accepting so much alteration. Yet I soon had evidence of considerable energy behind this dilapidated front. He beckoned me to a small chair beside his desk. A book lay on the seat. I recognized the pale green binding of James's *Theatricals, First Series,* 1894. I picked it up so as to be able to sit down. Laid into it was the long missing letter. Fullerton watched me with the mischievous little smile of a pleased child. He was keeping a fifteen-year-old promise.

I summoned some flowery French phrase of thanks for his thoughtfulness and generosity, and took the letter out of the book. It was written on James's embossed stationery, from De Vere Gardens in London. The handwriting was unmistakable—four pages covered with the rapid forward-plunging quasi-legible hand. Still in French, Fullerton said "*Allez, allez,* read it! I've plenty of time." I sat down and read it—read some of the phrases aloud to break the silence. The letter was clearly a response to the journalist's commiseration on the flop of James's play *Guy Domville* in 1895. When I finished scanning it, Fullerton emerged from behind the desk. He was bent and a bit shaky. He said the war had enabled him to find many missing letters and papers. He shuffled over to an old-fashioned revolving bookcase that stood in the middle of the room. Suddenly he stopped speaking French. He pulled himself up, and very clearly and dramatically announced, "There you have it—my life!"

Morton Fullerton had become an archive.

* * * * *

After this sudden fulfillment of his old promise, we talked briefly about the liberation of Paris. I asked him how he had managed to survive the Nazi occupation. He hadn't been bothered. "An old man like myself was hardly a threat to the German army," he said, his head making a gesture of dismissal. He had quietly sorted his old papers. It gave him something to do. As for money, he had scrabbled at times for funds, but he had lots of rare books to sell at inflated prices, and the black marketers were constantly looking for this kind of investment for their profits.

On top of his bookcase lay my old French book dealing with James's dramatic years—another gesture to show his memory was functioning. I asked him whether I might copy the letter. I was committed to the editing of James's complete plays, and it might be useful. "Of course. I intended it for you." Then with a laugh, "Didn't I promise it to you?" I told him I had a pen, but needed a sheet of paper. He shuffled back to his desk. I noticed his worn triangular shoes—street shoes—cracked and covered with dirt. He rummaged out two faded green quarter sheets of paper, and I copied the letter, using the volume of *Theatricals* as my prop. The letter wasn't long. James wrote that the British audience didn't appreciate an artistic and delicate work. Bernard Shaw had said as much to me one day, when describing nineteenth-century theater in England.

By the time I finished copying, Fullerton was again poised and musing over the bookcase that contained the relics of his little verbal empire, the empire of his ambitions. He stood there like some old dazed bedraggled bird. He had pulled out his early travelogue called *In Cairo*, the memories of his 1889 trip. Again he repeated that this was his life, although I was to learn that it wasn't. His writing had always been a way of showing himself a man of elegance, of wide political sagacity, while his real life was made up of the pursuit of women, and sometimes in his versatility, men. He drew out his *Terres Françaises,* a detailed account of out-of-the-way corners of the Republic, and the book of which he was perhaps proudest, for the French Academy had "crowned" it—as they used to say—for describing the glories of France. There was also his *Patriotism and Science,* a small book—his books were all small—containing several platitudinous articles about American-British similarities and differences. The prose struck me as stodgy and pompous. Years later, I read with amusement Edith Wharton's letter to Fullerton describing the book as "smothered in flabby tentacularities." She called it "a tired book." "You've read too much French and too much *Times,*" she scolded, "the most prolix and pedantic of all the dead languages. Go back to English . . . mow down every cliché, uproot all the dragging circumlocutions, compress, diversify, clarify, vivify."

He searched for and produced his *Problems of Power.* Teddy Roosevelt had reviewed the book, and spoken highly of Fullerton's political *savoir-faire.* Then he pointed to the clippings written during the Versailles Conference. Fullerton had been on good terms with General Pershing, as well as assorted statesmen of the time. Gesturing toward the funereal boxes, he said he had letters from ambassadors, diplomats, writers, and in France men like Charles Maurras. An identifying name—it spoke of Fullerton's involvement with the talented bigots of France, the royalists and the anti-Semites. Maurras was at that moment under arrest as a collaborator, and would die awaiting trial for treasonable adherence to France's enemies. It was inevitable that a seeker of the *beau monde* like Fullerton should be a high conservative. His *Figaro* pieces always spoke for the shoring up of the "old order," the moth-eaten aristocracy documented in Proust, and the world of which France had never wholly rid itself. He pointed to a box stuffed with George Santayana's letters, and another with letters from Bernard Berenson. They had been his classmates at Harvard.

Finally, he pointed to a box made not of cardboard but of metal, like a safety deposit box in a bank. "Edith Wharton's letters—and her verses," he said. Up to this time I was simply taking mental notes, trying to be sympathetic to this old man's past as I compared his ravaged state with his appearance years earlier. Now he aroused my curiosity. What singular value did Edith Wharton's letters have to be encased in metal, rather than in black cardboard like the others? And why would she have sent verses to this one-time dandy? Verses were for lovers, for romance, for communication of a particular kind. What kind of poetry could the laughing and usually amused lady I had known at the Pavillon Colombe have written to this self-proclaimed man-of-the-world?

There was a faint swagger in the way he waved his hand at the box, in his pause before the word "verses"—almost as if he were trying to arouse my curiosity. I made no comment, showed no particular curiosity. At the time it seemed I should be neutral—let him open up if he wished. I suppose today I might in a jocular voice ask, "What kind of verses did she write you?" We now know. That box must have contained the Whitmanesque poetry Edith wrote in the Charing Cross Hotel after her *rendez-vous* with her lover in London. But the mention of verses did touch an old memory of mine.

I had met Mrs. Wharton in 1930, and had spent several afternoons at her Pavillon Colombe during the ensuing years, traveling to the little town of Saint-Brice-sous-Forêt, twenty minutes outside the Gare du Nord, where she lived as the grand foreign lady. What surfaced at this moment, as I stood beside Fullerton, who looked as if he could be blown away by any little gust of wind, was a recollection of being led by Mrs. Wharton to her library at the far end of the Pavillon, to show me some of Henry James's books inscribed to her. She had pulled down *The Golden Bowl*, I think, and then *The Wings of the Dove*. They were indeed inscribed—but to W. Morton Fullerton. A small playful smile crossed Edith's face. She reached for another volume. It too was inscribed to Fullerton. "Oh dear," she said, "I guess the inscribed copies to me are at Hyères"—that is, at Saint-Clair-le-Château, her winter residence. She added that Morton had never picked up some of his books, left with her long ago, though she had asked him several times to do so.

This moment had aroused suspicions which Fullerton's knowing mention of verses only intensified. When I began in 1950 to work on the life of Henry James, I came on explicit references to a liaison between Edith and Morton. While pursuing the Paul Bourget letters, I met some residents of the old Fauborg-Saint-Germain, and eventually remarked in the fourth volume of my life that "Edith Wharton was charmed by Fullerton and for a time they would be intimate friends, perhaps even—gossips said—lovers." Aside from the details in the R. W. B. Lewis biography, the most important documentary evidence of the relationship emerged when the University of Texas acquired three hundred of Mrs. Wharton's letters to Fullerton. They could only have been the letters in the metal box.

By the time I took my leave, the autumn sun was setting. A golden shaft lit up the dust particles, and gilded the scattered books and papers. He gave me his shriveled hand once more. I told him I expected soon to leave for the front. The next day I went to the offices of the OSS, where I met for the first time Arthur Schlesinger, Jr., who was then a private in military intelligence. I asked him to inform Harvard about the important American archive I had come on so unexpectedly. Eventually Harvard did purchase a batch of the James letters, including the one I copied. This had certainly been Fullerton's hope. To LeRoy Phillips, his cousin and James's first bibliographer, Morton spoke of my wartime visit—

"Behold me, day in and day out, sorting my archives, with the vague hope of saving, from the flotsam and jetsam of the years, a respectable grist of documents that will be the legitimate provender for such fanatics as Edel and you (and me!) or for the library of my Alma Mater."

The rest of the material was widely scattered. Some of it is at Yale, some in Princeton, an important part in Texas. There are very fine James letters to Fullerton at the University of Virginia. I also imagine some bits of the Fullerton papers are still floating, like the dust in his rooms, in Parisian antiquarian shops and among autograph dealers—the journalist's collections of others' words, others' feelings and ideas.

Morton Fullerton achieved, in his journalistic role, a double identity. He had the ubiquity of a man of the world, and the secret life of a Victorian who liked to move in an aura of mystery. To be someone with the ability to recognize ideas, but without the ideas themselves; to spread himself from the particular to the panoramic; these were hints of a hollow man. When he died in 1952, the London *Times* obituary described him as having written "kilometric sentences"—prose so influenced by James's style as to involve "a very drastic process of sub-editing before it was suitable for publication in a daily newspaper."

INTERIORS

My social life in *bistro* and *boîte* had its counterpoint in private Parisian homes. The French tend to be less casual than the British or Americans in personal hospitality. Middle-class French homes are treated as if they were castles, to which select individuals may have access. However, certain friends of my Paris days, and certain particular acquaintances, were insistently welcoming, rejecting my argument that I could come after dinner, rather than deprive them of their rationed nourishment. They wanted to share their daily bread, even if it were only a crust. It would have been churlish to decline. I tried to make up for my presence by bringing otherwise unobtainable items, like soap, from the PX.

My first dining out was with the widow of my old Havas employer in New York. Madame Lemercier's younger daughter, Aimée, who had some minor office job at psychwar, one day asked me if I were the Leon Edel who had worked for her father in New York. I remembered Aimée at age five, curtseying with her older sister in a furnished flat off Park Avenue. The widow, who had remarried, insisted it was a privilege to bring together some of her late husband's staffers.

Aimée escorted me to an apartment somewhere near the Trocadéro. The revived metro still had its old damp smells, shabby wagons, and seats reserved for wounded veterans—a thoughtfulness that didn't exist on the clattering Manhattan subways. The apartment itself had sufficient space, with touches of elegance and taste. We were half a dozen at table. The new husband was a gentle scholar of a certain distinction. The former Havas guests were our captain at the Scribe, and Eugene Jolas.

I had known Jolas in New York, never having met him during the late twenties and early thirties in Paris. As the intimate of James Joyce, and an editor of the expatriate journal *transition,* with its striking jacket designs by Picasso, Arp, Klee, Duchamp, and others, Jolas had been a popular figure. The journal acquired its fame not only for its early publication of Hemingway, the Dadaists, the surrealists, and Kafka, but also for its serialization of Joyce's "work in progress"—the future *Finnegans Wake.* I met the Jolases, Maria and Eugene, during their exile in New

York after the fall of France, when they tried to create a fund for the Joyces, exiled in Zurich. Jolas was an attractive man, with a head that looked like that of a senator carved by a Roman sculptor. He had massive shoulders and a comfortable fullness, further emphasized by thick gray hair and a slow, thoughtful manner of speech. He was polyglot, learning his native French and German in Lorraine, and acquiring his English in the United States during his childhood. *Finnegans Wake* seemed made for him. He was a follower of the new, and an advocate of Verticalism—a recall of the human wish to be airborne, skybound, like Icarus and Daedalus, or Pegasus, or the winged horses of the North, or the magic carpets of the Orient, or saintly levitations. Jolas loved pyramids, temples, Gothic cathedrals, and the modern mania for skyscrapers.

Dining in France has its very special side. The French are solemn about their food, for they have never enjoyed the surfeit—or waste—of America's abundance. They have always insisted on quality at their table. Caution and even parsimony contributed to the development of the French national palate. The menu of this evening: *paté* on dry bread, meat balls (one per person), a quite decent salad, a sort of imitation cake, and tinned peaches. No wine. A distinct wartime repast.

We were anecdotal at table. Our captain, who had been in Algiers, described how André Gide in his exile kept himself cool in the tropical weather by periodically stepping into a wash bowl of cold water, and then walking about barefoot. Madame Lemercier talked of young girls in the Resistance who left home on mysterious missions, returning with their feet bloodied by wanderings through dark woods and stony creeks. Aimée told how much pleasure she derived during the occupation from pasting Pétain stamps upside down on envelopes. When I later mentioned this to Liane, she told me the Nazis threatened confiscation of all letters not treated decorously. We had a long discussion of what to do with the Germans once the war was won. We agreed that a more workable, but if possible tougher, peace than Versailles was needed.

I told Jolas of my visit with Sylvia Beach, and said she believed Joyce wanted to die once he reached Zurich and exile. Jolas, invoking other memories, claimed Joyce had been planning his next book—a book on oceans—and insisted that no man so creative seeks death before its time. I silently thought that while Joyce may have talked of his plans for the future, his writings, letters, and principal myth seemed pathologically depressed and self-destructive.

* * * * *

Somewhat later I visited a solid bourgeois interior with a former Havas colleague, Robert Rieffel. Eight years earlier he had been a novice reporter—wiry, alert, competent, married to a vivacious young woman, Cécile. They gave me an impression of Europe's dauntless young, confronting questions and decisions no Americans had to face. Security was not a word in their vocabulary; war was taken for granted. Since then, Rieffel had been tested by time in Warsaw after the invasions of Poland, by the flight of Cécile with her young child to Romania, by a period in Stockholm as refugees, and finally by their return to France, and to the Agence in its wartime offices at Clermont-Ferrand. He had learned I was in Paris. Could we meet at his aunt's for a meal? He was dining that evening at her flat in the Avenue de Neuilly.

A comfortable address: a solidly furnished, carpeted, picture-filled series of rooms that revealed upper middle class taste. Our hostess had weathered the occupation. Her husband had died. She carried on their textile business, making all the necessary compromises, knowing how to handle the Germans. She was from Alsace, and thus spoke their language. A practical no-nonsense woman in tweeds, she chain-smoked, and offered fine wines and liqueurs. She served no meat, but there were mushrooms and shredded bacon in the noodles, followed by a good cheese, fruit, and a delicious tart. She had obviously struck deals on the black market. *Il faut manger pour vivre,* she said in a practical way. She claimed to have been a resistant but did not say how—I think she meant she hadn't been passive. She had a set of the much sought "Midnight Editions," published by the underground during the occupation to show that literature could be kept alive in the midst of terror. She was happy to entertain an Allied soldier with her long-absent nephew.

Rieffel and I took advantage of that long evening in this genial flat to talk about the decade of history that was behind us. We talked of Maurice Schumann, whom I had glimpsed at the Arc de Triomphe with de Gaulle, and Rieffel told me a story which captured the essence of the man. Before the war, Rieffel and Schumann were sent by Havas to report the secular marriage of Wallis Simpson and the now abdicated Edward VIII at the Château de Condé. As the representative of one of Europe's oldest news agencies, Schumann would be admitted to the Château. Rieffel and other members of the press would be outside of the gate. The evening before the event, Schumann was downcast and ruminative. The American press had bought up all the vantage points. They had fast cars at the gates, and special wireless arrangements in the village. Havas would be scooped in its own territory.

"We must jump the news," said Schumann. "We will announce completion of the civil marriage at 11:47 a.m., although it's set for 11:30. The mayor will talk for at least three minutes, and he must formally verify the Duke's and Wallis's names. I'll add fourteen minutes to this three minutes. You'll send a message that the knot was tied at 11:47 a.m."

Why fourteen minutes? Schumann explained that when his cousin married, she was fourteen minutes late. Afterwards, she explained that women all over the world are this late for their weddings, and she didn't want to defy precedent. "Since we're guessing anyhow, it seems as good a figure as any," Schumann said, "A throw of the dice."

The next morning while the correspondents stood at the gates, waiting for word from inside, Rieffel stayed in the village. At 11:47, he sent out word that the knot had been tied. Then he waited for the Americans in their speedy automobiles. He heard them soon enough. They were shouting "11:47!"

Maurice Schumann's imagination had won the toss of the dice.

* * * * *

Still another kind of interior: Augier's love nest. One day I returned to the Hôtel Perey to find him impatiently waiting for me. He wanted me to come to dinner at his girlfriend's apartment. Albane received me in a smart flowery housecoat in her somewhat overstuffed flat in the Champs-Élysées. She was a typical mannequin—petite, with slender little feet, and a continued display of her small lithe body. Her friend Gilberte was also there—more hearty, and with a more alert mind. There was also a wan little servant, who seemed like an urchin out of Dickens. She supposedly suffered from tuberculosis, although Albane didn't pay much attention to this fact, for she kept her running back and forth. At one moment she had her crawling under the bed to retrieve a pair of shoes. There was also a little dog named Rabbit, who begged for his food in approved fashion, on his little haunches.

* * * * *

I've forgotten how I became entangled with a French "welcoming committee," which wanted American soldiers to have a taste of French hospitality. I pleaded that I had already had a considerable taste, stretching back many years. They argued I was just the person to give the thing a start.

I agreed to be "received" in the home of a French executive who lived in the fashionable Boulevard Malesherbes. The door was opened by my host himself, and I was ushered into an elegant apartment. The living room was paneled in light wood, well-lighted, with fresh flowers placed in discreet corners, and a thick carpet on the floor. There were bibelots and copies (I judged) of Impressionist paintings. Like his living room, my host was impeccably attired, conveying an air of comfort and suavity. He introduced me to his wife, sitting near a wide window that looked out on the boulevard, and two daughters, as buxom as she was, busy with their knitting. A third daughter sat some distance away, in a rigid posture that suggested she was an unwilling participant. A young son was also presented, an adolescent, who immediately disappeared.

From the moment we sat down I felt I was in for a monologue. In slowly spoken French, my host said he was certain I knew that France had food problems. He apologized for not inviting me to dine, and offered me a glass of Benedictine. He was bent on being objective; his goal however was political. France had suffered. The Germans were evil. This was the third time they had tried to conquer France, and twice they had been defeated with American help. His receiving me in his home was meant to convey the gratitude of the French people.

He had to admit that France had shown weakness at a crucial moment. It had been weakened by its radicals and revolutionaries, leaving the divided country ripe for conquest. He was against all forms of dictatorship, but you also couldn't tolerate communist anarchy. He said things hadn't been too bad with Marshal Pétain in Vichy, a genuine Frenchman, a great soldier of the old school. One could see from the very time of the Paris insurrection that the Communists wanted to take over. They had jumped the gun, started their attack too soon. Now one could expect strikes. There had already been signs of unrest in the south of France. He hoped, since I spoke French, that I would understand France's dilemma. A country has to have capital. I mustn't pay too much attention to the vacillating newspapers with their cries of "Resistance, Resistance."

I decided this was the moment to interrupt the sermon, and said I owed my life to the Resistance, when German tanks had prepared an ambush. Of course, he said, there had been heroic figures from all walks of French life. He was glad the fighters for freedom had aided me on the road to Paris. Still it was necessary to get down to business, and stop clamoring about the past. French capitalism believed in fair wages. He was certain France would take great strides to recovery, if it didn't become too vindictive with the so-called collaborators. I looked at the imposing grand piano, and asked whether his daughters played. They smiled mechanically and shook their heads. The executive said he himself played. He loved Debussy. No music was more perfect than Debussy's. It was purely French. Perhaps I would disagree, but there were no painters more wonderful than the French impressionists. They were so much better than the audacities of Picasso and his followers. He didn't like revolutions in the arts: in fact all revolutions ended up as negations of human achievement.

The distanced daughter grunted disapproval at her father's attack on Picasso. "You know how it is, no one understands modern art, especially one's parents," she said to me, raising her voice. I said this might be true of ideas too, each generation has to have its own. The mother, seeing possible controversy, immediately took over. She supposed in America we had no awareness of the bitter hardships suffered at the hands of the Germans. So many people starved. And they had to make their own clothes. She had even turned some old curtains into dresses for her daughters.

The Benedictine was good, but I declined to have my glass refilled. My duties called me, I said, and I told him I was glad to have been welcomed in this intimate way. I tried to speak without irony.

* * * * *

A few evenings later, I was introduced to a family at the opposite end of France's economic scale. I was in the rue Royale, and found myself looking at a trim sergeant. Our eyes met, and we shouted each other's name. It was Sagi, the former waiter who was our company clerk at Camp Ritchie. Smooth and civilized, with high manners and a seductive voice, his mustache was Barrymore, and his face had the polish of the old French screen star Adolph Menjou. Sagi was Hungarian to his fingertips. His uniform was well pressed, his necktie properly tied, his shoes highly polished. He was extremely agreeable to women, a Casanova in khaki. I remembered that during our long talks at Gettysburg, he used to entertain me with stories of sex in Budapest, and behind-the-scenes life in fashionable restaurants.

At this moment he had on his arm a woman who looked like a battered old prostitute, but whom he introduced as a countrywoman of his. He was in Paris on a forty-eight hour leave from his station in Nancy. He asked whether we mightn't meet in half an hour. He had to conduct his companion to her destination. I sat in Weber's over a glass of mediocre wine, remembering the life in camp the previous winter, when I used to stand guard facing flaming sunsets, or tramped for hours in snow and mud.

In exactly half an hour Sagi returned. I gathered he had paid off the prostitute. He gave me news of our company, and of the arrogance of some of the eastern Europeans. He described precious hours in Paris. He had picked up a charming girl, a working girl, on the Champs-Élysées, and she had gone to bed with him that very afternoon. He assured me it had been beautiful and romantic. He was invited to visit her home the next evening, before he left again for Lorraine. Would I come along? It would do me good, he said, to meet a working-class family, and I would help him, for his French wasn't good enough for civilized conversation.

The following evening we went by metro to the Place de la Nation. In a narrow street we climbed a series of stairways to reach Georgette's home. She was dark-haired, clear-skinned, poised, sophisticated, and clearly smitten with Sagi. We were introduced to a faded mother; a father, gnarled and rheumatic; and a slangy brother, just back from the *maquis*. They offered us small glasses of prune liqueur. The father talked with pride of his service in the first war, and showed us his decorations. The girl worked in a dress shop. The brother was an electrician. The home, in its shabbiness, reflected a life carefully fashioned on limited means and lack of space—a tiny kitchen, a tight series of steps leading to another room, a small rectangular parlor-bedroom. Sagi bade Georgette farewell with grace and affection, and said good-bye to her folks. Georgette soulfully wished he were stationed in Paris like me, and I was invited to come back and share a meal with them. She was obviously trying to please Sagi, whom she probably knew she would never see again.

* * * * *

The next week brought me to a more public interior, a very strange evening at the Catholic Institute in Paris. It was a social evening for American solders, and I fell in with a witty Monsignor, a tough-looking character who was rather discursive, and at moments eloquent. I suspected he had a liking for the Germans. He had dueled with German students in his youth, after their fashion, but bore no scars. He had a slight sneer in his tone when he spoke of de Gaulle, calling him an upstart, and claiming there were many regions of the country disobeying his orders. A loyal follower of Marshal Pétain, the Monsignor claimed to know him well, and believed he had handled his dilemma as spokesman for France to the Germans with dignity and resolution. The Monsignor argued with a curious twinkle in his eye that Pétain was perhaps, underneath his facade of compliance, one of the chief French resistants. One couldn't lose sight, he said, of the fact that our real enemy was Russia.

I suggested that he was committing a secular heresy. The Russians were losing millions of lives. With his perpetual smile and veneer of worldliness, the Monsignor replied "Ah, Sergeant Edel, we are bedfellows only to defeat Hitler. The Russians remain followers of the godless Marx." He said I had not seen the Marxist Spaniards and their influence —those who escaped from Franco and infected France. They had been received, he said, by the Jewish Marxist premier of France in the mid-1930s, Léon Blum.

The Monsignor's "line" was fascist and anti-Semitic. He admitted that the Jews had been persecuted, but suggested they should still be kept at a distance. Another young woman agreed—"Yes, they have suffered; but as far as I'm concerned, I have never received a Jew in my home and never will." This remark was the final chilling note of the *soirée*. Earlier, she had boasted that at the barricades she had managed to "get her German." Her candid remarks on Jews had the same aggressive quality. She would perhaps hang a Jew as readily as she shot her German.

I pleaded military duties, and withdrew from this unpleasant occasion. One could be anti-Stalin without being anti-Semitic.

FROM MY NOTEBOOK

Fragments drawn from an old notebook, written during the winter of 1944–1945 in Paris.

* * * * *

Curious little coincidence at *L'Aurore* when I went to get extra copies of this conservative paper. Familiar face of a young woman at the subscription desk. She reminded me that I had autographed her 100 franc note on the boulevard on the day of the liberation. She quoted me as having said the note would be worth little with my name on it. We were just beginning a conversation when she was interrupted by one of her superiors. I never saw her again.

* * * * *

An amusing advertisement in a newspaper: "Charles Brabant is looking for the commissioner or inspector of police who during a Franco-German search of his house on August 25, 1941 seized a fragment of his war journal very violent against Nazism and the government of Vichy, and courageously made it vanish."

* * * * *

Conversation in a bar with a French character who cursed Freemasons and Jesuits, claiming they caused the war. The man called himself an artisan: he is a picture-framer. He said the Nazis put a big flag on top of the Eiffel Tower, announcing, "The German Army is victorious on all fronts." A windstorm the next night blew it away.

* * * * *

Jazz at the Red Cross. Background music while the U.S. Military Police carried out one of their periodic checks of all persons in uniform.

* * * * *

William Royall Tyler came into our office, and I was introduced to him. He has been a State Department man and an ambassador. I placed him at once as the son of the heiress to Edith Wharton's estate. He handled the copyrights and certain valuable papers. (Coincidentally, I had been talking the previous afternoon with Morton Fullerton about Mrs. Wharton.) I mentioned my visits long ago to the Pavillon Colombe, and asked what became of her library. Tyler said a portion of it had been left by Edith to Kenneth Clark, the art historian. (I later learned some books were destroyed in a wartime bombing.)

*****

At the Perey late one evening, I found a crap game in the middle of the lobby. A big-eyed redhead from Ireland was seated on the floor beside one of the soldiers. We talked. She had been in a convent at Saint-Sauveur-le-Vicomte and had taken her vows. The Germans moved the nuns to Paris. She and several other nuns saw this as a chance for escape: a big city has so many hiding places. The Sister in charge said this would be anticipating the will of God, and urged obedience to the Germans. The nuns found someone who provided identity cards, and with these they became truants, traveling south into the unoccupied zone to another convent. With the coming of liberation, the Irishwoman returned to Paris, and hoped to get back to Eire. She had renounced her vows and enjoyed the company of American soldiers. The convent life was too rigid for her. Three of her brothers were priests. She had a sister who was a nun in Birmingham. Nine children in all, and five chose religion.

*****

Today I was at my typewriter; looking up, I found myself greeting Louis Rapkine's wide familiar grin.

A medical scientist who had left Montreal for Paris in the early 1920s, his genius had rapidly earned him the respect of the French scientific establishment. When I came to France, he was a mentor of sorts. I was attracted by his wit, his brooding seriousness, his capacity to work intensely, and then to relax. When France fell, he had drawn up a list of fifty-seven scientists he felt should be rescued. American foundations provided backing. With the Gaullists in New York and the Foreign Office in London, Rapkine worked like an accredited diplomat. He helped entire families escape to England and America, and found them jobs in exile. A lovable man, with X-ray eyes and a powerful sense of rectitude.

Rapkine brought a lot of news from Manhattan, where he lived in the apartment under mine. In a few sentences we caught up on two years. He had seen my wife, busy and well and awaiting my return. He had been crossing and recrossing the Atlantic in warplanes, a commuter in bucket seats. He was finding out how many of his old friends had died or disappeared.

"I'm dying for a smoke," he said. With a queer lift of his eyebrows he took a pack I offered: "I know they're coffin nails. But I have to have them." I reached into my desk and gave him two cartons.

I saw him again after he was decorated by de Gaulle, and given a laboratory in the Pasteur Institute. In 1948 he died as he predicted. Chain smoking—lung cancer.

* * * * *

16 December. Liane is back from Lille for four days. She looks more relaxed than at the time of the liberation, says it's because she leads a quiet boring life and works hard. She is still *première danseuse* at the Théâtre Sébastopol in Lille. She dances in operettas, and does Hungarian czardas, the Faust ballet, and generally a lot of hackneyed stuff. She wore a hand-me-down fur coat, quite stylish, and has let her hair grow longer. She is as striking and intense as ever.

The same old tight quarters—the couch on which the girls sat, a chair for me, a large wardrobe that takes up lots of space with a full-length mirror, a little table in the corner with an odd assortment of books and photos of French and American stars cut out of magazines—Gary Cooper, William Powell, Edwige Feuillère. And the family snapshots. Liane sat in the middle of the couch in her fur coat, her black hair falling in disorder on the collar framing her face. Kay, with her mop of hair and doll-like look, still wearing a skiing outfit, sat on the edge of the sofa, Irene beside her. "The Princess Liane with her hand-maidens," I said. "Attended by her intellectual," she promptly rejoined.

We talked of small things at first—daily ennuis and the weather. A fierce winter. Cold, cold, cold. Liane described the cold in Lille, north of Paris. She speaks disparagingly of her bourgeois audiences, and the sorts of things she has to dance for them. She criticizes fellow-dancers who change the music to suit their techniques. Liane said one must dance to the music; she didn't believe in making the music serve the dance.

And then an outburst of eloquence, which makes her seem so full of life. The false and the true in art. How to teach this? How to think of art amid the hatreds unloosed in the world? Suddenly she is revealing how much she suffers in the provincial environment to which her work had taken her—

"The French are decadent, full of hate. Art has no hatreds. The French have no cosmopolitan feeling. They're provincial; what's worse, they hate! They do not understand that what is true in art has nothing to do with nationality. I, who have every reason to hate Germans, don't hate them. I can't hate anyone."

Something has happened in Lille to put her out of sorts and tarnish her idealism. She wants more acclaim and more importance than she has found in the audiences brutalized by winter cold and hunger. She has the intolerance of her youth, the impatience of someone who had hoped to dazzle. The light in the tiny room falls on her face; her lipstick put on as carelessly as always. The words come out in a torrent. She is filled with sincerity and frustration.

She has some photos of herself dancing, and she inscribes one for me—

Au cher intellectuel mister Edel en souvenir d'une insupportable danseuse with my plus sincère friendly for always Lia— Schubert. Paris 20 December 1944.

A PARACHUTIST'S STORY

Christmas 1944 offered few promises. There had been a night of snow, and the sidewalks were icy. The luxury hotels mustered a few decorations, and even some warmth, when a small shipment of coal reached the capital. In the shabby little hotels and old warehouse where the GIs were housed, the men dressed their holiday feelings with scraps of colored wrapping paper from their Christmas parcels and stray bits of tinsel. The Paris churches would offer midnight services; the Infant of Peace would be celebrated by congregations wearing overcoats and every available bit of woolen underwear. On cloudless nights, when the moon was doing its monthly turn, the blackout changed color. The city was dipped in a magical, chaste, blue-green whiteness.

* * * * *

The soldier who sat near me in the bar—he was a second lieutenant and wore the airborne insignia—was "tanked up." I tried to explain the epithet to the bartender, who wore a long white apron and liked to play with words. He suggested the equivalent probably was *plein comme un oeuf*—full like an egg.

The lieutenant slowly slid from the barstool, and grabbed my lapels. I looked into a pair of young blood-shot blue eyes and a silly grin. "Sarge," he said, and then he straightened up. He extended his arms, and pulled himself up—as if he were about to recite Shakespeare. The heavy throaty alcoholic voice sounded jubilant. It shouted at me, and everyone took notice—

"At Christmas, I die!"

His liquored breath blew his anguish full into my face. I pulled away, but showed little surprise.

"Are you talking about suicide, sir?" I said lightly. "Are you scheduling it for Christmas?"

His grin gave way to astonishment. I reckoned he had expected I would hug him in sympathy, or at least respond to his future rendezvous with death with, "I'm sorry."

"Hell no, Sarge. That's crazy. I'm just going the way of my teammates, and they're all dead."

Turning to his small audience he shouted again, with a touch of anxiety—

"At Christmas, I die!"

I kept up my cool approach.

"Why at Christmas?"

"We're going to jump across the Rhine, as soon as Patton gets across."

I showed a bit of impatience.

"Do you think Patton announces such plans in advance?"

He put his arms around me. Then he whispered, as if ashamed—

"Sarge, I'm scared—for the first time I'm scared!"

"Come now. There won't be a jump at Christmas."

Again lowering his voice, he confided he felt awful. He said he needed another drink. The bartender pretended to be busy.

The lieutenant seemed like a burn-out case. He wouldn't be much use in a jump, I supposed. Maybe he was putting on a bar act—showing off—but still, he had used the word "scared." I thanked God I wasn't in that kind of outfit. There was nothing like being on *terra firma*. You can dive for a foxhole if there's one around. Cloud journeys weren't for me.

I handed over some francs as I left the bar. They wouldn't bounce the soldier. As I walked the wet sidewalks, the moon dove in and out of the creamy clouds.

THE PERFORMING ARTS

That autumn the Hôtel Scribe became an American crossroads. Federal and state legislators, industrialists, media folk, movie stars, entrepreneurs, and columnists crossed the Atlantic, courtesy of Army transport, to be given a look at the liberated city. The columnists tried to convey a sense of having risked their lives to keep America informed. The businessmen quietly went their way; they had much ground to cover, for Hitler had enjoyed a four-year monopoly over the French economy. The other well-fed and carefully entertained visitors chatted with a few rear-line soldiers, contemplated the motorless boulevards of Paris, and agreed that our boys were being splendidly taken care of.

In my private hours, I distanced myself from the hubbub. I was busy rediscovering the re-emerging arts in Paris. A big retrospective Picasso exhibition was speedily opened in the Grand Palais. I attended the reopening of the Paris Opera to see *Boris Godunov,* a choice which paid tribute to the Russian armies that were at the moment sweeping the Nazis across the steppes. The theaters opened up as soon as they had electricity, demonstrating anew that the French art of acting and sophisticated direction can be exercised with distinction in spite of minimal resources. There was endless entertainment in the troop theaters. Heifetz was flown over to supply us, as he remarked, with "musical meat and mashed potatoes"— a serious movement from a concerto, followed by Paganini or Kreisler. We had abridged Shakespeare by an English company. We also had Bob Hope's wisecracks.

I returned to the Théâtre Français. It was good to have a refresher course in Molière, Victor Hugo, and some of the nineteenth century comedies. And I went to the reopening of the hastily refurbished Théâtre Sarah Bernhardt. Reclaiming the name of the great Jewish actress, the cavernous theater seemed an enormous frigidaire. We sat wrapped in our overcoats, but the evening was heart-warming, if punctuated by coughing and nose blowing. Charles Dullin restaged his modernized production of Ben Jonson's *Volpone,* using the adaptation by Stefan

Zweig. I had seen the original production—four times!—fifteen years earlier. The actors wore many thicknesses of wool beneath their flimsy Venetian costumes. When they spoke their lines, their breath hung before us, as if in Arctic air.

Older, bulkier, yet in full possession of his mimic genius, Dullin portrayed the Venetian fox with many sublime touches. At the end of the play, Volpone, defeated in all his predatory escapades, makes a tragicomic exit. Dullin changed this exit each time. In this newest and chilliest version, he walked off into the wings throwing a scarf—as if it were flung by the hand of fate—around his face. His stride was long and carefree, as capricious as all his actions. To me it suggested also that he was in a hurry for a drink of whiskey.

On another evening I went to Dullin's old theater in Montmartre to see Jean Anouilh's adaptation of Sophocles' *Antigone*. Paying scant attention to Antigone's defiant poetic argument for human freedom, during the occupation the Nazi censors had approved the play, apparently because of Creon's speeches on the power of the state and the validity of dictatorship. I remember standing on the little rise in front of the Atelier, smoking cigarettes and discussing with friends the excitement the play created. The debate between the fated Antigone and the imperial Creon suggested that the German censors had been blind, stupid, or simply bureaucrats, who felt that half a loaf of tyranny was sufficiently valuable to permit the poetry of response to remain. I have never forgotten the electric atmosphere of that evening, nor the glimpse I had, as I walked up the aisle, of Gertrude Stein, massively seated in the very middle of the theater, looking like a Buddhist statue, with her closely cropped hair and her fine strong features.

One afternoon I came to my room to change my clothes. A chambermaid named Madeleine was moving the dust around, her hands blue with cold. In a low voice, as if it were a great secret, she confided there was hot water flowing from the tap. There might be enough coal to enjoy this luxury once a week. According to my notes, "I tore off my clothes as I tore into the bathroom." The water was only—but delightfully—lukewarm. Within minutes I was lathered and soaking. I put on a fresh uniform, and walked with long vigorous strides up the rue du Faubourg-Saint-Honoré. I was on my way to a concert of the Pasdeloup Orchestra at the Salle Pleyel.

When I first knew it in 1928, the Salle Pleyel had just been built. Now I enjoyed once more its *art nouveau* architecture—its long curved walls, as if it were a giant megaphone; its sunken lights in the high sloping ceiling. Listening to César Franck and Debussy, I told myself that the older we grow, the more we find life composed of memories. Living in 1944, I was steeped in the emotions and sensations of 1929. I had sat here with my old friend A. J. M. Smith, the gifted Canadian poet, and his wife Jeannie, to hear Stravinsky's *Sacre du Printemps.* Paris had given me a valuable musical education, and my finest sense of the modern, when "modern" was still contemporary.

HOSPITALS

In November a clinging laryngitis drove me to the rue du Helder infirmary, where an Army doctor signed my hospitalization because "What with the cold, you won't ever get rid of that voice." I was transported to the Hôpital Beaujon—a modern glassed building, warm and sleep-inducing. The place was silent, white, spotless, antiseptic. No one had bothered to remove the German signs. *Unkleideraum FRZ. Bad Abort. Besenraum.* A great sense of lassitude as I got into bed. I fell asleep almost at once.

The lights came on at 6:30 the next morning. The soldiers mostly slept on, some snoring rhythmically. A few sat up, stretched, lit cigarettes they were soon told to extinguish. The nurse brought me aspirin, tea, and toast. I watched her administering pills, saying in French, "Simpson, here's your ration of cognac; Caldwell, I've brought you a bloody Mary; Marshall, you're getting a martini."

I listened to the complaints of a sturdy cleaning woman from the Basque country. She has been ordered to wax the long hall outside and wanted to know why she was being given inferior wax to put on a floor that would best be cleaned with soap and water. I asked her if she was afraid we might slip on the wax. She rejoined, "We have plenty of beds to put you in if you do."

After two or three days I asked to be discharged. The nurse said I might as well relax. They were in no hurry to let me go, unless there was a big battle and more beds were needed. Now ambulatory, I began to explore the hospital. I glanced into the ward below, packed with VD cases. I went to the ground floor, to the Red Cross lounge. Here I talked with some British airmen who had been burned when their plane crashed. Still bandaged, they spoke of getting back into action. The Americans had the usual army gripes, and many complained about the "limeys." The British were unfamiliar to the boys from middle America; to me they seemed like the British-Canadians I'd known since childhood.

The Americans weren't interested in politics, or even the progress of the war. Many had had their rendezvous with death, as an old First World War poem put it, and felt a sense of release. The most wretched case I encountered was that of a soldier who had enlisted when he was fifteen. Now eighteen, he seemed to have a bad case of nerves. He was a Kentucky boy, not very bright, and in his present condition living mostly in a daydream. He had seen a man's head blown off on D-Day, spoke of walking on German entrails in the dark, and now complained of being constantly sick to the stomach. He had fought at Saint-Lô, where he was wounded in the hip.

On the eighth day I was promised release the next day. During the night, however, there was a shipment of wounded, and we were packed into a couple of trucks and moved to the First General Hospital at Vitry. The rooms were cold and smelled of fresh paint. Large sections of broken glass had just been replaced. The hospital beds had white blankets instead of khaki. They looked immaculate, and were stamped "M.D. U.S. Army." Fresh pajamas were issued, and new wine-colored robes. I was chilly, and crept between the crisp sheets. As warmth returned, lying in my narrow space, I meditated on how small people looked in bed—or in their graves.

It was getting dark when I awoke—time for supper. I put on my robe and went to the washroom. It seemed to me as if I had entered the land of Lilliput. The toilets, two inches off the floor, looked like little chamber pots. The showers were miniature and the taps were so low I had to lean down to turn them on. A bench behind each row of sinks was about six inches off the floor. There were no mirrors for shaving. I went down for my meal, and noticed that the fire alarms in the hall were also extremely low. I stopped one of the French workers, who explained that this was the State orphanage before the Germans had arrived.

It made perfect sense. Children were precious: France had been worried for years about its declining population.

ROMANCES AND SHOW BIZ

I stayed in the Lilliputian hospital that one night. The next day, I was ferried back to the rue du Helder and released. It was a chilly November day. The trees had shed their leaves, and the boulevards seemed naked and forlorn. Before returning to the Hôtel Perey, I walked to the Rainbow Corner, and in its deserted lounge drank a cup of coffee. I was holding back from returning to the chill of the hotel room or of my office. My mind kept drifting back to the hospitals, and the torn bodies of the wounded. I thought of Walt Whitman, and the way in which he haunted the Civil War hospitals and comforted the wounded.

Back at the Perey, I was distressed by the quantity of mail and parcels that had accumulated during my ten-day absence. My room seemed to have shrunk in size. I looked out at the familiar rooftops and smokeless chimneys—the cold hearths of Paris. Our shabby furniture, the chill, and loneliness made me want to return to the streets. The maid told me Augier had been spending nights in our room, which seemed strange. Presently he arrived, pale and hollow-eyed, as if he had been shedding tears. His manner was nevertheless histrionically cheerful, almost excessively so. He threw the news at me, as if to get it out as quickly as possible. "Albane has locked me out," he said, a quaver in his voice.

He had arrived at the Champs-Élysées apartment one day, and the concierge, whom he had plied for weeks with candy and cigarettes, told him Albane wasn't home. This was unusual, and when he questioned the concierge, she admitted she was told to say Albane wasn't at home to *him*. He wheedled his way upstairs, and rang the bell for a long time. Finally the little maid, with the dog Rabbit sniffing at her heels, opened a vertical crack. She repeated the news. Albane simply didn't want to see her wartime boyfriend anymore. When the hurt and surprised Augier pleaded for a reason, the maid blurted out, "*Elle est enceinte.*"

Albane's morning sickness hadn't been due to food poisoning. The doctor had confirmed it. "So I'm supposed to be a father," Augier said, with a grin and more sadness than he intended. He had talked with

Gilberte, and learned that Albane was busy swallowing all the nostrums of midwifery to induce a miscarriage.

Augier delivered flowers and sweets to her every day. The maid received them through the crack in the door, with Rabbit sticking his wet little snout at him. But he got no thanks, he said. Albane would never see him again. It was like one of the old operas—the courtesan heroine, the baffled hero, the love that had withered. Albane's career depended on remaining childless. In due course Augier told me that a miscarriage had been induced. But the romance was over.

* * * * *

Our brain trust at the Perey was functioning as usual, and I was promptly cross-examined about my experiences in the military hospitals. I described the horror of treating individuals wounded not by life but by man's inventions, and the repairing of bodies to be sent back to the front for a second chance. Morris Janowitz changed the subject to his latest intelligence from the icy front. The Nazis were fighting hard, and we were in for a fierce winter. He also predicted that "brain rear" was likely to become "brain forward," and we could all expect a move to the front. Our time was running out.

Though my colonel apparently was insisting on the return of men like me who had been loaned to other units, the head of the press section told me he had distinct plans for me. Like a baseball player, I was sitting on the sidelines for awhile. I spent part of my mornings at the rue d'Aguesseau; my afternoons and evenings were free. I frequently joined young Paul Dombrowski, a chubby private first class in psychwar who seemed to have as much leisure as I had. A relaxed, good-natured New Yorker, Paul had owned a hole-in-the-wall gramophone shop. In Paris he had made himself at home backstage. Paul introduced me to vaudeville comedians, singers, and ballerinas. I felt I was a sort of Degas or Toulouse-Lautrec, taking them in as they put on make-up and flexed their toes. Paul had cultivated in particular a singer named Anne Chapelle, an angular young woman with a homely face and a raucous voice, who was loved by the audiences for her songs about seamstresses and mannequins—their long hours, their snatched moments of love, their chronic melancholy. Distinctly masculine in body movement, but feminine in her overflow of feeling, she had a genuine streak of art. A kind of unplaintive and defiant Édith Piaf, she had a small motorcycle, and would take Paul with her to do errands—some bit of shopping, or sometimes a visit to the hairdresser or dressmaker. Her true genius, Paul said, lay in her comic improvisations, but management soon suppressed these because she didn't know when to stop. Paul would have gladly devoted all his days to her. With her scrappy English and his scrappy French, his rotund shortness and her generous height, they were a show team, and the affection she bestowed on me because I was Paul's friend gave me a suggestion of the affection she showered on him.

One evening I guided Paul through Montparnasse. It had remained in my memory as a series of cafés crowded with Americans of the 1920s and travelers from many lands. But the old cafés were deserted. At the Dôme there were a few GIs and WACs indulging in non-talk at the bar. The *dame du comptoir* at the Select was the same woman I used to see in 1929, much amplified. The Coupole, which seemed huge and gloomy, offered oysters and other seafood. Its black market connections were obviously good. After a sinful supper, I took Paul to the Boule Blanche, a small *bôite* in the rue Vavin, which was agreeably frequented by natives of Haiti, Martinique, and Guadeloupe. We drank red wine, and Paul danced with some of the young girls to music supplied by a small band. Between numbers, the entertainers joined their small audience, and were lively and conversational. The Haitians were particularly good company. Some time later, I would read Edmund Wilson's notes on Haiti, where he found the educated Haitians quick, polite, and with no sense of inferiority. As Wilson put it, "You have only to see them to realize what a wretched life we have made for the Negroes in the United States."

I met a Haitian poet, a small man with a soft way of speech, who spoke a bookish sort of French. His verse was influenced by the French surrealists. We covered much ground. He talked of voodoo, his African roots, and the quality of writing in Haiti, describing the different kinds of poetry in the people of these starved and politically violated islands.

One of the entertainers was a young woman known as Moune, who came from Martinique, where a somber volcano bears the name of Mount Pelée. (In far away Hawai'i, where I live, Pele is the goddess of the volcano.) She sang her little songs in a small bell-like voice. They referred to *Monsieur-le-curé* and *Monsieur-le-maire,* and had in them fairy tale fantasies of childhood. She also sang current boulevard songs.

Paul was in rapture. He whispered to me, "I must teach her some American songs; they'd sound wonderful with her French accent." He spent the rest of the evening in deep talk with Moune, using a great deal of sign language. "I told her she belonged in Café Society" (a popular Manhattan night club), he told me.

Moune was eager to go, and so this fantasy became a serious undertaking. Paul found that he could get passage for Moune under the rubric of "cultural relations," that constant ferrying of visitors from the U.S. to Paris and vice-versa. A letter from the manager of Café Society told Paul he'd be delighted to audition Moune if she could get to New York. By this time Paul had been adopted into her extended family. They lived near Montparnasse, and when *Life* ran a picture of Moune surrounded by her family, Paul was beaming beside her.

A year or so later, when I reached New York, Moune was singing in Café Society. But she seemed frozen behind a grand piano and a microphone. Eventually, Moune returned to France, where she had her own little *bôite,* thanks to her Manhattan adventure.

RÉVEILLON 1944

On December 24, 1944, a notice was suddenly pinned to our bulletin board. Its cold official words told us we were confined to quarters for that evening, Christmas Eve, from 6 p.m. to the next morning at 8 a.m. There were no explanations.

Some of the soldiers had dates, but couldn't get word to their girlfriends. Out on the boulevards when the confinement was announced, the men were brought to their hotel without comment or reprimand. The MPs were painfully silent. The brain trust guessed that something must have gone wrong in the forested Ardennes. The Hitler offensive—which many of us considered his last gasp—had in one day broken through the Allied lines, and pushed fifty miles toward Antwerp along the old lines of earlier wars—1870, 1914, and again in 1940.

We settled down to our gloomy evening. We played cards and chess, or threw dice. Some read. Many of us kept up a meandering conversation. Morris Janowitz, who read the communiqués with full knowledge of Army doublespeak, thought our troops were in for a rough time. He said the situation at the front was sticky, and that if I was sent there, I might find myself in tight situations. He seemed reluctant to say more. I was very nervous. My days in Paris seemed numbered. When we came down for breakfast there was a new notice. Though we could roam the city on Christmas day, we were to be confined again that night. Indeed, night after night we remained in the Perey.

Barkeepers in the boulevards were curious. Where were all the American soldiers during these Yule nights? Instructed not to talk about our confinement, we shrugged: "You know, Army stuff." It would be some weeks before the mystery was solved. The Ardennes offensive had included a secret Nazi plan to parachute German troops to the rear of our lines, and as close to Paris as possible. These Germans all spoke English, and wore American uniforms taken from our dead soldiers or from prisoners of war. The soldiers were ordered to roam the countryside and the Paris streets. They were to commit sabotage at every opportunity. Once our intelligence learned of this plan, the simplest expedient was to confine all Americans. The MPs then took into custody anyone in uniform. Several hundred of these bogus soldiers were rapidly swept into confinement quite different from ours.

As we anxiously waited to know whether we might be freed for New Year's eve, I received a call from Madame Rieffel, the textile lady I had visited with her nephew. She and some friends were having a *réveillon* that evening. They were pooling their food, and planned a foray into the black market. Would I be free to join them? I told her I was delighted, but I had to accept conditionally. When word came that we were released that night from our bondage, I phoned my acceptance to Madame Rieffel.

* * * * *

I stepped out of the Hôtel Perey into a city lit by a full moon (electricity was rationed.) I reached Madame Rieffel's at seven, and entered a warm, bright, candle-lit interior. My hostess beamed. I was to be a showpiece, a real American, clad in excellent textiles, who could communicate with her guests in their language. I noted with pleasure that my hostess was violating the rationing; she had a couple of electric heaters going. A table was set up in the large sitting-and-dining room adjoining the parlor. The glassware gleamed, the porcelain was exquisite, the silver polished. There would be fourteen guests, including me. One or two were already in the drawing room, sipping vermouth cassis. As I approached them, I noted how the fine leather volumes on Madame Rieffel's bookshelves reflected the candlelight.

As one might expect, the talk ran at first to the weather, food, the black market, and the Battle of the Bulge. A man with a spade beard who had the air of a diplomat parceled out little facts, as if from a secret cache. He claimed the Ritz and the Crillon received special coal rations, so that the high American military who lived there could have hot water. The same all-knowing gentleman said some of the Anglo-American correspondents were taking advantage of military transportation between London and Paris. They flew to the British capital for a bath, and then returned to their chilled Parisian habitats. There was a discussion of the lucid editorials of Albert Camus in *Combat,* which most of the guests praised. A young Frenchman from Algiers, he was very withdrawn in conversation, but marvelously assured—and concise—in his journalism. Some however considered him a rank communist.

No one bothered to introduce me: my uniform was enough. I was the sole—and welcome—outsider in a hotbed of French arts, especially music—alert minds, crisp wits, fountains of Parisian gossip, and constant aggressive repartee. There were more men than women. The males were in dark suits; the women wore black, set off by colored shawls. There was a fat lady named Carmen, in a black dress trimmed with lace and sequins: a jovial anecdotist who taught violin at the Conservatoire. I saw a display of rosettes in buttonholes. The Supreme Headquarters, Allied Expeditionary Force symbol of the sword on my shoulder was unknown to the French, and they kept asking what it stood for. They attached importance to my wearing it. Not knowing what my Tech Sergeant's stripes meant, they addressed me as Colonel. I accepted the promotion.

We sat down at table after an hour of pleasant drinking. Amid kitchen sounds and agreeable herbal smells, our hostess brought on the feast. A quiet man—slim, with dark and penetrating eyes—sat on our hostess's right. He spoke a few words of English, garnered in the United States, but preferred to speak French. On the other side were a couple of businessmen. One of them spoke of the shortage of newsprint, and asked whether we had noticed that the news sheets were being sliced to even smaller size. I had noticed, and was able to participate in the discussion of the press.

The charming man next to me began to talk of his trip before the war to the United States. I told him I hadn't caught his name. He said it was Honegger, and that he was Swiss. I told him the only Swiss Honegger known to me by reputation was a composer, Arthur Honegger, whose work I admired. He said his name was Arthur. I told him I had heard and greatly enjoyed his *Roi David,* during my student days in Paris. I had also heard his diverting piece of incidental music called *Pacific 231,* an evocation of an American train chugging through the mountains amid great walls of rock. I told him of my devotion to Stravinsky. Honegger spoke of his friendship with Jean Cocteau.

I made my way through a *jambon d'York* with melon and a splendid stew—one didn't ask what kind of meat had been used. I drank the fine wines. Carmen across the table began to talk about Maurice Ravel, whom Honegger had known. She had been a close friend of Ravel for many years, and spoke of how awful his death had been. He had been in a car accident, and suffered from a brain injury for four years before the end. Seven years had gone by, and she still wept when she spoke of him. I said I had been present the night he introduced his "Bolero"—danced at the opera by the aging Ida Rubenstein of the Russian Ballet. I had a vivid memory of the thin little man, with his long face and sunken eyes, beating time for the large orchestra in its slow-paced reiteration of the single theme.

And so, dropping musical names and memories of performances, we made our way through a salad and some sorbet. We were still at table when the midnight hour neared. We exchanged kisses in the French manner—one on each cheek—and then a single one added for good measure. We drank champagne to a quick end of the war and to everyone's good health. Then we started on after dinner drinks, circulating in the dining room and the parlor. I lingered well into the early hours of the new year, feeling myself duty-bound to do so as the displayed stranger. Honegger, our hostess, and I and the fleshly Carmen kept up our talk of the performing arts. When 1945 seemed well encradled, Carmen announced it was time for her to leave. She lived a short distance away, and Honegger and I offered her to see her home. I gave our hostess a new year's kiss under the mistletoe, and the three of us stepped into the moonlight, a freezing bath of marble whiteness. Honegger took one of Carmen's arms, and I took the other. There was still some ice in her street, and we had to support her rather considerable weight. We inched along, she with tentative footsteps. She talked about the "Group of Six," to which Honegger belonged. I had recently attended a concert given by these innovators—Milhaud, Auric, Poulenc, Germaine Tailleferre and Louis Durey. Finally we were at Carmen's door, and we bade her an elaborate farewell. She called me *"un grave américain,"* and I saluted her as the Muse of the Violin. Then Honegger and I set off.

It was pleasant walking briskly after the evening of culinary excess. At the Place de l'Étoile, we paused to take in the length of central Paris. The Champs-Élysées was deserted. Not a vehicle, rare humans. The city seemed chaste and pure, wrapped in enchanting silence. All the tawdriness of neon, all the commerce of the boulevard, were extinguished. There were no illuminated windows to display the motorcars of the world, and no solicitations for grand luxuries. But the general blackout was totally undermined by the moon. A single bomber, if it could break through the anti-aircraft, would have found all its targets clearly displayed. Names of dead cities wove their way through my mind. Nineveh somehow, though I had no sense of what it might have looked like, and more obviously Alexandria, Athens, Rome. I imagined mosques and minarets everywhere. A kind of sepulchral beauty. Translate that into music, Honegger said, and I said that he mustn't make a composer out of me. All I could do was invoke Beethoven's so-called Moonlight Sonata. Good enough, he said.

The *lune* cast its dramatic shadows over the entire landscape as Honegger spoke of his childhood. Of Swiss origin, he was born in France at Le Havre, but had lived the war years in Paris. His studio was high in Montmartre. He talked of his old teachers—Vincent d'Indy, whom I had met long before, and Widor the organist. He remembered Satie. He praised Fauré. He had kept his connections with Switzerland, though he was essentially a part of the French modern school. He had set some of Apollinaire to music. He grew nostalgic about his work with Cocteau in 1922, on a version of *Antigone* for which Picasso did the sets. And he talked too of what it had meant for him to have his early career truncated by the first war. Now this second war—French musicians had seldom been produced, since they refused participation in the Vichy-sponsored arts.

We walked out into the center of the Place de la Concorde to take in the scene, and stood in the narrow shadow of the obelisk. At the corner of the rue du Faubourg-Saint-Honoré we parted.

PART FIVE

STRASBOURG

A Sudden Panic
Farewells
A Winter Journey
Strasbourg Besieged
Street of the Blue Sky
Briefings
Story of Claude
Siege Notes
Cannonade
A Didactic Moment

À la Population de Strasbourg!

La situation militaire n'a rien d'inquiétant.

Que les habitants se rassurent et restent paisiblement chez eux.

Strasbourg et l'Alsace seront défendus par les Armées Alliées qui ne songent pas à se replier.

Vive l'Alsace!
Vive la France!

signé:
LE GÉNÉRAL AMÉRICAIN
Commandant de Strasbourg

À la Population de Strasbourg!

    La situation militaire n'a rien d'inquiétant.

    Que les habitants se rassurent et restent paisiblement chez eux.

    Strasbourg et l'Alsace seront défendus par les Armées Alliées qui ne songent pas à se replier.

    Vive l'Alsace!
    Vive la France!

signé:

Le Général Americain
Commandant de Strasbourg.

A SUDDEN PANIC

I was lifted out of my contentment in Paris and sent in mid-winter 1944–1945 to Strasbourg, France's proud city on the lower Rhine, the capital of Alsace. With its asymmetrical cathedral—the highest spire in all Europe—and its complex of ancient fortifications, the city had passed back and forth between France and Germany during the preceding centuries. Alsace and Lorraine were annexed by the old Germany in the Franco-Prussian war of 1870. In 1920, under the Treaty of Versailles, the provinces had been restored to France. Hitler's conquest of France in 1940 took over Alsace as German "occupied" territory. All Nazi laws instantly applied. A concentration camp was set up for political prisoners and undesirables, including inevitably such Jews as remained. French activists were executed.

Though still under Nazi siege on three sides, the city had been liberated the previous November, when General Leclerc swiftly crossed the Vosges mountains, and caught the German garrison in Stras-bourg napping. He took sixteen thousand prisoners. General de Gaulle arrived, and was acclaimed. But three weeks later, Hitler sprang his surprise offensive in the Ardennes, two-hundred miles northeast of Stras-bourg, and the city's joy turned into acute fear and anxiety. The enemy had established a bridgehead at Gambsheim, four miles north of Stras-bourg's center. Now German artillery pounded the city. Strasbourg feared a sudden return of vengeful Nazis and a new regime of terror.

On the morning of January 3, the population went into a violent state of panic. Some sixty thousand crowded onto the main highway heading toward interior France, driving motor vehicles, horse-drawn farm wagons, scooters, and even bicycles. At the railroad station, ten thousand filled the streets, hoping to escape. There were no trains.

One fact was known: that Eisenhower himself, having insufficient information about Strasbourg's morale, had issued an order for residual units and war *matériel* to be moved from Strasbourg to the Vosges mountains. The citizens quite rightly interpreted the order to mean that he no longer planned to defend the city. De Gaulle recognized that Eisenhower had military reasons for his decisions, but as a noble "Daughter of France," Strasbourg could not be allowed to fall back into German hands. The General wrote and telephoned Eisenhower. He called Churchill. He apparently sent a cable to Roosevelt. These moves must have deeply disturbed Eisenhower. "The Strasbourg question was to plague me throughout the duration of the Ardennes battle," he would write four years later in his memoirs, and the "plague" was General de Gaulle.

Snaking in and out of the long procession fleeing the city on the highway, two British public address vans helped the Strasbourg police cope with the general alarm. The leader of this British unit was a Captain bearing a famous Russian aristocratic name—Galitzin—though he proved to be a chubby, red-cheeked Englishman, reared and educated in Britain, when I met him two weeks later. "I was called out of bed early," he wrote in his official report of the incident, "summoned to headquarters, and told we were intending to withdraw. The news came as a dreadful surprise." Broadcasting both in French and German, the loudspeaker vans tried to be reassuring, but there was no let up in the panic, as the exodus continued for six hours or more. Then at 3 p.m., Galitzin received a sudden summons to headquarters. Eisenhower had just rescinded his order. Strasbourg would be defended after all.

Galitzin sent word to the two vans on the highway. He took his van to the railroad station; encountering a French officer, he yielded the microphone to him. It would sound better to have a French voice address the frightened crowd. "It was moving," Galitzin said, "to see this straggling, bewildered crowd suddenly realize that everything would be all right." The crowd seemed to have complete faith in Eisenhower: "By nightfall, everyone was either moving back into the city or under shelter for the night." The next morning, Strasbourg's walls carried enormous signs in large black letters, reassuring the population. I translate from a copy I still possess:

To the Population of Strasbourg!

The military situation is completely under control. The inhabitants should rest assured of this and should remain quietly in their homes. Strasbourg and Alsace will be defended by the Allied Armies. They have no plans for a withdrawal.

The poster was signed "The American General in Command of Strasbourg." That general was Jacob Devers, head of the Sixth U.S. Army Group.

American Psychological Warfare had failed to be a presence during the Strasbourg panic. It had not grasped the jittery state of the city. Now that the panic had been short-circuited, it was important for psychwar headquarters to analyze its mistakes and undertake appropriate remedial action. Our commander, General Robert A. McClure, was intelligent, shy, and mostly invisible. Directly responsible to Eisenhower, he kept running smoothly an operation made up of a few highly disciplined soldiers and many temperamental media civilians. How he had maintained the delicate balance between the broadcasting professionals, and those who were strictly Army, was a mystery to us all. It was an open secret that the media moguls who had been given high army ranks were proving extremely useful in handling Allied propaganda. We heard they were provided with extraordinary comforts while they pretended to be soldiers. If there were military officers who resented these arrangements, we did not know it. They probably realized how special psychwar was, a strange hybrid of the Tower of Babel and show biz.

Even before the panic, I had sufficient hints I would be sent to a forward position. I hung around the rue d'Aguesseau offices that afternoon, hoping to get some signal. My regular duties were being taken over by an Office of War Information official. I was on hold. In late afternoon, I received word that Luther Conant, still my boss in the psychwar press section, wanted to see me. The winter dark had set in. The office was icy. Conant looked crushed. He told me it had been a grueling day: he needed a few martinis and wouldn't detain me long. He then announced I was to be a member of the team assigned to Strasbourg. There were several problems to solve. He had to find someone to monitor the German broadcasts. We needed to know why the Strasbourg press had failed to maintain morale. And we had to find out what the Gaullists were up to. Conant told me to keep in touch daily with his office. I asked him about our essential mission. He looked a bit puzzled. I said I wanted some definition. The city could fall to the Germans at any time. We might find ourselves involved in the action, or even taken prisoners. I was worried about our safety. What were our specific goals, besides priming the French press and helping Radio Strasbourg get back on the air?

Conant said that if I wanted a general statement, he would have to say, "You must make an effort to improve the morale of Strasbourg."

I laughed. If Conant had been military I would simply have replied, "Yes, sir." But with a fellow pressman I could laugh, and I remarked that the best answer to morale would be a few American tanks in the city's streets. Conant said I was forgetting that American tanks were all at the Bulge, and then shifted ground. I had been chosen to head up the press team of enlisted men, whose jobs would be to handle communications. I would also be a liaison with the local editors. In other words, I was to continue being a French linguist with news experience. Conant was sorry he couldn't tell me anything more—"The exact picture of what's happening to the media in Strasbourg probably won't be known till we get into the city."

In 1945, we were still using the telegraph, and would have some Morse men on our team. If the city's power remained unavailable, we would need a generator. I told Conant I would need to know the situation along the front from hour to hour. I could not wait for the official communiqués. Conant assured me precautions would be taken, but added, "You'll be expected to use your soldierly training if necessary."

I walked away from the rue d'Aguesseau feeling half depressed, half exhilarated, and a bit scared. Luther Conant had told me to hold myself ready to leave for the front at a moment's notice, but that moment would stretch itself out to two weeks. A German linguist was assigned to us. Telegraphists were supplied. There would be vehicles and drivers on the spot, and the generator. We would be an independent unit attached to other freewheeling units. We would have to recognize that we were going to a threatened city, to be exposed to the unexpected situations of war.

FAREWELLS

Waiting in Paris for an uncertain departure was hard on my nerves. I had wild fantasies. I studied the daily communiqués. They weren't helpful. I appealed constantly to Morris Janowitz for every scrap of intelligence he could supply. I recognized he was trying to tell me as little as possible. He usually said the situation was "a bit sticky." I must have suffered from what psychologists call separation anxiety—a rather acute case. The thought of leaving my little niche and finding myself within a battle scene, as I had in Normandy, gave me spasms of worry. I wasn't made for war or the army, and was well past the age of vigorous death-dealing action. I did not have the soldier mentality.

During this period, Augier, my companion since the liberation, was whisked away to Nancy, where my former mobile broadcasting company was immured for the winter. I would never see him again. Now he belongs with the soldiers who remain arrested in memory, as they were in 1944.

* * * * *

In the middle of January, Janowitz decided I deserved a send-off. He knew some of the young women in OSS and OWI, billeted in a midtown luxury hotel at the Rond-Point des Champs-Élysées. He was sure they would want to meet me; I ungratefully said it sounded as if he was announcing a party for a condemned man on his way to execution. Janowitz persisted. We gathered in a lounge on one of the hotel floors, a comfortable room with soft armchairs. There seemed to be some central heating; in fact, the women said they had hot water in their bathrooms, which they put at my disposal. We were a mixed group, but I felt very much an outsider because I was at least a dozen years older than the men and women who were sending me off. Silent and solemn, I was an object of sympathy. Some of the girls had colds and left early. A few hardy drinkers remained. I left as soon as I could decently do so, apologizing to Janowitz for my seeming ingratitude. In a sepulchral tone he said he understood how I felt. I sensed he believed I was in for a rough time.

*****

Five days before my departure, I wandered in Montparnasse. The place had sunk into winter deadness. Chilled stragglers sat in café corners, imbibing hot drinks that fast became cold. Restless and preoccupied, I walked down the Boulevard Raspail till I reached the rue de Rennes. I turned past the Vieux Colombier and found myself in the rue du Cherche-Midi—the Street of the Sundial. It was still a typical neighborhood of an older time—the grocer, wine merchant, shoemaker, and two or three other shops. In 1936–1937, I had lived at No. 15—a comfortable apartment with a small bedroom, tiny kitchen, and large-windowed living room furnished with a few fine old pieces. It was a sublet from an American opera singer, and I had a six months lease. This was sufficient, for I planned to go on the Guggenheim Fellowship I had been given to edit James's plays.

I stood in the blackout in front of No. 15, thinking of the time I spent there when I was working for the Agence Havas. I remembered the intensities of that period, and the vivid cables that crossed my desk. The evidence was mounting that we were moving toward war. Democratic forces were being defeated in Spain's civil war, in which Hitler and Mussolini tested Western Europe, and found it vulnerable and ready for their horrors. I read the foreign affairs analyses, which generally regarded Russia's Marxism as the West's greatest enemy, greater even than Hitler's hysterical Napoleonic dreams.

Standing in front of my former apartment that night in 1945, I found myself in a reverie about a young French journalist at Havas who introduced himself to me nine years earlier. His name was Robert Mengin. He spoke excellent English, acquired in a British school, and he felt we could have conversations in English that would be useful to him. He proved a charming friend—cultivated, literary, with British habits of friendliness and hospitality. Early in the summer of 1936, he suggested I might find it interesting to meet his father, who had spent much of his youth in England. Urbain Mengin was a sturdy man of about seventy, short, vigorous, with a neatly trimmed beard. Recently attached to the French Institute in Florence, he talked about Italian art and British writers. He knew Berenson, and was skeptical about some of his attributions to the old masters of painting.

In the midst of this amusing talk, I noticed on a bookshelf a plump red volume I recognized at once as Henry James's *The American Scene*. I asked him how he liked James. At this, he set down his knife and fork, dropped his formality, and launched into enthusiastic praise of the Master and his works. He considered James an American genius, a man of generosity and warmth. I said he was speaking as if he had known him. He had indeed known him fifty years earlier, and beamed at me when I told him my doctorate had been devoted to James's playwriting years. It was a magical coincidence, one that I have always cherished, that the young Mengin should have approached me, and that I should find myself at lunch with his father, who produced later an autographed photo of James, and a bundle of letters. Mengin had been very young when he came to the British capital in the 1880s, with a letter of introduction from the French novelist Paul Bourget to James. The elder Mengin said his entire life in London had been irradiated by James's charming presence. They had become good friends.

Mengin read me bits out of James's letters, but apologized for not showing me the correspondence. The letters contained allusions to Bourget which Mengin regarded as too personal to be shown. I told him how in 1931 I had tried to meet Bourget. Mengin said that by then the novelist had become old and sour. His rigid conservatism apparently stiffened the differences between him and Mengin. He was "politically impossible," anti-Semitic, and frosty. With these words, Mengin suggested his own liberality. He read to me from a letter dealing with one of James's plays. In formal French, James wrote that the "thirst for gold" had pushed him into "the dishonorable road" of writing for the stage.

Mengin sent me to visit another old Parisian friend of James's, who lived in a flat at No. 88 rue de Varenne. A. Mary F. Robinson, as she first signed her books, was a distinguished English lady of letters, who published works in English and French on both sides of the Channel. She had married an eminent French orientalist, James Darmsteter. He was a hunchback who cherished her. When widowed, she married Émile Duclaux, who succeeded Pasteur at the Institute. She was a close friend of Vernon Lee (Violet Paget), the essayist and novelist.

The first time I met her and her novelist sister Mabel, she was having a weekly tea reception. I found myself in an assemblage of elderly Victorian ladies, drinking endless cups of tea with an abundance of cakes and cookies, and indulging in ancient gossip. On a second occasion I saw her alone. She sat under a portrait of herself at twenty, painted by Sargent, and talked as if Walter Pater had tipped his hat to her in Oxford that very morning, or she had seen Browning the day before yesterday. She described him after Elizabeth Barrett's death, always convinced she was in the next room. "At any moment she may walk in," he used to say. Then a few minutes later, "but she never does." Mrs. Robinson was amusing about Henry James when he lived in Rye, in Sussex, where grocers used to flourish extravagantly worded autograph letters ordering a pound of coffee or cheese. When asked to put away the silver for the summer, the servants in the house she rented at Rye said, "But you will need it when Mr. James comes for tea."

On the eve of Strasbourg, in the damp cold and the dark, I had no difficulty recovering the old warm ambiance of the rue du Cherche-Midi. I tore myself away, and crossed the rue de Sèvres to the rue du Dragon. Somewhere in the dark, in some nearby house, a flute fell on the night air in the deserted streets with particular melancholy. A cat watched me as I walked along the curving narrow sidewalk. The cat was near a butcher shop. I could see a thin knife-edge of light down one door, and heard chopping and sawing sounds, as if some side of beef was being trimmed for morning customers into small rations.

I reached the Boulevard Saint-Germain, and went down a narrow street to the Seine. At the river's edge I witnessed a procession of ambulances, gliding like a ghostly train, with their lights blazing yet almost soundless. These grim vehicles, with their fierce illumination, sent me to my sleep with a shudder which led to fantastic, unremembered dreams.

A WINTER JOURNEY

We left for the front early on January 20, a cold crisp sunny winter's day. I managed to get an early breakfast at the Hôtel Perey before my usual companions came downstairs, and avoided painful good-byes. The jeep arrived punctually. It was open and had flapping plastic curtains—a slight protection against the wind. I met for the first time the members of my team. A sad-eyed corporal with a small-trimmed mustache named Pryor, an expert in communications; two Morse operators, Manhattan youngsters of nineteen or twenty eager to be off; a young, slender private first class named Warren Manshel, a German refugee schooled in the U.S., who would monitor the Nazi broadcasts. The jeep, a limousine, and a truck made up our little procession destined for the Rhine. In the truck, carefully packaged, was our generator.

The wind bit into us. We drank coffee from a thermos; it didn't help much. The captain, whom I accompanied, soon ran out of jokes and stories, and we continued in chill and silence. All I remember was that in the late afternoon we came to the village of Domrémy, the birthplace of Joan of Arc. It had been a farm village in the middle ages, and still looked medieval. The tiny houses in the street seemed walled in by fortifications: in reality, piles of frozen cow dung, to be plowed into the fields in the spring. We quickly skidded through the town where the Maid of Orléans heard her mystic voices and put on armor to rally the French armies around a reluctant king in Reims, about seventy-five miles to the north.

At Vittel, our stopover, brawny monks in brown cassocks gave us huge bowls of soup and large crusts of peasant bread. I felt myself thawing out. Distant memories came to me of how, as a boy in Saskatchewan, I pushed through blizzardy streets in fifty below weather, and of that pleasurable feeling of creeping warmth in the classrooms that restored my frozen body.

The next morning we had another eight hours of travel, along the straight road across the plain behind Strasbourg. There was heavy army traffic. Other roads were still under enemy fire. We moved slowly and steadily, again with a feeling of chronic refrigeration. The wind-chill factor, as we would now say, was considerable. The sky looked sullen; the white-covered land seemed endless. It was still dark in the early morning, and on the horizon there were occasional flashes of flame. Somewhere, shells were seeking invisible targets.

In Strasbourg, low houses and business buildings emerged out of snow heaped in front of them to considerable height, sometimes ten feet or more. By this time it was pitch dark. The driver of the leading vehicle seemed lost. I was exhausted—stiff from so much sitting. Suddenly we came to a stop. I saw a sign over a doorway which read *Die Zauberflöte*—the Magic Flute, though this was hardly an operatic setting. A door flew open, and I got a glimpse of a large café, lit by candles stuck in wine or beer bottles under a haze of tobacco smoke.

Half a dozen hearty French soldiers practically lifted us out of our vehicles and rushed us into the café. They asked what took us so long. They had expected us at 6 p.m. It was now 9. The room seemed warm, probably because of human presence: there were about a hundred officers, soldiers, civilians. The tables looked festive. They were covered with checkered cloths, and we found ourselves holding glasses of wine or Armagnac. Two energetic waitresses wrapped in big white aprons, one ample and soft, the other thin and assertive, told us to sit anywhere, and we were in a few minutes eating hot food from large bowls.

A civilian at our table told us in his Alsatian accent that his missing arm was in Estonia. He had been among thousands of Alsatians conscripted by the Germans to fight the Russians. While in the hospital, wondering where he would be shipped next, he learned from a clandestine radio that Strasbourg had been liberated. He slipped out of the building and rode freight trains to the French frontier. He decided to remain in his German uniform. His missing arm was his best identification. At the frontier, he obtained civilian clothes so that he would not be shot by Allied soldiers, and surrendered to the French. U.S. Army intelligence cleared him.

As we ate our stew and drank a coarse wine, I heard a great deal of gossip about the situation in Strasbourg. The French regional commissioner was described as having "siege psychosis." He kept his bags packed for flight. He had made no attempt to stiffen morale. The Communists were the ones encouraging the city. They had plastered the walls with posters telling the citizens to keep in mind that other populations— London under the bombs, the insurrection in Paris, the fighters in

Warsaw and Stalingrad—had not fled, but had taken up the battle. I couldn't tell from what they said whether this strategy frightened the population or stimulated it. I later sent one of these posters to the rue d'Aguesseau, as an example of our strange bedfellow in psychwar.

After a while we only half-listened, groggy and exhausted. Captain Yurka Galitzin of the British psychwar team, the man with the loudspeaker vans, came to my team's rescue. He marched us through a narrow path in the snow to our quarters, a large house the Nazis had renovated for their stay. One long narrow room had sinks and sufficient toilets. Wide beds in each room assured us of comfortable rest. The house was decorated with the same kind of macho Nazi art I had seen in Paris. On the wall facing our beds were two huge nude figures, giant and giantess. In the room across the way, an Amazonian woman with huge breasts filled the entire curve of a wall painted lemon yellow. The house was solidly built. A little heat, and we would have been insulated against the cold; as it was, it seemed to retain the city's frosts. Still, what with the wine and hot food and the seemingly endless journey, I was instantly asleep. At various times during the night, however, the chatter of small arms awakened me. There was an occasional belch of a large gun. Dropping in and out of consciousness, I felt sure that the doors would open in the morning on a fighting front.

STRASBOURG BESIEGED

In the morning, I plunged into the freezing bathroom, with its ridiculous murals, to wash and shave. Presently the others joined me. Young animals, released from two days' confinement in a truck, suddenly they became songbirds. In love with Lili Marlene, they jumped from one song to another, in falsetto voices. They talked like tourists, newly arrived in a city. I chilled their exuberance, reminding them this is the Army. Duty first, sightseeing after. Meanwhile, I kept brooding on the Rhine, just two miles away, and all the Nazi soldiers who surrounded us.

Soon we were walking along the icy path between high snowdrifts back to the Zauberflöte down the street. A young French mess sergeant tried to convince us that oatmeal doesn't need to be cooked. All it requires is milk; he offered to heat the milk. We settled for dry cereal, tinned orange juice, our own Nescafé. Then Captain Galitzin arrived. He looked this morning like a British schoolboy, wearing a funny peaked cap, quite unmilitary, and wrapped in a heavy coat. He was short, bulky, dark-haired, with a pair of schoolmasterly gold-rimmed spectacles on his bridgeless nose. I ask him whether he belonged to the princely Galitzins of the time of Peter the Great, whose descendants figured in Tolstoy, or the opera *Prince Igor*. He told me his family came to England long ago, then switched our talk to the effectiveness of his loudspeaker vans. The people of Strasbourg were hungry for news; they turned up in large numbers at street corners to listen to bulletins. I promised to supply him with a news report especially written for street broadcast. He also told me I would be under command of a captain staying at the Hôtel de France. I had better report to him.

He marched us to the offices of the former German women's labor service. We crossed a small courtyard in the building. Our truck awaited us. We climbed some stairs, and Galitzin ushered us into a suite of offices arranged around a central reception room. The place was a shambles. A picture of Adolf Hitler filled one wall, his eyes seeming to follow us wherever we stood. There were pictures of Goering and Goebbels, Hess and others, and the lesser fry. The floor was heaped with directories, papers scattered out of filing cabinets, and boxes, from which swastika armbands had been spilled. Our communications expert was in ecstasy. There were two fine radios: he would have excellent reception from all parts of Germany. Another office would serve the Morse operators; I would preside from the reception room, where a large worktable in the center had a droplight hanging directly over it. There was enough electricity for all our technical equipment and twenty light bulbs.

The men seemed delighted; the idea of being ensconced in offices gave them a sense of importance. They brought in furniture from other empty offices, to make our little world seem as if it had always existed in upholstered comfort. Adjoining us was the office of the French Information Services. Down the hall, Agence France-Presse was preparing to move in. Our goal was to serve as liaison with de Gaulle's information deputy and the local press. We would have a French and German file as well as the one in English. The French were willing, indeed eager, to use any news we would supply.

I reported to the captain in charge at the Hôtel de France. He was an easy-going Irishman who expressed interest in our welfare, but clearly didn't want to be bothered. He would forget about roll call, calisthenics, and other duties, so long as I assured him that all my men were on the job. When I asked about censoring the men's mail, he told me to sign his name in a corner of the envelope. I balked at this. Sergeants weren't supposed to read their men's mail. "You don't have to read it," he replied, "All it needs is a signature." We compromised. He would take care of the mail unless he was away. Then I would put his initials on the envelopes.

STREET OF THE BLUE SKY

The principal newspaper in Strasbourg was *Les Dernières Nouvelles,* "The Latest News." It was located in the rue de la Nuée Bleue—"The Street of the Blue Sky." The newspaper was installed in a solid brick building, whose glassed front displayed the well-oiled, shining presses. Inside, the building seemed cluttered and crowded. Five other journals had moved in temporarily, and were being printed on the one press. This was a union of right and center. Those of the left—the Socialist and Communist papers—and the Catholic papers as well, were ignored.

The managing editor of *Les Dernières Nouvelles* received me with a show of cordiality. He was a sharply dressed yet pudgy little man who was filled with self-importance. He professed his love for the American army, and immediately promoted me to colonel. Instead of objecting, I attempted a witticism, saying that the siege had unfortunately turned "The Latest News" into "The Late News."

"*Mon colonel,*" he said, with a sweep of his arms, "*que voulez-vous?* We're doing the best we can." I apologized, and acknowledged the achievement of getting any of the city's papers out in spite of the siege. I complimented him on the modernity of his presses, the excellent typography of *Les Dernières Nouvelles,* and the precision of the editing. In reality, the leading papers had got themselves into a rut. Since the curfew was at 6:30 p.m., the reporters and printer set up the papers by 6 p.m. then went home. Twelve hours later, they ran them off and delivered them to the news stands, but by this time the news was stale. A whole new set of communiqués was already available. Despite this problem, the papers had clearly not attempted to revise the timing of their editions, stagger their staffs, or make provision for stop-press news. Their customers got the news once every twenty-four hours, or had to satisfy themselves with whatever radio stations were available—and the German stations were succeeding in confusing and frightening the populace.

I asked whether the newspapers had considered leaving space for last minute bulletins. I said my sources could supply the latest military news, and it could be set up overnight. Then I would hand-carry this file every evening here to the rue de la Nuée Bleue. The managing editor grew red-faced—

"*Mon colonel,* you seem not to have been told we are subject also to double censorship. Even if the papers were printed on a different schedule, the news would always be late. There is the army censorship; then there is the local political censor. He is a trouble-making man, who refuses to heed our deadlines."

I said the news would be be entirely official, precensored, and ready for the front page.

BRIEFINGS

In the late afternoon of my second day in Strasbourg, I set off for Saverne, about twenty-five miles distant, where I was to attend the daily briefings at General Devers' forward headquarters. Saverne was the hub of a number of roads—even in the time of horses and carriages, it had been a posting center. Jefferson visited this region in the spring of 1788, when he was studying European husbandry and vineyards. (He would have been astonished that the young revolutionary country he helped found had spread a mighty army across Europe and penetrated the Vosges mountains.) He described "waving hills and hollows; red, rich enough; mostly in small grain, but some vines." It didn't look like that during late January and February of 1945. Winter choked the hills and hollows. Only the tall wire frames for the hop vines harkened back to Jefferson's time.

A smart-looking youth of twenty-two named Claude, who had packed into his few years a good deal of adventure and warfare, was assigned to me on occasion as a driver from the French army. The first time he came into my office he clicked his heels, German style, and gave me a snappy salute. He might have come out of a Hollywood movie.

We usually set out at curfew time. Our first and absolutely essential call was to the local command for the night's password. Names and geography were used a great deal in the interest of simplicity. The challenging soldier would plant himself in front of our vehicle at a checkpoint, grasping his rifle. He might whisper "Casablanca." Our answer would be "Eisenhower," or some other familiar name, proving we belonged to the same army.

We would pass through Strasbourg's darkening squares and streets, already empty of humans—old streets with names such as the Blauwolkengasse or the Judengasse, or with fancy geographical names like Istria. I have only to close my eyes and think of the name Saverne to see us in our vehicle, chains rattling against the paved road partially cleared by heavy tank traffic. Each night had its own sky, its own fireworks, its own sounds of war. The sky was most often overcast. Stars rarely appeared. Suddenly we would be stopped at some roadblock, and have to go through our word-signals. Usually an ominous tank or two would be tucked away in some corner.

The on-record briefing in Saverne was often concise, limited, and vague. An officer with decorations and a pointer explained the military situation to newsmen and Army staff. It was the bare bones. The press mostly asked banal or obvious questions, which usually elicited ambiguous answers. My main purpose in being there was to assuage my chronic anxiety. I had to know how close the enemy was, and whether there had been any changes. By 8 p.m., we were on our way back in the total blackness.

One night proved to be singular. It had begun to snow, and the flakes were large and moist. We arrived at a checkpoint on the freshly-whitened road, and an American soldier poked his face into the vehicle.

"Telegraph," he said. His gun was pointed at us.

I experienced an inner shudder. This wasn't the evening's password. We had received something quite different half an hour earlier in Strasbourg. I looked blankly at the face. The guard moved his gun slightly.

"How about it?"

I told him we had another word. The word telegraph had no meaning to me. He repeated the word, dividing it into syllables for my comprehension. He looked at me hard.

"Are you sure that's the right word?" I said. "I have a reply but it's not to your word."

His next move was a surprise.

"What's the capital of New York State?"

I had lived much in Manhattan and was about to say New York—New Yorkers think their city is the capital of the state, and maybe the world. But something stopped me.

"Albany."

"Yep," he said, "Give you an A for that." He lowered his gun. Then he asked me about some ball team—maybe the Dodgers.

"Not baseball," I said, "I'm better on hockey."

He touched me lightly with the gun, as if it were a sniffing dog.

"I guess you'd better surrender your weapons."

I handed him my M-3, and Claude gave him his French weapon.

The guard said he'd take care of our vehicle, and marched us to a nearby doorway. The door opened into what looked like a garage. We stamped the snow off our feet, and approached a U.S. Army first lieutenant sitting at a card table beside a French officer. Both officers were in fatigues. I decided to take the initiative. I offered a snappy salute, and said—

"Sir, your guard has the wrong password."

The lieutenant snapped back that he didn't think so. His chin jutting out, he asked for our dogtags, and told us to strip.

I took an instant dislike to him. He was nasty and put on airs. I told myself the less said the better. We stood there, cold and damp, in our underwear, as he studied our dog tags and every scrap of paper we carried. The French officer asked why we were going to Saverne. I said I was on my way to a briefing. The American lieutenant interposed—

"Why? You ain't correspondents. You're GIs, unless you're Germans in our uniforms."

I explained we belonged to Psychological Warfare, which was attached to General Eisenhower's headquarters. We were part of crowd control. We worked with the military police. To the French officer I said in English I was a French linguist, used by the Army to talk to French civilians on loudspeaker trucks.

"Your knowing French makes me even more suspicious," he replied. I said in French I recognized they had to be suspicious, but the facts of the case were that in Psychological Warfare we spoke all kinds of languages.

The American lieutenant tried to put a call through on the field telephone sitting on his card table. He got no reply. He asked me if I could speak German. I said I knew a few words.

"I might say that if I were a German soldier captured by the enemy," he said.

I said if I were a German I'd probably have a German accent when I spoke English. He said I might be a German-American helping Hitler. He had a grim way of twisting his mouth. He tried phoning again, without success. Then he exchanged whispers with the French officer. Finally he turned to me and asked me to give him the password I was given in Strasbourg. I gave it to him. Did I know, he asked, why that password was no longer useful? I said I knew. Obviously someone had leaked it to the enemy. Exactly, he said. He then told me that the answer to the new password "Telegraph" was "Fifi"—he spelled it out and drew it out long—"Fee-fee."

We were allowed to put our clothes on again. He gave us back our papers and dogtags. I thanked the officer, saluting him as smartly as possible. Claude's salute was smarter. The big soft flakes were still falling. The guard led us back to our vehicle. He turned and said "Telegraph."

I answered "Fee-fee."

"Good," he said, "Take care."

By the time we reached Saverne, the briefing was over. We started back to Strasbourg. The evening now seemed eerie—the moist snowfall, the ghostly guard station, those two officers full of suspicion. Claude could speak German, but he had decided to stick to the French that went with his uniform. He told me the French officer had thrown a few quiet questions in French at him while I was talking to the lieutenant. They were easy to answer. I reported our problem the next day, when we picked up the newest password. I was told that it was simply too bad if a password was leaked and you had the wrong one. We must expect to be treated as if we were the enemy.

STORY OF CLAUDE

I never asked for, nor learned, Claude's last name. A blond, blue-eyed Strasbourg youth who spoke both German and French, he made a good —even startling—impression, for he looked like a Nazi who had crawled into a French uniform. He was cautious, grateful, smiling, disciplined, with none of the severity of the average iron-featured German soldier. I suppose this was because he was more French than German. After one of our drives, I invited him to come some evening to our offices and tell me more about his military service with the German army. I wanted to know what it was like to be a soldier for Hitler.

Arriving one night, he faced me across a desk. The solitary bulb set in the green droplight fixture threw a pool of yellow across the cluttered surface. "A Frenchman wearing a German mask," I thought. He smiled, settled into his chair, and said, as if he were reading my thoughts—

"I suppose you're wondering about me. I happen to be a Strasbourg Jew who has managed to pass as a German."

I tried not to look astonished. Many Europeans wore Nazi disguises during the regime of Hitler. Then I said, "Maybe you're pulling my leg." I had to explain what that meant in English. He said he wasn't.

"I became the enemy in order to escape from him."

His voice was low, almost a whisper, as if he feared someone might be listening. He shared recollections, starting with his experiences along the Russian front, and then swinging back to life among the *maquis* around Vichy. He had no indoctrination, knew little about the Resistance, only that he must remain, at every minute of the day, under his cover. He soon recognized he was being drilled for the German army. There was a great deal of malingering among the men—duty-shirking and displays of fatigue on the parade ground. Borrowing language from the American soldiers, Claude explained that they "played at being fuck-ups."

That was just like the French, the Germans said; they would never make good soldiers. Men were sent to the Russian front. If they would not learn, they could serve as cannon fodder. Claude by his very nature couldn't offer a display of ineptness, so he decided he would demonstrate limited kinds of efficiency. He mastered engines, becoming an expert in vehicle maintenance. He made a point of clicking his heels and saluting, even when salutes weren't necessary. When sent to the Russian front, he served as a driver for a Prussian colonel who was as hard as nails. Later Claude was attached to a captain, a decent man, who spoke constantly about the cold. Claude often slept in his vehicle, covering himself with purloined rugs and every bit of wool he could find. He feared the Russian partisans, who moved like ghosts in a snow-world, raiding supplies, stealing vehicles or setting them on fire, killing. No German soldier dared to be alone: those who walked near an encampment often never returned.

A shell exploded near the car, killing the captain. Claude received some flesh wounds. He was taken to a base hospital, where he learned that as soon as he became ambulatory he would be returned to the front. He hoarded cigarettes and cookies supplied by the Red Cross. Wearing some stolen civilian clothes, he disappeared into the night. He had been in Russia little more than a year.

The story suddenly shifted back to his Vichy training. Claude had turned seventeen in 1939, when the war began. He was attending high school when the German armies swept into France. He had planned to become a pharmacist, but he dropped his studies and worked in his father's small clothing factory, which had a contract to produce French army uniforms. Then the Germans reorganized the factory and promulgated their racist laws. The daughter went to live with a friend in the unoccupied zone; the parents felt they should wait to see what happened.

In July 1942, after Claude had returned from the front, the Nazis forced the Strasbourg Jews to wear the yellow Star of David, created a curfew that kept them indoors from 7 p.m. to 7 a.m., and ordered them to stay out of parks and movies. With his blond hair and blue eyes, Claude obtained forged passports and identification papers for his parents and himself. His parents couldn't make up their minds. They clung to a fantasy that things might change. One evening they bitterly quarreled; he left never to return. In due course his parents were sent off to the camps.

Though a member of the youth ranks, Claude feared constantly he might be discovered and deported. He was also solicited to join the French underground, the "Franc-tireurs et Partisans" (FTP). They were actively proselytizing the Vichy recruits. When he could get away from the training camp, he helped these partisans smuggle clothing and automatic weapons to pre-arranged hideouts.

A Spaniard, a baker who had fought in the Spanish Civil War, took Claude under his wing and indoctrinated him into the politics of living under German occupation. This baker had set up an underground escape route for some of the young in the factories. A few would be smuggled out under piles of French bread in the bakery truck.

As Claude gained greater freedom of movement in the youth ranks, he found himself driving a brand new delivery truck. One day a group of partisans took him prisoner. They said his truck was too new and shiny to be anything but in the service of the Germans. "You must become one of us," they said. Claude did, and he took the truck with him.

Becoming "one of us" meant you were a guerrilla. You fought with hate and the determination to kill, to rid yourself of an enemy that killed civilians, that threatened the land you marched or crawled on, that obeyed the dictate of a strange murderous fanaticism. To survive, the *maquis* had to be fanatics as well.

Claude was a part of a group of highly motivated killers. They moved swiftly, shadow-like, and his deceptive truck gave him a particular responsibility, involving him in hair-raising chases and shoot-outs. One of his stories was about a train, which the *maquis* captured in a shoot-out. It was taking almost a hundred Jews and Communists to a death camp. Eleven of the enemy were killed; the twelfth got away. The *maquis* brought the train into a town, liberated the prisoners, and discovered that the attached freight cars were filled with tinned sardines. They lived on them for weeks.

Claude made his way back to Strasbourg after it was liberated. One day he found himself face to face with a collaborationist who was wearing a familiar camel hair coat. He recognized it at once: it had been especially tailored for his father in his factory.

"I wanted to shoot the bastard then and there. Instead I went to the police. They shrugged my story off with 'There are too many Jews in the French army.'"

Claude talked far into the night. Some of his adventures reminded me of those I had heard from Liane and her friends, who fought to survive on the civilian front. Like them, Claude had a strong will to live, and to resist the exterminators of his own race. If you had to kill to save your own skin, you killed. If you had to lie, you lied. This was his philosophy. He had learned to cheat, dissimulate, betray—and yet he clung to the truth.

SIEGE NOTES

So there we lived, in an area bounded by a few streets and icy pathways, dark and deserted at night and claustrophobic by day. For the first time I knew what it felt like to be near the front, to be aware that there was an enemy four miles away, to be in a city cut off to the north and south, and under bombardment periodically. A state of siege.

I use the word siege cautiously. There was no comparison with the great sieges of history—the legendary decade of Troy's anguish, resolved by the fabled wooden horse; the dramatic siege of Paris during the Franco-Prussian war; or the nine-hundred day siege of Leningrad, in the same war that had brought me to the Rhine. We never choked on our own rubbish, or faced mounds of gathered dead. Our siege was one of chronic malaise, with moments of shock and fear at occasional bursting shells in our neighborhood.

Sometimes when I slept lightly, I woke up at three or four in the morning, and listened to the gunfire at Gambsheim. Wrapped in the reveries of my body, I tried to sort out the dialogue of the guns. Sometimes they sounded like furniture being dragged across an upstairs floor. At times there was a sharp snap, and then a reverberating boom. One cannon sounded like an operatic basso. It seemed to hold itself in reserve.

In some ways a siege possesses more human interest than huge battles, which are affairs of single days or hours, matters of direct human slaughter, kill or be killed. Sieges call for endurance above all—patience, stealth, intelligence. An army settles down before a fortified place, and tries to undermine the surrounded enemy and fortifications by a series of ongoing attacks and skirmishes. Whether a small castle, or a massive fortified city like Strasbourg, the place doggedly strains to hold out. You are playing cat-and-mouse with the enemy; the enemy does the same with you. It's a waiting game. One reads with nausea stories of those sieges when the enemies cut the supplies, and the inhabitants, having consumed their pets, move on to rodents. Our mini-siege spared us such horrors. Thus far, it was comparatively short—from November to February.

There were moments when I liked the situation in which I found myself. Some nights, when I tramped the pathways bounded by snowdrifts, the sky was star-filled, with the particular sparkle stars have in a cold atmosphere. I listened as I walked to the crunch of my boots. At other times there was thick snow, or a cutting wind. I felt exhilaration. But guerrillas, and sometimes even German patrols, roamed the streets. At times I felt like a child, scared of the dark. As I walked, I had nightmares of the unexpected. I clutched my M-3; it could protect me. An excellent automatic weapon—it could empty twenty shots at my enemies. But that was a two-way street: my enemy had weapons too. And I was alone; they might have three or four or more. When most the victim of my fancies, I saw myself lying on a virgin-white snowdrift, spread-eagled, my blood anointing the whiteness. These forebodings occurred each night, and each one ended with me pounding the snow off my boots in the newspaper office as I handed over the dispatches, the day's continuing histories of blood and death.

My young teammates showed no external signs of fear. They seemed happy, secure, and full of fun. They spent their free hours in the big square near the famous cathedral, which seems to touch the sky, its famous spire on the right. There young Strasbourg females, in dark winter clothes enlivened by colored scarves, engaged in monosyllabics with Britons, Americans, Moroccans. If words were lacking, the universal language of sex was eloquent. Our young males said they had nowhere encountered so much sexual acquiescence.

I didn't join the young often in their sexual quests, and when I went along it was rather as an older uncle, or even a surrogate father. I have spoken of the diminished libido I experienced in Paris. Here I seemed wholly relieved of sexual intrusions. Paul Fussell, in his appraisal of human behavior during the two big wars of our century, asserts that sexual deprivation "didn't trouble men on the front line." "The front," he says, "was the one wartime place that was sexless."

One incident offers a kind of sociological testimony about love and war, and the conflicts of some of the men. Corporal Pryor came into the office late one evening when I was alone. His lips were twitching, and there was a strange grim look on his face. I saw he was on the verge of tears. He began to talk but was incoherent; he stuttered, choking back what he wanted to say, and then broke into heavy sobbing. At first he uttered almost meaningless words. I caught enough to realize he was talking about himself as a survivor. He had seen so many of his buddies die in Italy. It was horrible, he said. Why them? Why not himself? Why was he spared?

He began to fumble in his pocket. He pulled out a wrinkled letter from his girl friend back home, and grasped it tightly in his fist, as if he were crushing her. She had given up waiting for him. The war was lasting too long; she had just gotten married. At first I said nothing. Then I said that we must blame no one but the politicians and generals who make wars, even "just wars" like ours. The confrontation with the fascists could have taken place earlier, when they were weaker. I did not see that we could blame his former sweetheart. She was a victim like us. And certainly he couldn't blame himself. We were caught up in this tremendous dislocation of husbands and wives, sweethearts and lovers.

"She wants kids," he said. That was understandable, I responded. The young women in the Place Kléber wanted kids too. After a while he was more composed. He stood and apologized for having made me a party to his feelings. Then, as he was turning to leave, he dropped the crumpled letter on my desk, as if he was ridding himself of her and the hurt she had inflicted.

After he was gone, I smoothed out and read the letter. It must have cut like a knife. She was truthful about her envy of girls who were getting married and having children. "I couldn't stand it," she wrote, "and without looking into things very much I decided to get married." The rest of her letter seemed to involve her guilt at having betrayed him. "How rotten I have acted towards you," she wrote, "I wish to hell I'd never been born. I seem to have lost the last bit of sense I had."

These words were of a piece with the dilemmas enacted every day in the nearby Strasbourg square—the quest for new love to replace the deprivations of the war. Pryor was feeling like a discarded and worthless survivor; misery derived from his loss of his fiancée, joined with guilt over losing his comrades. He faced up to the realities very quickly. A few days later I met him in the Place Kléber. Of medium height, Pryor had with him a Valkyrie who gazed at him with soft gray eyes. Some days later, he confided that she was pregnant. The baby he had been supposed to

CANNONADE

Anxieties disappeared overnight. Suddenly Strasbourg was free. As if spring were at hand, the Allied flags bloomed in the stiff winter breeze. The population had a feeling that all France had been liberated; the last portions of Alsace were once again part of the restored nation. Shells were still falling on Strasbourg, but the outbursts were spaced, and seemed to be gestures of defeat, rather than a strategy of terror. The talk was of the ultimate Allied crossing of the Rhine. The fictions initiated by our black stations now were genuine. Hitler would not have Strasbourg as an offering from the bloody hands of Himmler. As for de Gaulle, he had a new triumph, local indeed, but significant for the citizens of Alsace and Lorraine.

A week after the liberation of Colmar, Claude appeared in the doorway of my office. He was like a frisky colt. He wore a fresh French uniform, and was full of news about the Colmar battle, where he had driven a jeep. He had dispatches to deliver, and would drop me off at the press camp outside Colmar, then pick me up on his way back. I was eager to go. It might be useful to have a visual image of Colmar to complete the Strasbourg Incident. I picked up my helmet and my M-3. Claude said I needn't worry; I told him I preferred to have them with me. His own gun I noticed was beside his seat in the jeep. We took the southern road. There was fresh snow everywhere, and the morning light gave a jeweled effect to the landscape. His excitement mounted as we sped along—

"Wait till you see Ostheim. It looks like the flattened towns near Stalingrad."

We soon passed from the glittering snow world to an area of mud and slime. The highway disappeared. Claude was navigating a wilderness, a chaos of burnt-out tanks, when the stench of death hit. A cow lay near a sagging fence. It seemed to be asleep. Beyond I saw horses, their feet pointing to the sky. Squads had apparently removed all the human remains. Ostheim indeed had disappeared from the face of the earth.

There was rubble in the mud, and a beheaded house, with furniture still clinging to a single wall. Army engineers had created an improvised bridge to replace one that lay crushed like a large insect in a narrow half-frozen river. I wondered why I had wanted to come to see this. The pockmarked earth, the bulldozers wandering like dazed antediluvian creatures, the scarred skeletons of vehicles—a mix of dead mechanical animals and those created by millions of years of evolution.

Claude set me down at a barracks a few miles away. I lunched with some rather weary correspondents. They passed a whiskey bottle around, and I took a couple of swigs. It helped. The mess sergeant asked no questions—he accepted my presence among the officers and newsmen. As always, they talked shop. One or two were mildly curious about the siege of Strasbourg. I described what psychwar was doing. They were amused when I described how the black station helped undermine the morale of the city.

Claude brought me back to the rue de Castlenau late in the afternoon. As we parted, he told me he was moving to another part of the front. He hoped to go with the French Army into Germany. We said good-bye, leaving his life without an ending for me. I could not even try to invent what his future held for him.

*****

The erratic shelling of Strasbourg that followed the German withdrawal seemed a mocking, tormenting farewell. Periods of calm were followed by intense cannonade. Shells fell in the center of the city, and in adjacent neighborhoods. The briefings at Saverne described the attacks as "dispersed hostile artillery." The word *hostile* struck me as curious. Was shelling a city ever anything but hostile? The communiqués also played down the damage, calling it insubstantial. I suppose nothing less than devastation was the headquarters' idea of substantiality. On one day I set down some notes about a particular bombardment, to show how this dry language of war might be translated into human terms. I recorded what headquarters had reported, and then what I knew really had happened.

The center and outskirts of Strasbourg received dispersed hostile artillery . . .

The first shells whistled in at about 6:30 p.m. The day had been quiet. We were in our offices. My doors were closed. I had my familiar pool of light on the center of my desk. The shells came over. One, two, the third with a peculiar shrillness. The explosions seemed near. Then three more. A couple fell very close, shaking our building. The team members burst into my office, as if I could order the shells to go away. Galitzin came in just behind them. He had a startled air, as if the enemy wasn't supposed to disturb us at the dinner hour. I spoke a bit sharply to the men, asking them whether they thought my office was an air raid shelter. Galitzin said, "If this goes on, we may have another problem on our hands." He was worried about a repeat of the panic.

I suggested we go to the Zauberflöte for supper. There was really nothing we could do, and we'd be best off if we went about our usual business. I walked with Galitzin, and the men followed behind. They were twitting Manshel, who had offered bets that "they'll never shell Strasbourg center." I stepped into our billet to wash up. Corporal Pryor greeted us with, "Yep, those were pretty close." I decided to wear my helmet. We came downstairs, stumbling in the darkness. At the foot of the stairs we ran into our landlady, whom we rarely saw. She spoke a mixture of French and German: she was now was cursing the Nazis in French.

. . . without suffering substantial damage.

Four more shells plowed into our neighborhood. A French soldier breathing heavily burst into the house.

"Looking for someone?" I asked.

"Just for shelter. Three landed in our barracks. One hit a row of windows."

The barracks was an enormous building at the far end of the street.

We walked along Castlenau, past silent shuttered buildings, and entered the Zauberflöte, pushing ourselves through the smallest possible crack. The café was dark except for one table, where some soldiers were drinking wine around a solitary candle. We lit our own candle and sat down. There was a faint buzz of talk, the sound of suppressed excitement and fear. There was much joking at wearing helmets indoors. An officer and some enlisted men who had been eating at the Frankenhof Hotel—now the Hôtel de France—said a shell hit the adjoining lot, amid the rubble of a building. It had shaken the dining room like an earthquake.

A young straight-limbed French soldier entered, sitting down casually.

"Good thing I decided to shave, or I'd have been in the Place Broglie. Two landed there. Smashed the bank. Heaps of rubble. Lots of broken glass. A young Frenchman and his companion, a young woman, were in front of the bank. The man hit the ground. He's fine, just a bit scratched. The young woman died instantly."

Eight dead were counted by the time I came to the newspapers in Blue Sky Street. The people of Strasbourg shrugged. They remembered a U.S. bombing, when shells destined for the other side of the Rhine fell on a Strasbourg suburb. Some 2,000, or maybe 3,000, died. As the communiqué said, this time there wasn't substantial damage.

A DIDACTIC MOMENT

One night during my last couple of weeks in Strasbourg, I was on my way to the *Dernières Nouvelles,* in the rue de la Nuée Bleue, with the latest batch of news from London. I turned the familiar corner of a short cut and surveyed the star-filled winter sky. My thoughts were on the great stellar spaces and my impending return to Paris. I thought of myself back in the capital during the spring. The chestnut trees, their splendor and beauty. The war should be over by then.

As I turned the next corner, three young men in ragged uniforms stood in my path. The one in the center had an automatic weapon that looked like a Sten gun: we were dropping them by air for the partisans. Suddenly, the gun was stuck against my ribs. The men were stocky, unshaven. They stared at me with squinting eyes.

"The password," said the man with the gun.

"Here we go again," I thought. These men weren't soldiers, and they didn't know the protocols. Out of my frozen self, in a voice I thought dim and far away, I heard myself saying—

"Yes, it consists of two words. I know them and you know them. Challenge me with the first word and I'll answer with the second. That's the way it works."

My weapon hung on my shoulder, but I didn't dare touch it. The partisans had a reputation for being trigger-happy.

The spokesman said I should quit kidding and give them the password. The Sten gun moved from my ribs to my belly, nudging me insistently. Instead, I asked whether they were in the French Underground.

"How come you talk French so fluently?" he asked, which made me feel a bit better, in spite of his nudging me with his gun. I told him that some of us Americans were sent to Strasbourg precisely because we could speak French.

In the snow-reflected light, I looked into a bewildered boyish face, mouth firm, jaw set. I tried again.

"Look—the first word tells me whether you're friendly or the enemy. The second word shows I'm not the enemy."

"Where are you going?"

"To the newspaper, *Les Dernières Nouvelles*."

Then he got my message. He spit out the word, as if to get rid of it—

"Algiers."

I shouted—and the word rang through the streets—

"Patton!"

Suddenly the gun was gone from my belly. The men had melted into the darkness.

The stars were shining high above. I was lying on my back looking up at them. My feet had given way. I was spread-eagled on an icy snowdrift, still clutching my weapon. I stared into the glorious congeries of piercing diamonds, and after a bit, discerned the Big Dipper—Ursa Major. I used to see it among the northern lights in Saskatchewan.

What if he'd pulled the trigger? It had all taken place in slow motion. Those damned fools should be given the password properly. It should be explained to them. Then I thought how foolish it was of me to have insisted on explaining the routine. I might have pronounced the two words. That would have been the safest thing to do.

I slowly, shakily found my feet again, and walked to the newspaper. The security man opened the door.

"Hey," he said, "you've taken a tumble in the snow." He brushed me off.

I told him yes, I had fallen into the big drift across the way.

PART SIX
INFORMAL FURLOUGH

Return from the Front
The Avenue Rapp
Plans and Proposals
An Informal Furlough
A Soldier's Tale
Miss Nausicaa
Reverie in the Avenue Montaigne
Terminations

Summer 1945: Detached to Supreme Headquarters, Allied Expeditionary Force, heading to Germany with the occupying forces.

RETURN FROM THE FRONT

I was recalled to the rue d'Aguesseau a fortnight after the end of Strasbourg's siege. When the hour came for my departure I felt empty and bereft. We had worked at such a pitch of intensity that the lifting of the burden gave me a sense of collapse. I felt disinherited. Leave taking was always a termination.

My travel orders took ten days to reach me. Before I left I interviewed two job candidates, both French Army men. They were bilinguals, and wanted the monitoring job. As if they were members of a trade union rather than an army, they asked for details of work hours. I also carried out a request from Luther Conant, which he wrote in capitals in his recall letter: "GET SOME SWISS CHEESE FOR THE GENERAL AND A TIN OR TWO OF PATÉ." I thus left the city on February 19, 1945, a month after I arrived, with a sizable chunk of a *gruyère* wheel, and half a dozen tins of Strasbourg's renowned goose liver *paté*. My stay on the Rhine had been the finale of the Battle of France.

A jeep ride to Nancy would get me to the overnight train for Paris. The day began gray and unpromising, then the sun broke through. We were in gently rolling country, filled with hints of a still distant spring. An early thaw had melted some of the snow, exposing relics of combat. There were skeletons of vehicles, and of rusty German and Allied tanks —lying on their side, burned black. As always, I thought of the men who had died in these little infernos, and for some reason, my memory brought forward images of those horses with their feet in the air. I remember one spot where the snow had been carefully cleared away, and the frozen ground broken to create a row of graves. I counted nine small wooden crosses. Dried flowers still clung to them.

Staring at the panorama of extinction, I found myself recalling the troops I had watched as a small boy, training on the Canadian prairie in 1914, and how my elders later talked of trenches and the heaped up dead. Now heaps of dead had shifted from the war sites to the cities— civilians bombed and destroyed at centers of urban life. Hiroshima still lay ahead, and so too did the remaining half-century, with its series of needless wars.

I told myself that the shelling of Strasbourg was more easily endured than the air raids on the cities of Europe. London, Dresden, Berlin, Warsaw—a long list, blotted out by new generations facing the problems we confronted all over again. There must have been saturated bombing of the enemy on the day we drove from Strasbourg, for south of Nancy we passed the largest airfield I had seen. Few planes were visible. They were in the air. At intervals I saw stacks of large-bellied bombs, gleaming metal weapons. They reminded me of rows of tuna from the Bay of Biscay I had seen in Concarneau long ago.

The psychwar post near my destination was in a village outside Lunéville. My train would leave in six hours. The village consisted of farmhouses widely spaced, each with their piles of frozen cow turds heaped as neatly as the bombs, ready for spring sowing. I trudged through the long street until I came to a small café. A broadly proportioned, gray-haired Frenchwoman became pleasantly hospitable when I addressed her in French. She poured me a glass of white wine, and set me down at a cleared table in a room with a fireplace. I sat contentedly reading, smoking, and writing. My thoughts kept returning to the little Strasbourg lane where I had been stopped by the FTP. I wondered again whether I wouldn't have been better off if I had simply given those youths the entire password. Why did I have to insist they play the game according to its rules? By their very nature partisans defy rules.

As arranged, the friendly *dame du comptoir* fed me at 6. She didn't envy my going to Paris. The Parisians were having a rude winter. I said, "So are we all." She replied it wasn't so bad out here in the countryside. She insisted I drink a *digestif* after my meal, and gave me some Armagnac and well-brewed U.S. coffee. I kissed her on both cheeks, thanking her for having eased my long wait.

The train was made up when I reached the station. The first-class cars were reserved for some American nurses, who were going on leaves in Paris. Officers were in second class; GIs and French civilians were in third, where I found an empty compartment. I recognized the old-time wagons of my student days, with their curved, polished, yellow wooden seats, like elongated park benches. After a bit, an American GI arrived with two neatly-dressed French girls. They waited on the platform while he sought a place for them. He told me he had met the girls earlier that day, and wondered whether I might vacate my compartment briefly till the train started. Lowering his voice, he said he hoped he might "throw in a quickie."

I was willing to be helpful, but didn't want to lose my place. He guaranteed he would protect it for me, so I walked down the platform. When I came back after about twenty minutes, the soldier was gone and the girls were saving my seat. They smiled. I smiled back. Then they looked at each other and giggled. They continued to giggle in spasms for some time after the train had started. The soldier's sexual strategy had clearly been unsuccessful.

The only other person in the compartment was a French soldier from the fortified seaport of Lorient. He sat next to me, and we carried on our conversation in the dark. France needed a dictator, he said. I rejoined we were fighting a war against dictators. He said de Gaulle was pussyfooting with the politicians. I said he had to confront them. The soldier didn't like Americans. He was jealous of our well-supplied existence. I felt he talked not so much out of dislike as out of envy. He said it would take France a long time to recover from the trauma of 1940. I agreed. Then we ran out of conversation.

We pulled into the dawn-filtered Gare de l'Est half an hour late. My scheduled vehicle from SHAEF didn't turn up. Recalling how this station used to swarm with blue-bloused porters, I took possession of a small luggage cart, took my baggage to a checkroom, then went down into the metro's damp morning smell. I was quickly conveyed to the Place de la Concorde, and felt an acute pleasure when I stepped into the great square. A morning haze hung over it. The heads of the majestic statues seemed to fade up into the fog. The sun was creeping into the street when I passed under the old archway to the Retiro. The place was deserted. I had a sudden gloomy feeling. What if we were no longer at the Perey? I hurried into the hotel, my M-3 dangling from my shoulder. No welcoming smells of bacon and coffee. The kitchen and dining area were gone. A tall thin man with a long face emerged from behind the desk, and spoke to me in English with a heavy French accent. The American troops had moved out. The hotel had reverted to civilian use. He scribbled the new address for me. I had never heard of the Avenue Rapp. Easy to reach by metro, he said. It was a short ride to the other side of the Alma bridge.

THE AVENUE RAPP

The Avenue Rapp's main feature was a huge barn-like warehouse, or retired factory, that had probably housed members of the German garrison in Paris. A fussy second lieutenant made me sign in, and talked to me as if I were a new recruit. I asked for a high bunk, and he led me to one. I could smell the fermented dampness of its straw. "We have nightly bed checks," he told me in a low voice, as if he were sounding a warning of doom.

I was back in the world of communal toilets and improvised showers, surrounded by the chattering young. There must have been a thousand men billeted there, but at this morning hour the place wasn't crowded. My dream of hotcakes and coffee melted away when I learned the mess hall was two blocks away. I ate a couple of my ration biscuits, and fell asleep staring at a huge unwashed window. When I awoke a couple of hours later, Paul, the stage-door johnny from the Perey, was sitting at one end of my bunk. "We've been expecting you," he said.

He poured out his news. The men from the Perey were scattered, the brain trust dissolved. Janowitz was on some hush-hush mission, studying the morale of the German Army at the front. And then in his usual satirical manner, Paul waved at our surroundings. "Luxury bedroom, eh?" He offered to escort me to the mess hall. There was still time for lunch. We ate in a kind of monkish refectory; religious paintings and a few crucifixes scattered in strategic places.

My companion told me the circumstances of our leaving the Perey. It was a "disaster, a regression," the consequence of a December 4, 1944, article in *Life* which said there were too many officers in too many hotels in Paris. The targets were high brass in the luxury hotels. After deliberating for several weeks, the Army responded by systematically emptying the small shabby commercial hotels like the Perey. Meanwhile, the officers remained in their luxurious quarters, sleeping on mattresses between laundered sheets, and dining nearby. Paul said I'd find our new residence drafty and dreary. I'd be living again out of my duffel bag. He also talked of wasted man-hours and the perquisites of rank. He had been on guard duty a few nights earlier at the Army garage. All evening, officers were being ferried to the nightspots of Paris. Many were driven to the Folies.

After Paul left, I surveyed the neighborhood. The streets surrounding the drab Avenue Rapp had a certain charm. I was particularly impressed by the Boulevard de la Tour-Marbourg, which harbored the usual little shops that made the old Parisian quarters seem domestic and civilized. I stopped in front of the small Hôtel des Ministères. At some time in its history, it had probably catered to government officials. Looking at its neat little windows and clear curtains, I decided to go in. I found a concierge with innumerable keys, friendly and business-like. Yes, she could give me a comfortable small room—Number 13, for a few dollars a night. Was I superstitious? Without waiting for my answer, she warned me I could expect no hot water and no heat. I said I wanted it anyway. I paid a deposit, and later that evening returned with adequate luggage to let my Strasbourg memories sink in. The bed check didn't trouble me. Paul had told me to make a friendly arrangement with the orderlies.

I stayed only a few days in the Hôtel des Ministères, though I returned for a second period some time later. My residence was a useful withdrawal into myself. I read, I wrote, I had long hours of sleep—my first hours of complete privacy in many months. Though the hotel was cold, the silence and solitude were almost as pleasant as those mornings in Normandy—it seemed now long ago—when I awoke with the dawn and the birdsong, plunged into the icy stream amid the lowing of the cows, and felt the fresh wind that blew over the hedgerows.

PLANS AND PROPOSALS

In Strasbourg, on the edge of the war, I had lived between fears and explosions, with scattered moments of reverie and profound sleep. I now escaped to the lively metropolis. There seemed to be more vehicles than when I had left; apparently more black market gasoline was available. The Seine had been at flood height; it now was receding. The quays rose slowly out of the water, and the city's perpetual fishermen moved back to their usual places on the bridges. There were tales that during the street fighting in August, a number of fishermen had remained in their spots, ignoring the sniper fire and civilian terror.

In due course, I went back to the rue d'Aguesseau, to report to my chief. I deposited on his desk the tins of *paté de foie gras* and the *gruyère*, which was beginning to offer a certain fragrance. Luther Conant was pleased—so pleased, he insisted on paying me twice what they had cost. He invited me to dine with him that very evening at his hotel—the first such invitation, and a defiance of the Army's caste system. My sense of military propriety made me go at once to a barbershop. I had not had my hair cut in Strasbourg. I weighed myself on a scale in the shop. I had lost sixteen pounds. Once in the barber's chair I ordered the entire menu, so that I emerged trimmed, shampooed, shaved, and manicured, with my mustache clipped to permissible military size. I then recalled that one of the young women at my farewell party had given me a standing invitation to use her bathroom in the hotel at the Rond-Point. I telephoned her, and inquired whether the invitation was still valid. She replied that the line formed daily at 6 p.m. I performed my ablutions there as if I were Odysseus, welcomed by the young Nausicaa. But I wasn't a shipboard voyager—simply a survivor of a mini-siege.

* * * * *

Luther Conant led me to a corner table in the dining room and promptly ordered dry martinis. I took note of the starched tablecloths and white napkins, but noticed also that the Astor had some of the shabbiness of the Perey. Its rugs were worn, its china chipped. The waiters were French

—very professional—and the bartender was expert. By the second round of martinis, my head was pleasantly swimming. The food was good, a *chateaubriand à point* with tinned vegetables, crisp baguettes, and excellent coffee served in a cup with a broken handle. Above all, we had a very good bottle of claret.

Conant raised his glass. He said he was drinking to my impending promotion to officer rank. I thought he was joking, until Conant said, "General McClure has ordered your promotion. He said you carried out a difficult job, highly important to psychological warfare, in a very soldierly way." I found this hard to believe. Then came the catch. The promotion was based on the assumption that I would go on to Germany. After a rush of pride, I felt burdened. I had assumed that I was fixed in my role as tech sergeant, and expected to be demobilized rapidly once the fighting ended. To rise from the ranks was a dazzling prospect, but did I want to remain in the Army, perhaps for another year? Did I want to stay on in Europe once the fighting was over? These thoughts unrolled rapidly, while Conant beamed at me.

I thanked him for what he had done. I was sure he had played a significant part in my impending promotion. He said the General had been genuinely impressed by my reports. I asked what plans were being developed, and Conant said the overall idea was "denazification"—candidly remarking, "As if you can swallow a pill and be declared a democrat." We would be concerned exclusively with information control; that is, restoring some kind of objective press to a country that had been fed lies for a dozen years. It would be difficult to find clean German journalists. I said my German was not very good. Conant said German wasn't essential for the position he had in mind. I had demonstrated in Strasbourg my ability to insure that individual newspapers had full use of our resources. He was thinking of me as head of some sort of German Associated Press, a news agency that would service the entire U.S. Zone. We would create a series of bureaus to replace the Goebbels newsgathering machine. Conant promised I would have plenty of German linguists, skillful bureau personnel, proper offices, and the full support of the General's staff.

"All of them taking orders from a second lieutenant?" I asked, a bit mockingly.

"Don't worry about that. They will all be civilians. You may have to deal with colonels and majors in communications matters, and I'm sure that won't be easy, but you have the know-how, and we'll see you have the clout. Remember, we're all still part of Supreme Headquarters."

The proposal was tempting. I would have an intimate view of Germany after the war, although the idea of contact with the country did not greatly appeal to me. Save for some intellectuals of the pre-Hitlerian culture—its writers, philosophers, and composers—I had never found the Germans sympathetic. Despite certain reservations about its conservatism and anti-Semitism, my partiality for French culture was considerable, and my hostility toward the Reich was one shared by many French citizens. I finally told Conant that since I was in the Army, I'd have to go wherever I was ordered, and that I would just as soon go to Germany with Information Control as be reassigned to my old Third Mobile Broadcasting Company. I would be available for the position he offered me, but only if my commission came through. A noncom could not undertake such a big job. He thought this was reasonable, though he was certain that I would be an officer before the war ended.

AN INFORMAL FURLOUGH

And so I found myself on an unofficial furlough from the rue d'Aguesseau, bestowed by the press chief in psychwar. My body still belonged to army discipline and the morning's roll call, but from breakfast to evening I was a free agent. At times I actually chose to spend time in the Avenue Rapp barracks. Though it was inevitable that the soldiers spent minimal time in our quarters, some groups were always comfortably idling there —playing cards or craps, listening to the radio, and talking endlessly. There was also a certain amount of surreptitious drinking. Some soldiers had no difficulty establishing miniature wine cellars. Liquor came from other sources as well, some from overseas. One day a soldier displayed a large can of apple juice he had just received in a parcel. "Sarge," he said, "this is a strange can of juice," and pointed to a small spot on the bottom, where a puncture hole had been carefully soldered. He opened the can to pour me a drink of Kentucky bourbon.

Still struggling from the effects of their four-year captivity, the French were now beginning to find the honeymoon with their American liberators was also wearing thin. We were tolerated because our pockets were stuffed with soap, sugar, candies—items they had done without for a long time. The French however wanted not only to be rid of the Germans along their frontier, but of the Americans and their war machinery as well. The French wanted to repossess themselves, and yet feared what lay ahead. Outwardly they were as clear, jocular, and sardonic as ever, but behind their linguistic fortifications were crevices of guilt, division, and hatred, fascistic streaks that had contributed to their swift and humiliating defeat. I was aware of the undercurrents of anti-Semitism; others were haunted by Vichy's treatment of the Jews. The horrors of the Holocaust would soon be revealed, and the people would come to know the extent to which France had helped Hitler in his final solution.

At times I found myself deeply depressed. While intrigued by the projected adventure in Germany, I really didn't want to go. My mind went back to my earliest visits to the Reich in its pre-Hitler days—it was 1930—when I had traveled along the Rhine for a brief sojourn in

Freiburg-in-Breisgau, where my brother was studying German. I was surprised at the smallness of the castles. They had seemed more enchanting in opera books. I wandered with eyes only half-opened in the galleries of Munich, where I ate sausages and drank beer. I looked at Breughels and heard *Don Giovanni* for the first time. I melted into the music rather than into the life around me. I heard Hitler's name, without paying attention to what he advocated.

In a German pension in Freiburg I sat at table with assorted travelers, and listened to a peevish, thin-faced man referred to as a Count snarl at a fat ex-army captain—a Fascist snarling at a Nazi. My landlady became agitated as their voices rose. As she ladled soup swimming with fat, in an icy German tone she said, "Gentlemen, please, no politics at this table."

Before leaving Germany, I had attended the 1930 Passion Play at Oberammergau, where I was lodged in a tourist room in a peasant house. An angular big-boned landlady provided a soft, down-filled bed, and a breakfast of cheese and coffee amid compulsive cleanliness and German clichés. I also went to Vienna that summer, finding the latter more like Paris—lighter, happier, the cafés filled with beautiful women and well-dressed men smoking cigars. I carried away from Germany the impression of a heavy-handed gluttonous people treasuring their little rococo *schlosses* and their middle-class lives. I suppose I had absorbed the universal antagonism as a child, during the first war.

I have told how provincial I was—a child of the prairies, reared intellectually to be a Puritan—and how little I was prepared for the more instinctual things of life: intimate relations between men and women, the deeper soundings of passion. I grew up in a male-centered society among domineering women. Like many in my generation, I had been instructed in traditional storybook virtues. At the threshold of my twenties, certain adolescent residues persisted. Even when just a little older than myself, most men I sought out were cast in the role of surrogate fathers. Women used to smile at me, but I did not have the courage to go beyond smiling back.

Only later did I come to understand the never-never land of my youth. Moving in an aesthetic-intellectual world, the education of my emotions was blocked and slow—a kind of blundering into life, in spite of a veneer of sophistication. My little journeys were innocent, lonely, anxious, artistic, and mindless—or perhaps too much mind. I did not follow the signals of my senses.

* * * * *

Sometimes during that Paris spring, when I was sauntering in bright sunshine along the Seine, I fell into deep reveries about my old quest for Henry James. When at eighteen I proposed a study on stream of consciousness in James Joyce, my favorite professor at McGill, George Latham, had told me in the friendliest of ways that the graduate school wouldn't accept dissertations on living authors. "You're supposed to read the moderns yourselves," he said, "They belong to your generation. You're supposed to stay in the past, and use the past for your future. Leave the new authors to the reviewers and the babblers." I thought this rather stuffy on Latham's part. However, I had too much respect for him to argue. Showing that he was more up to date than he sounded, Latham then remarked, "I've felt that a lot of these moderns you talk about derive from Henry James. He's been dead since 1916. You can use him if you want as an umbrella for your subject, and then bring in your Joycean readings. Your core subject however must remain someone whose work is finished, whom you can deal with as a totality in his time."

That was how my quest began. I went to the library. I wandered, as I always did, in the different alcoves, savoring the musty smell of old books, looking at the complete sets of the Victorians—the many-volumed Ruskin, Stevenson, Pater, Wilde—the works of Ibsen, and in the French section, of Flaubert and Zola. Among the Americans I found Henry James. I remember his name displeased me. Both his names were given to the kings of England, or to butlers and valets and chauffeurs. I had in me a goodly quantity of snobbishness, picked up from my mother. The wealthy had dazzled her profoundly bourgeois makeup. Eventually I got over the name, and wrote an immature, if forward-looking, attempt at describing "Henry James and Some Recent Psychological Fiction." It was written in my best reportorial style, acquired during my summers on the *Montreal Star,* and my professors approved it. But when I first went abroad in 1928, I thought I had finished with James.

Working on the *Montreal Star* was a way of earning money, but I wanted to move out of having to meddle in other people's lives and misfortunes. I had chased fires and accidents, and I had covered the magistrate's court. That was the school of journalism from which I wanted to graduate as soon as possible. I preferred political journalism, and best of all would have liked simply to be a writer. I did try my hand at short stories, and dreamed about a novel set in Montreal. Others would write such novels later on. I was "literary" in my readings, but too young to understand that serious writing was a lifelong task. I had enough imagination, without the aptitudes. I therefore looked forward to my impending three years in Paris, funded by a special scholarship, as the chance to assume some sort of character as a man of letters. I would still write for the *Montreal Star* on aesthetic matters in Paris, and on Canadian gossip, gathered at the Canadian ministry in the Cours Albert 1er. It may indeed be that a part of my attachment to the Avenue Montaigne belonged to my old regular visits to the Canadian embassy, where the secretary of the legation took care of the press.

The following years, my Parisian years of music and the other arts, flew by like a dream. After some indecision, I settled down to a serious reading of James's works. I found them in the American Library near the Élysées, in the pristine pages of the New York Edition. In the English Institute of the Sorbonne, I also found the familiar thirty-five volumes, blue and gold, of the Macmillan edition of James's complete fiction, edited by Percy Lubbock. Lubbock had also edited two stout volumes of James's letters, with very few from his earlier days. I began thinking about James's plays. Where were they? I knew something of *Guy Domville*. That play had been booed; a letter from Henry to William James described briefly that debacle. Some other plays proved to be in the Lord Chamberlain's Office in London.

Censorship still existed: all plays had to be sent to the Lord Chamberlain before they could be produced. Four of the plays were in this archive. I would have to go to London to read them. I would find more. My *Dramatic Years* was published in 1932, but the great economic depression thrust me back where I had started in 1928. I had emerged from the University of Paris with a *docteur-ès-lettres* degree, but in those times it counted for little, except as a certain academic qualification and honor. On my return I could find no position. Universities were dropping teachers, not hiring them, and Jews weren't wanted in English departments. I tumbled back into journalism and a certain amount of tutoring of academic delinquents. I managed to squeeze out $25 a week. I was lucky to have that.

Now, in March 1945, I found myself back in what I used to call my other life. Academe reached out—for a brief moment. The Catholic Institute cordially asked me to give a talk on literature to a small group, and the Sorbonne's Center for English and American Studies sent me a message through Professor Le Breton, a scholar who came after my time there, that the Center would welcome my talking to its young Americanists on the works of Henry James. I spoke to the young Catholics about James's French literary connections—how he absorbed Zola's "naturalism"; how he filled his hours with Flaubert, Zola, Daudet, and Maupassant; how greatly he admired Flaubert, who growled passages of French poetry at him when they spent an afternoon together. I also alluded to James's friendship with Turgenev, Russia's expatriate novelist, especially since Russia was our ally at that moment. The English Institute lecture was less formal. I talked out of my old dissertation, which dealt with James's attempt to become a playwright. I found Le Breton urbane and well-read in Americana—more so than most American professors. Occasionally, I fumbled for English words, taking refuge in French phrases.

* * * * *

In the middle of March, Morris Janowitz turned up in Paris. Like me, he had had a taste of the front, and like me, he had been promised a promotion if he accompanied his superior to Germany. He had heard early rumblings about the genocide of the Jews, just beginning to be unveiled in all its horrors. Now that the Russians were advancing on Berlin, and we were plunging deep into the heart of Hitler's Reich, I kept trying to pin Janowitz down. When would the war be over? He refused to prophesy. One couldn't speed up the process. It depended on the enemy as well as ourselves. At the front, he had not felt that the war was nearing its end.

I would see Janowitz again years later, when he was a distinguished professor of sociology at the University of Chicago. He achieved a considerable reputation by writing about the nature of the American soldier. Indeed, his book *The Professional Soldier* dealt with the relations between military and civilian society. Janowitz believed that the army should reflect enlightened ideas. In the early 1980s, he became the first American scholar to occupy the Marshall Chair at the U.S. Army's Research Institute for Behavioral and Social Sciences. He died at sixty-nine of Parkinson's. From his brother I learned that he had asked to be buried with full military honors.

* * * * *

A few days later, the process of converting me into an officer began. I was ordered to report for X-rays and a physical. I was then interviewed by a psychwar board, which would judge my fitness for promotion. Two colonels and two lieutenant colonels allowed me to sit down, and asked me about Strasbourg. I answered as tersely as possible, focusing on relations with the French and the efficiency of our operation—its coherence, purpose, and dispatch. I had a feeling that the board was eager to get specialists like myself into Germany once the fighting ended, but I was actually in for eight weeks of suspense.

Shortly after appearing before the board, I developed laryngitis. I went to the familiar infirmary near the Opera, where a doctor inspected my throat, saw nothing, then handed me a bottle of cough medicine and some lozenges. I stayed in my bunk for the rest of the day in confused sleep, with some coughing. The next day I tried the infirmary again. Now I had a bit of fever, and was conveyed with a bunch of respiratory cases to a small hospital run by Catholic nuns. After twenty-four hours of bed rest and quiet I felt much better. On the fifth day—March 31—I asked the nurse if she intended to keep me much longer: my temperature had been normal for three days. She would arrange for my discharge the next day. "It will be Easter Sunday," she said.

A SOLDIER'S TALE

I went down to the hospital mess for lunch. I was eating alone when a soldier who looked like a mere schoolboy sat down beside me. He had heard me speaking to one of the nurses in French, and asked me to write a letter for him to a French girl named Yvonne. He had tried to phone her before he left for the hospital but did not reach her.

His name was Roger. He was from Illinois. I noticed he was a private, first class, and wore a purple heart. When he grinned I saw wide spaces between his teeth, and his lips curved up, as if he were a comic strip yokel. He had cat-like ears and he talked in a whisper, as if he was telling secrets. I told him he looked under-age for the army. He said he was twenty-five. He pulled out his wallet and showed me a snapshot of a five-year-old boy holding a baseball bat. This was his son back home.

He said he was getting a divorce and was going to marry the French girl to whom I was to write a letter. He had been wounded the previous autumn near Aachen, and was sent to a hospital in Paris. The wound healed fast, but he remained unwell, and began to suffer episodes of panic. The doctors decided to give him a quiet job back of the lines. He was assigned to a postal unit not far from Le Mans. They had a nice whorehouse there. At first he had a Spanish girl. He didn't speak much Spanish, but she was good company, and they made out all right. Then he took up with Yvonne, one of the nicest girls in the house. He fell in love with her right away, and she with him. She refused to take his money. Later, when she heard how little he made, she began to share her money with him.

"It sounds funny, Sarge, but she gave me thousands of francs. Imagine my being in the pay of a whore. But she's real special. We rented a couple of rooms. She cooked wonderful meals when I came home from duty, and after a while I stopped worrying about the money. She said she had plenty, and I spent most of it on her."

He said he found it thrilling when she sang in English with a nice French accent "Roll Me Over and Zigzig Me Again," one of the popular army songs of the time. She had obviously been a success in the brothel, and had saved up a great deal. He knew he couldn't leave her, and he didn't want to go home. He wrote his wife, and she agreed to a divorce if she could have custody of their son. He said that after a bit he got accustomed to the idea. He was expecting to be discharged early after the war ended, what with his Purple Heart. Yvonne said he mustn't worry about their future. She would always take care of him.

The young soldier was clearly a naive American youth—I had seen so many during the previous winter in Paris. Yvonne seemed like one of de Maupassant's hearty whores. I did ask him whether he still had panic attacks. He said he no longer thought about them.

MISS NAUSICAA

I left the hospital amid the sound of the bells of Paris chiming the Resurrection. The Lord's handmaidens, the nuns, were busy with their patients and their rejoicings. During my few days in the hospital the trees of Paris had burst into leaf. I had an acute and delicious feeling of strolling in a garden city. The warehouse in the Avenue Rapp was virtually empty. The soldiers were on the town. I telephoned the Nausicaa girl, and asked whether she was still having open house in her bathroom. She sounded low but said I was welcome to come that evening. She planned to go to some Easter bash, if she got rid of her headache. She'd leave the key under the doormat, and her hospitality would include a brandy bottle on the coffee table.

She didn't resemble the beauteous Princess Nausicaa who picked up Ulysses on the beach after his stormy voyage. Doubtless she considered me a father figure, since I was an old soldier among the youths I encountered during her organized bath hours. I wondered at her strange impulse to be a hostess to a line of Army bathers, for I was struck also by her Victorian aloofness. After a warm shower, I tasted the brandy and ate a few sweet biscuits. For the first time, I took in from her balcony the splendid view of the Seine, meandering all the way to Notre Dame. Under the dark clouds at twilight on that Easter day, Paris looked placid and countrified. I wondered how soon the French capital would become the City of Light that it called itself. I sat contentedly, sipping my brandy until darkness descended, and the city took back its regular countenance of war.

Feeling that I owed her some return for her generosity, I got to know Nausicaa better during my informal furlough. She was a mid-western girl, from some town in Kansas. She was lively but dispassionate, always up-to-date like the other girls on the Army gossip emerging from the network of offices in which they worked. The Office of Strategic Services team was situated in the Champs-Élysées; the Office of War Information was in the *grands boulevards*. When in their residences, these civilian women wore cotton dresses, or some Parisian fantasies, or slacks. Nausicaa was different. She clung to the uniform of an assimilated officer—the field green jacket and skirt, with their brass buttons. When I got to know her better, I had to listen to her set speech about how wonderful it was to have the Army decide what she should wear. What I also discovered was that her small-town rearing, as the only daughter of a local bank clerk and a conforming rigid mother, had contributed to an entire series of anxieties about clothes, manners, small-talk. She wanted to be like the other girls, independent and free, but she didn't have the requisite conditioning.

The uniform gratified her masculine aspirations. She felt however she had to show a certain respect to her own gender. This she did by going to the hair dresser for a fancy arrangement of her brown hair. Piled high above her forehead, it helped to offset an aggressive chin and a featureless face. She had pale blond eyebrows and pallid eyes. Her face was dominated by her prim pursed lips. She used no make-up, except for a thin line of lipstick. She was like a traditional country schoolmarm—genteel enough, and even bookish.

I offered to thank her by taking her to a Stravinsky concert. Although she said she loved music, this was too highbrow, and she politely declined. She had played the trumpet in the town band, and said she was summoned often to sound taps at the local cemetery. I could almost hear her, clinging to each melancholy note and each teardrop. I soon discovered that the best amenity I could offer was to take her on a walk through the Latin Quarter, to see my old student haunts along Boulevard Saint-Michel or at Saint-Germain-des-Prés. She became animated when I showed her the hangouts of Hemingway and Fitzgerald. I took her once to Montparnasse, which had faded considerably from what it was in the 1920s. I used to like the Dôme, but now I preferred the Deux Magots. The expensive Brasserie Lipp I couldn't explore, for I avoided places that relied on the black market.

One evening, when I stayed on after the bath, she asked me to stay for a drink, and she launched into an autobiographical account of what she termed her "escape" from the middle west. She was an only child, and her parents had given her the status of a queen. They were impressed by their daughter's education, the things she picked up from the radio, her reputation for trumpet playing. I said a trumpet was a good instrument to wake up a sleepy town. She told me I was pulling her leg. She remembered her high school days with precision, and at college she had set out to be a doctor. She found math and chemistry trying, and went to Washington as au pair to the family of a favorite history professor. There she obtained a job with the OSS. Her parents raised a rumpus, but Nausicaa was by this time twenty. She knew what she wanted.

She applied to go overseas in 1944. After being interviewed by an eminent psychiatrist attached to OSS—a woman who helped her with her self-assertion and desire for independence—Nausicaa landed in the House of Girls on the Champs-Élysées. As she told these rambling stories of her life, her eyes evaded me and the room, as if she was seeing instead the little town, its wooden buildings, her parents. She brought out the trumpet and showed it to me—the treasured scepter of her rural power. I asked her to blow a few notes for me. She was tempted but resisted. She said her neighbors wouldn't like it.

One evening we walked from Place de la Concorde to Saint-Germain-des-Prés and then to Boul' Mich. They seemed to her like new worlds, and I realized that she had been living entirely within the few blocks that lay between her hotel and her office. We sat for a while in the Deux Magots, which she studied with awe. I was amused when a few days later she told me she had escorted some of the girls on the same Latin Quarter stroll. She quickly made it a part of her particular Paris, and turned herself into a guide. Later she showed me an article she had written for her hometown paper about life in Paris. Her sentences were good, her manner cajoling, her viewpoint unsophisticated. It was Paris by her Kansas yardstick.

I soon realized that she was one of the young in Paris who like Thomas Wolfe couldn't go home again. I myself remembered what it had felt like to leave Europe in 1932, turning my face toward Montreal after four years in the French capital. A short vacation she took to the Riviera with some of the girls added to Nausicaa's veneer of sophistication. She came back from her spring visit to Nice and Cannes touched by the sun of the Midi.

*****

During her travels she had picked up a picture book about French cathedrals. On her return to Paris, she exacted a promise that I would take her on a tour of Notre Dame in Chartres. She said we could spend the day there, for there was much to see. We could picnic by the Eure after sightseeing, and she offered a list of available trains. I replied that the precious stained glass was laid away, concealed for the duration, but I liked the idea on the whole, for I remembered my glimpse of the sandbagged cathedral eight months earlier, before our entry into Paris. With the removal of that wondrous stained glass, Proust's "positive jewel of stone" seemed a ghostly broken mansion, a tattered House of God suddenly made decrepit, even while it cried out that if the glass were restored all would be redeemed.

On a Sunday in late April, Nausicaa and I set out. We carried several boxes of K rations for our picnic. I saw what the press meant when it said France's railroads were damaged goods. The cars were dirty and unkempt. Some of the windows had not been replaced, and the jagged glass was boarded over. Throughout the interminable trip, Nausicaa read her guide book like a bible. She told me Chartres was fifty-five miles southwest of Paris, on the left bank of the Eure river. I added that yes, the city was in the heart of the granary of France, situated on the quiet plain of Beauce. I had a vision of brilliant yellow mustard fields and lush green grain. As we pulled into the city, I could see the cathedral in the middle distance—sufficient distance to obliterate its current poverty. It was the way I had seen it during the 1920s and 30s, when a Sunday at Chartres seemed a glorious holiday, a medieval feast for the eyes.

We walked through the steep, narrow streets of the old town. The sun gave us occasional splashes of pale yellow for our viewing, and a sense of springtime warmth. Nausicaa pointed to the simple southern spire of the late twelfth century, and its robust companion to the north —complex, ornate, and completed three hundred years later, in 1506. One thinks of Gothic not in decades but in centuries. Nausicaa showed emotion at the spectacle. Her history professor would be thrilled to know that she was actually seeing these stony concretions, three dimensional against the cloud-scattered sky, rather than as flat pictures in books. We spent some time examining carvings and statuary, trying to distinguish between the ravages of time and of the war.

We entered the cathedral, weaving our way between piles of sandbags. Astonishingly, my old visual memories of the immortal stained glass tried to assert themselves and paste over the daylight blanks that invaded the ancient chiaroscuro I had known in times of peace. Nausicaa, having plunged back into the guide book, was reeling off in whispers the heights of the spires, but I no longer listened. My eyes were filled with the remembered blue-blue, that extraordinary transparency that Diane de Margerie describes in her lyrical *La Femme en Pierre*.

A mass was ending. I sat down, overcome by the fusion of old and new—the awe and wonder of my youth, and this middle-aged soldierly attempt to take in the differences of decades and history. I reminded myself that the "jewel in stone" had seen many more wars than those of modern times, and had probably not been as protected as it now was. I wondered whether in other times the stained glass had been removed and hidden in great secrecy, to keep sacred its historic representations of legends, parables, donors, and saints.

Nausicaa sat beside me. I was surveying the lined faces of the worshipers. There was an absence of young people, as if they no longer lived in old Chartres. A few veterans displayed decorations and medals on their ill-fitting jackets. Some limped. I saw two amputees struggling awkwardly when they rose or resumed their seats. The music of the mass swelled into the immense invading out-of-doors, and seemed to emphasize a mourning for the cruelties, the terrors, and the war dead. One woman dressed in black, with a frozen hard face, clutched a bunch of keys, as if she carried with her for her prayers these symbols of possession or administration. She may have been a concierge, who felt safe only if her keys were coiled in her hand.

The mass seemed out of tune with my memories of the cathedral's chiaroscuro. I missed its air of mystic reverence. The daylight, bold and brash, seemed to want to overcome its centuries of exclusion. I saw a man in deep prayer, one hand covering his eyes, as if to hide behind his darkened visions. A younger woman, perhaps in her late thirties, slowly peeled off a pair of long gray gloves that covered her arms to their elbows. She did this gracefully, and the whiteness that was revealed extended to her delicate fingers. Uncovered, her right hand clutched her prayer book, as tightly as the other woman clutched her keys. Nearby, a pale nun with intense eyes followed the service, her head nodding to the rhythm of the chanting.

We walked the length of the cathedral. The great altar seemed bare, and the candles lit in alcoves and shrines swayed with the intruding gusts of air. I pondered the strangeness of an enclosing cathedral suddenly open to weather. It would continue nude and derelict until the war's end. My thoughts wandered to Proust and his Illiers. I had been in his Normandy a year earlier. This was very close to the scenes of his childhood, the Combray of his magnificent fiction.

We descended to the Eure, crossing a little bridge and passing a few bombed-out houses. Nausicaa gasped with delight at seeing the flying buttresses. We ate our supply of rations on the bank of the river in the warm sunshine. We had come on a woman who was selling small fruit tarts. They made an admirable dessert to the corned beef and the biscuits.

Nausicaa and I talked as if by soliloquy—hers the tourist approach, mine a tangle of memories and a painful recognition of war's cruelties. Yet I was glad she had prodded me into this little adventure. We caught a late afternoon train, and were back in Paris by early evening.

REVERIE IN THE AVENUE MONTAIGNE

April 24, 1945. I sit on a bench in the artistic and aristocratic Avenue Montaigne, with its fresh-leaved elegant trees and its wide sidewalks. I have been in Paris since its liberation the previous August, with a few weeks out for service in besieged Strasbourg. Now I wait for the ultimate victory that would take me into Germany.

The Avenue Montaigne is named for Michel de Montaigne, who invented the enduring form of the essay. Nearby is a street called Goethe, and another called Bizet. Over by the Champs-Élysées, there are streets for Balzac and Lord Byron. The *élite* makes itself a part of poetry and music by having streets named after geniuses who stir French feelings. The *élite* sings their songs, subsidizes their operas, supports a national theater. Now the French are selecting old names that can be scratched out. Streets will be renamed for the heroes of this new era of freedom.

I am sentimental about this street. It was here that in my younger years I went to see the last of the famous Ballets Russes, and to hear the modernism of Stravinsky. I went again and again to the Comédie des Champs-Élysées, to see Louis Jouvet's productions of the plays of Jean Giraudoux. Giraudoux died in January 1944, a few months before the liberation. The plays were usually on classical subjects, but the actors talked about modern problems. His *Amphitryon 38* drew on a charming and characteristic Greek legend; the number was Giraudoux's way of suggesting that thirty-seven dramatic versions existed before the one he wrought with his light pen. I saw *Siegfried,* his play about Franco-German relations, three times. I couldn't have enough of this small theater. Its few hundred seats were red or pink. A warm rosy atmosphere, a refined intimacy prevailed. I admired Louis Jouvet as the producer and director, and relished him when he took parts himself, such as the darting Mercury of *Amphitryon.* I also remember Pierre Renoir, Michel Simon, Valentine Tessier. There was something magical in Jouvet's disciplined theater.

It was in the Théâtre des Champs-Élysées that Stravinsky's *Le Sacre du Printemps* caused a memorable riot early in the century. Here I heard Stravinsky's *Psalm Symphony* at its premiere many years later—quite a different occasion, received with thunderous applause. Thoughts of the theater bring me back to Stravinsky, conducting his own works, in two concerts in the early 1930s. He was then as always wispy, bouncy, quick, and intense, displaying his genius with ineffable delight in performance. I heard his memorial on Debussy's death; just a few instruments that wandered in and expressed their doleful feelings to the conductor. A highly original evocation of the state of mourning.

I also love the Avenue Montaigne because of its associations with my early research, when I was editing some of Henry James's hitherto lost plays. Once I came to the Avenue to call on a former Ambassador to Washington, who lived in one of the very fine stone houses. When in the French ministry in London, he had been a friend of James. I remember climbing a solid stone staircase to be greeted by the aged envoy. Ambassador Jusserand talked for an hour in his large study, where his papers were piled on a series of desks. Occasionally he picked up a letter by Browning or Tennyson, but he couldn't find James's letters. There weren't many, and I ran them down later. He recalled going to Hampstead Heath on Sundays with James to be with George du Maurier. Jusserand was a delightful little man—as small and as energetic, even in old age, as Stravinsky.

At this moment in my reverie, my eye fell on a man of medium height who was detaching himself from the area in front of the theater. A solitary figure, there was something familiar about him—the walk, the body movement. As if in a state of somnambulism, he came toward my bench. He wore gray flannel slacks, and a dazzlingly blue windjacket. His head was sunk into a white foulard that looked rather silky. His face was bronzed, lined, and he seemed melancholy, lost.

Suddenly I recognize him. It is Louis Jouvet, fifteen years older than when I first watched him on stage. I feel as if I have performed an act of magic, calling him up from the vasty deep of other years. He belongs in this street, and near his old theater, where I spent so many rare evenings when I was twenty-one or twenty-two. I tell myself that I might stop him and tell him of my admiration for his work long ago, pour out to him the pleasure he gave me when I was young. He would appreciate having an American in uniform say flattering things to him. But I decide this would be wrong. Instead, I follow the deep blue of the windbreaker until it melts into other figures down the avenue.

Later, I asked myself where Jouvet had been during the German occupation. The answer would fill a book. When the Germans arrived in Paris, they laid down their ground rules for French theater. The plays of Giraudoux were forbidden, since he had been a subtle anti-fascist. But Jouvet was permitted to perform the French classics, especially Molière. Indeed, he had no difficulty convincing Vichy that he should fulfill an engagement to play Molière in Switzerland. From Switzerland he fled to Portugal, and crossed the South Atlantic to Latin America, where he was welcomed with open arms. During the next four years he played in fifteen Latin countries and thirty-three of their biggest cities. Audiences came to watch the French players even when they didn't know French. The power of the acting was sufficient.

There is now a street in Paris named after Jean Giraudoux, not far from the landmark Théâtre des Champs-Élysées.

TERMINATIONS

Some days before my ruminations in the Avenue Montaigne, I had gone to a Stravinsky concert at the Théâtre des Champs-Élysées—the concert Nausicaa declined. It was a thrill to find myself once again in the theater, and to have Ernest Ansermet, the Swiss conductor who made a specialty of Stravinsky, offer a choice program. I was exhilarated by the music, a delightful combination of irregular, interrupted rhythms, dissonances, and cacophonies, with lapses into the classic mode. My ears had long become accustomed to them.

I walked from the concert in the blackout to the Avenue Rapp. The warehouse was uncommonly silent and dark. The place was filled with shadows rather than the usual sounds. On my floor, a young sergeant approached me with a whisper. There was a tearful look in his eyes. Had I heard the news? Franklin D. Roosevelt had died a few hours ago. Harry Truman had just been sworn in as President. Immediately, I felt the full shock of the news. Roosevelt had recently been re-elected for a fourth term. He had passed away on the edge of our victory, deprived of this final triumph. I said I didn't find the news surprising, for FDR looked like death in all the photos of the Yalta Conference. We agreed his old bounce and energy had been disappearing, particularly when put beside that of Churchill, de Gaulle, Eisenhower, and Stalin. They would see the war to its end.

We talked of FDR. He had been long at the helm, a remarkable, creative president who had many enemies, and who made human mistakes, yet seemed always to be a guide—the voice of a father to the entire nation. The American rightists couldn't abide him. But what fresh air could they abide? I told the sergeant that if he went into politics, I would vote for him. He said he might try for vice-president first. We joked clumsily to hide our feelings. The sergeant spoke pleasantly of the folksy way in which Truman stepped into FDR's shoes, which he could never fill. I confessed to being snobbish about his career, wondering what this former haberdasher had in the way of imagination beyond buying and selling. Would he summon sufficient vision to prepare the world for peace? A great change was needed to reverse the iniquities of the European fascists. We were still a few months from the dropping of the atom bomb on Japan—for which Truman would have to shoulder responsibility.

I had liked FDR, his quest for reform, his political adroitness, his grasp of the domestic American picture. He had redefined democracy for the rest of our century. As Labour did in England after Churchill, the Republicans would in due course take power, as if the second war hadn't defined anything.

Roosevelt had died in the midst of the final offensive in Germany, a drive from the Seine to the Baltic in the west, with the Russians slicing across the east. At this moment, Luther Conant asked me to attend some off-the-record international press briefings by Eisenhower's Chief of Staff, General Walter Bedell Smith. It was he who had negotiated the surrender of Italy in 1943, and would in due course negotiate the final surrender of Germany. The psychwar newsroom in London wanted a summary of the Bedell Smith briefings, and Conant had agreed to have them covered. I was the most available party for this job. Promptly accredited as a war correspondent, I found myself in the very midst of the news funnels from various fronts. The Information Room at the Hôtel Scribe had enormous maps on its walls. They helped make everything fairly clear, insofar as headquarters was letting us know what was happening. The maps seemed oppressive, with the great pointed arrows showing the two fronts closing in on the German armies. Bedell Smith was a seasoned diplomat as well as a soldier. He had served in the other war as an infantry lieutenant. In this war, he had been appointed secretary of the joint chiefs of staff in 1942, and moved speedily to the position of chief of staff of European theater operations—Eisenhower's chief of staff. He was a compact man of medium height, straightforward, easy in his give and take with the press, with all his information at his fingertips. We had a feeling that these special briefings at this late hour were whispers from Supreme Headquarters—a kind of inner track.

He began by setting forth the Allied positions across Europe. There was no question that the Germans were at last thoroughly hemmed in. We pressed him to tell us how much longer it would take. He shrugged off this question. It wasn't something he could answer. He wanted us to be certain not to make any premature announcements of victory. That would be most unfortunate, and those of us who had been close to the Battle of the Bulge knew why. Hitler had pulled that offensive out of his hat and caught us unawares. Did he have other tricks up his by now tattered sleeves? Finally Bedell Smith "guessed" the war could last three or four months. We thought his estimate was related to his demand that there be no premature soundings of the trumpets of triumph.

Things happened far more quickly. As accounts flooded into the Hôtel Scribe, the finale of the war seemed a mix of Grand Opera and Shakespeare. In Wagner it had been the Twilight of the Gods, but when the Götterdämmerung came for the Nazis, there was no twilight. They had made their great gamble for glory and conquest, and lost. Death was hurried and unphilosophical. Hitler died in the Chancellery bunker when the Russians came to Berlin. It was April 30. Mussolini had died at the hands of the partisans near Lake Como two nights before. Bedell Smith accepted the surrenders on various fronts of those German generals who wanted peace, and who gave up loyalty to their Hitlerian oaths. In a state of shock and relief, the Allies celebrated from the night of May 7–8, when the peace became official.

Scribbled in old copy-books, my own notes of those days show that I somehow couldn't feel any of the exhilaration that swept through Paris. My pleasure came from the city itself. The beauty of the weather was haunting. The chestnut trees had flowered in profusion, and cast their petals along the streets. The city's warm leafiness filled me with joy; the Tuileries Gardens were never more magnificent. The lights now came on, as the last alert was sounded. The fountains surged up. The Arc de Triomphe suddenly had its peacetime floodlighting, as did the Place de la Concorde. Crowds filled the Champs-Élysées and various quarters of the French metropolis.

"Well it's over," I wrote May 7, "A series of capitulations with the final unconditional surrender early today in Rheims." Walter Bedell Smith had accepted the surrender. It became official at 12:01 a.m. on May 9.

I felt numb.

"There has been too heavy a burden for us to throw it off at the mention of victory in Europe," I decided.

"There is the Pacific war."

It would end in August.

"There is the occupation of the Reich."

I would be a part of that.

"The war for peace hasn't yet begun."